ORGANISATIONAL GROWTH AND SUSTAINABILITY

An Organisational Development and
Change Approach

Endorsements

This book is a testament to Dr Rica Viljoen's ability to unite academic rigour with heartfelt humanity. It beautifully demonstrates the true meaning of an Integral Way, bringing together insights gleaned from real-world experiences and groundbreaking research. The book captures what it means to guide organisations, leaders and teams through meaningful change, showcasing Rica's unique talent for drawing out the voices within a system – encouraging inclusivity, empathy, and shared purpose on every page.

May this book inspire its readers to cultivate workplaces where respect, collaboration and adaptability serve as cornerstones of enduring success. And may Dr. Viljoen's passion continue to spark new conversations, new ideas and new ways of thinking about how we care for our organisations – and each other – on this shared journey toward a brighter future.

Dr Khaled ElSherbini, Consciousness Academy Egypt

I feel a humble sense of pride on being asked to reflect not only on the content of Rica's new book but most importantly on the contribution of her work over an illustrious and incredibly interesting career to date, on how her knowledge of and teaching on organisational design had developed and evolved and on the immense value of the work she had done and the contribution she had made in understanding ourselves and our people.

As a doctor, an academic and an aspiring fashion designer, every aspect of the subject of organisational design and transformation resonates deeply. I am a huge fan of complex problem-solving and the critical importance contextual relevance plays in doing so. I have such appreciation for how Rica's work informs an understanding of how strategy plays out in systems and structures, how it deals with the understanding of complex situations and systems, and reading and understanding that, and weaving it into the tapestry of a plan.

I have many personal stories to tell of how her innate grasp on the people part of business has mentored and saved people, teams and organisations and has shaped complex and challenging situations into opportunities for growth and learning. The work is always systemic and sustainable, and the learnings are kept after the situation, enabling the people to be more developed and more apt leaders.

Rica understands that the world is always changing. That seismic shifts and pandemics occur. And that leadership must develop alongside these changes and in tandem with all other geopolitical shifts. Work on people is never complete and never in vain. It adds eternal value through developing emotional intelligence and emotional mobility. Its education is never complete and hence my excitement about new content to make my own, in my journey and ambition to be a better human and a better leader.

Dr Anchen Laubscher, Group Medical Director Netcare Limited

Dr Rica Viljoen's work reaches a new level of sophistication in this book. Her own voice is heard and without losing the academic rigour that characterised her other publications, her experience of helping leaders to navigate complex change initiatives while cultivating cultures characterised by trust and collaboration becomes clear. This book reaches a degree of simplicity that is easily palatable for a wider audience and can help practitioners and leaders to implement effective change strategies in their relative spaces.

Dr Jan Bosman, MD TDI

In our rapidly developing global economy, African leaders are tasked with the challenge of integrating indigenous African concepts into their decision making while operating within western contexts. In addition, African concepts and philosophies have gained traction globally for their focus on collective well-being, interconnectedness and community. This has put storytelling at the very core of transformation, reminding us that organisations are not just systems, but they are living communities where interconnectedness shapes both individual and collective outcomes. African philosophies also teach us that identity is communal, whereby people find meaning in connecting with others. Storytelling can help in addressing how people and organisations experience change while creating a sense of belonging.

Dr Rica Viljoen has taken this narrative approach and applied it to systems at all levels – individuals, teams and organisations. For organisations to truly be resilient and adaptable in the face of uncertainty, change initiatives, including elements that deepen understanding (not just drive action) must be implemented. Through designing immersive experiences of African life, Dr Viljoen has created opportunities for experiential learning to compound on practical insights, fostering a deeper understanding of diverse cultures and inspiring innovative approaches to organisational challenges.

Thando Ikaneng, M-student Industrial Psychology

In many ways this text reflects the mind of someone deeply human and compassionate. Someone who continues to be fascinated with whom Homo Sapiens is becoming and how it shows up in life, amongst peers and in particular at work. The text takes one on a journey to explore different possibilities and ways of being amongst each other in an attempt to potentially turn the tide and make a meaningful, yet sustainable, contribution towards society and life at large.

Prof Benjamin Anderson, The Da Vinci Institute

Dedication For

The gift of space:
Carina and Bernard
Giselle and Mark

The gift of roots:
Loraine Laubscher
Don Beck
George Lindeque
Jan Nel

The gift of support:
Jan Bosman
Eirinaki
Ansie
Mia

The gift of reason:
Piet

The gift of containment:
Cecil

"And the crux of the reality of ODC – no true definition – context defines it"

First published in 2025.

ISBN: 978-1-991272-27-0 (Printed)
eISBN: 978-1-991272-28-7 (PDF eBook)

Published by KR Publishing
Tel: (011) 706-6009
E-mail: orders@knowres.co.za
Website: www.kr.co.za

Typesetting, layout and design: Cia Joubert, cia@knowledgekr.co.za
Cover design: Marlene De Lorme, marlene@knowledgekr.co.za
The mandala images: Eirene Kristas, erene9@hotmail.com
Editing & proofreading: KR Publishing Team
Project management: Cia Joubert, cia@ knowledgekr.co.za

ORGANISATIONAL GROWTH AND SUSTAINABILITY

An Organisational Development
and Change Approach

Edited by

Dr Rica C Viljoen

kr
publishing

2025

Table of Contents

List of Figures

List of Tables

Foreword

We stand at a unique crossroad – a space where the luminous threads of African heritage, modern organisational transformation and the timeless wisdom of our ancestors converge.

For nearly two decades, alongside my dear friend and co-traveller, Dr Rica Viljoen, at the Centre of Human Emergence Africa, I have witnessed firsthand the transformative power of inclusivity. Our shared journey has been one of profound exploration – a quest to reshape organisations, and to rekindle the collective soul of humanity.

Don Beck, revered as the father of Spiral Dynamics, once challenged us to bridge the vast expanse between the contemporary world and Africa's vibrant heritage. His vision was to create a mosaic of ideas – a dynamic interplay of "meshworks" that weave together the multifaceted experiences of our time. We have been told that our work resonates with an integral quality, one that honours the complexity of our inner lives and the myriad voices within our communities. This book is born from that shared vision, a bold endeavour to bring the wisdom of old and the insights of modernity into a dance of I, WE, US, THEM.

At its heart, the unique contribution of our work lies in inclusivity – deep listening, ensuring that every voice is heard, that every story finds its space, and that the spectrum of human experience is celebrated. In a world that often seems fragmented by its differences, we have seen that true transformation begins when we create environments where individuals are acknowledged and actively empowered to contribute their full selves. This is the transformative power of inclusivity and the heart: it is both a philosophy and a practice, a way of uniting disparate elements into a coherent, sustainable whole.

In our journeys, we have discovered that the process of change is much like the ancient dance of existence described by Graves in 1974[1] – a leap into the unknown, a transcendent moment where old patterns dissolve to make way for something entirely new. Graves taught us that the existential leap for humanity is a theoretical possibility and an imperative, a call to venture beyond the familiar in order to embrace a more profound, collective awakening. In many ways, this book is our way of answering that call.

Our work is woven from the vibrant tapestry of African philosophy and myth – a rich heritage of story and song that speaks to the eternal truths of human existence. We draw on the wisdom of the past and the clarity of empirical evidence, and the capacity to work with emergence, showing how interventions across diverse contexts have ignited transformative change. Whether it is in boardrooms, on factory floors, or within communities and networks, we see the unfolding of a new narrative – one in which every individual's contribution forms a vital part of the collective whole.

This foreword is an invitation – a call to leaders, practitioners and seekers from all walks of life to join us in this shared exploration. It challenges us to look beyond conventional paradigms and to embrace a vision that is as much about heart and soul as it is about structure and strategy. Here, the dance between the inner self (the I), the relational space we share (the WE), the collective identity (the US), and the broader societal context (the THEM) is celebrated as the very essence of transformation.

The journey ahead is one of courage and creativity – a journey that requires us to dismantle the barriers that prevent true dialogue and genuine inclusion. It is a journey that honours both the scientific rigour of empirical research and the poetic resonance of myth and legend. In these pages, you will encounter stories of transformation that are as much about numbers and outcomes as they are about the human spirit – a spirit that, when unleashed, has the power to transform organisations, networks and societies in balance with nature.

As you read, allow yourself to be drawn into the narrative – a narrative that challenges you to reimagine the future of work, leadership, and community. **Let it be a reminder that change is not merely a process to be managed, but a living, breathing phenomenon that requires our active participation**. Just as a dance evolves with every step, so too does the process of organisational and societal transformation. In this dance, every individual's voice is essential, every contribution valuable, and every moment an opportunity to create something truly new.

I invite you to join us in this bold quest – to take up the mantle of transformation, to embrace the call of inclusivity, to listen to the heart and to contribute to a future where every voice matters. This book is more than an academic treatise or a practical guide; it is a manifesto for a new era of human emergence, one **where the boundaries of traditional thinking are transcended in favour of a holistic and integrative approach**. A call is made to leaders and their organisations, to take on the hero's journey to a more hopeful future – much as the 1977 inspirational song Heroes of David Bowie challenges us to.

May these pages inspire you to listen deeply, to engage courageously, and to dance with the full spectrum of human possibility. The interplay of our individual and collective energies holds the power to create a sustainable and profoundly just world – one where striving for human betterment is both the journey and the destination, benefiting all life.

Drs Anne-Marie Voorhoeve, *Co-founder, The Hague Center for Global Governance, Innovation and Human Emergence, The Hag/Vreeland, The Netherlands*

About the Editor

Dr Rica Viljoen is a globally recognised Master Organisational Development and Change (ODC) practitioner with a distinguished career spanning over 25 years. Her work, which has taken her to 53 countries across sectors, including mining, banking, healthcare, and energy, is anchored in systems thinking, behavioural science, and a deep commitment to inclusivity and human transformation within complex organisational ecosystems.

Dr Viljoen is renowned for her ability to partner with executive and strategic human resource teams to co-create purposeful strategy, culture, and talent architectures rooted in integral thinking. Her work is characterised by a multi-level, participative approach that enables the human spirit within systems to emerge. Through the application of inclusive organisational design and culture methodologies, she has consistently facilitated systemic interventions that lead to measurable improvements in leadership maturity, employee engagement, and organisational performance.

In one published case, Dr Viljoen's approach to inclusive transformation contributed to a complete offset of the annual Learning and Development budget when a national union strike was averted in an organisation where her methods had been applied. In another, despite the global challenges posed by the COVID-19 pandemic, the leadership capacity within an industrial operation increased significantly – as measured by the BarOn Emotional Quotient Inventory – leading to the achievement of record production targets. These examples underscore her conviction that inclusive, values-driven systems generate not only human well-being but tangible organisational sustainability.

Dr Viljoen serves on the boards of several internationally respected professional bodies, including the **International Society for the Psychoanalytic Study of Organisations (ISPSO)**, the **Don Beck Spiral Dynamics Integral Foundation**, the **Integral Scholar Consortium**, and the **Clare W. Graves Foundation**. She is the **founding director of the Centre for Human Emergence: Africa**, a thought leadership platform committed to enabling conscious transformation on the continent. Her work has been cited for its unique integration of African indigenous wisdom, Jungian depth psychology, and Spiral Dynamics, offering an integral lens for engaging with organisational complexity in both local and global contexts.

Dr Viljoen is also a prolific author. *Spiral Dynamics in Action*, her ninth book, has been translated into nine languages and is used globally as a key text in organisational transformation and leadership development. This current volume marks her tenth publication of this nature, extending her legacy of contributing reflective, practice-based scholarship to the evolving field of Organisational Development and Change.

She continues to publish, lecture, and consult internationally, contributing to the academic and practical advancement of the ODC field. Her praxis remains guided by the belief that sustainable organisations are those that create space for people to find their voice, participate meaningfully, and align individual purpose with collective destiny.

About the Contributors

Chrisna Ashforth

Chrisna is the founder and principal instructor at Eagles View Yoga Studio, nestled in Winston Park, Gillitts, KwaZulu-Natal. With a degree in Physical Education from the University of Pretoria and a background as a competitive beach volleyball player, she discovered Kundalini Yoga while recovering from sports-related injuries – finding not only physical healing but a deeper journey into self-awareness .

In 2010, Chrisna completed her international certifications in Kundalini Yoga, as well as training in Hatha and Restorative yoga styles. That same year, she opened Eagles View Yoga Studio, where she now teaches both in-person and via Zoom, five days a week .

Her approach blends movement, breath, and meditation to support people managing the pressures of daily life – from careers to family responsibilities. She also offers complementary modalities like applied kinesiology, Bach flower remedies, and "Hidden Mind" sessions, embracing holistic well-being .

Outside the studio, Chrisna teams up with her sister, Salomie (a psychologist), to host retreats in Bela-Bela and the Drakensberg, weaving in raw-food awareness, inner-child work, and nature-based healing. She's also passionate about guiding creative workshops inspired by The Artist's Way – offering these twice yearly to help people nurture their inner artist. Chrisna's work is quiet but heartfelt: she offers a steady space for people to heal, grow, and reconnect – with their bodies, minds, creative instincts, and the natural world.

Alice Prazeres Pereira Coelho

Alice is a registered Clinical Psychologist with over 20 years of experience in private practice, education, and organisational development. Her therapeutic approach fosters sacred and creative spaces for personal transformation, helping individuals reconnect with hope and soulfulness.

Alice has designed and facilitated programmes in Emotional Intelligence, Diversity, Change Management, Mindfulness, and Organisational Culture, and recently developed a proprietary Emotional Intelligence tool used in both private and corporate settings. She has served as a lead psychologist for reality TV productions and has supported capacity-building initiatives in South Africa's Water Sector. As the lead psychologist for the Angolan Embassy, she provides psychotherapeutic support to Portuguese-speaking clients and healthcare professionals.

A Reiki practitioner and IxCacao Kuchina, Alice also leads mindfulness and cacao ceremonies. Her work spans individuals, families, and leadership teams, and reflects a deep passion for healing and transformation.

Helga Coetzer

Helga – Holistic Healing Practitioner and Self-Discovery Guide.

She is passionate about the journey of self-discovery and unlocking human potential. With 35 years dedicated to holistic healing, she integrates diverse methodologies, including BodyTalk, Cranio-Sacral Therapy, Psych-K, Breathwork, and Bio-geometry, to facilitate transformation.

Rooted in personal experience, she holds the belief that every individual has untapped power awaiting revelation. She guides others towards profound inner growth by embracing discomfort and rewriting personal narratives.

Having overcome traumas and limitations, Helga stands as a living testament to the power of self-realisation. Her approach centres on the wisdom stored in our bodies and stories, empowering individuals to break free from repetitive patterns and shape the reality they choose to perceive. More than a practitioner, she serves as a guide, mentor, and advocate for transformation through deep connection and inner work.

Giselle Courtney

Giselle is an organisational development and culinary Fynbos specialist based in the Cape Winelands of South Africa.

She is the founder of South African Fynbos®, a nature-based approach to people development and the creator of an indigenous range of ancient gourmet herbs unique to the southern tip of Africa. These herbs of origin predate humanity and comprised the landscape at the time of cognitive evolution in modern humans. Their aromatic scents and novel flavours are, in essence, a primal sensory connection to the 'flowering' of human consciousness at the Cape.

By rooting leadership development in humanity's shared origins and leveraging the power of sensory exploration, this approach transforms the understanding of individuality and collective identity. It introduces an environment where participants can interact with authenticity and creativity in the shared symbolic journey that unites all humans across time.

Signature interventions are the Cape Town Fynbos Experience®, the South African Fynbos® Origins Retreat and the Get to the Point® Origins Leadership Journey.

Dr Ajay Jivan

Ajay is a Director at Vantage Lab, and he leads the thought leadership, research, alliances, and quality assurance at the HR professional body, the South African Board for People Practices (SABPP). He co-facilitated and co-authored the revised National HRM Standards with Dr Penny Abbott. The revised Standards was launched as the National People Practices and Governance Standards. He is an experienced senior manager in human capital management with board, policy, and strategy-level experience. He previously served on the Ministerial Task Team on Professionalisation of the Public Service and as an Independent Non-Executive Director of the South African coaching and mentoring professional body, Coaches and Mentors of South Africa (COMENSA). He attained his Masters in Clinical Psychology, Masters in Management, and Phd at the University of Witwatersrand. He has published in peer-reviewed journals and other academic publications, and he has authored the Fact Sheets of the SABPP. He is registered as a Chartered Fellow with Chartered Institute of Personnel and Development (CIPD, UK), Master HR Practitioner with the SABPP, and Clinical Psychologist with the Health Professional Council of SA (HPCSA).

Mark Klinkert, CA and MD More Cor

Mark is foremost a dad and husband. Professionally, a South African Chartered Accountant focused on delivering management and CFO services – driven by a passion for helping businesses and people succeed (keen for South Africa to grow in a strong, positive direction).

On the flip side: part-time poet, workshop tinkerer, motorcyclist, rock climber, archer, dog lover, and grounded by the quiet simplicity of the bushveld.

Dr Anna-Rosa le Roux

Anna-Rosa is a registered Industrial/Organisational Psychologist (HPCSA) with postgraduate qualifications in Psychology and a DPhil in Leadership, Performance, and Change. With a career spanning corporate leadership, consulting, coaching, and academia, she embodies a scientific-practitioner approach to addressing complex organisational challenges.

Anna-Rosa's work is rooted in an organisational development philosophy, emphasizing systemic, transformative growth. Her expertise lies in delivering projects in culture, leadership, well-being, and sustainable performance in an era of rapid change. She has contributed to academic books, presented at international conferences, and delivered impactful consulting assignments across Africa, Europe, and the Middle East for corporate, government, and non-profit sectors.

Anna-Rosa has held senior roles, including Head of Organisational Effectiveness at Woolworths Financial Services and Head of Talent Management for Gold Fields' Africa region. She has also served on the executive committees of professional bodies such as SIOPSA and ACMP Africa and is an honorary Vice President and Fellow of the International Society for Coaching Psychology.

Currently, Anna-Rosa collaborates with various thought leaders to deliver solutions for creating people-first organisations for sustainable impact and profit.

Dr Calum McComb

Calum is an organisational psychologist specialising in systems psychodynamics, with expertise in psychoanalysis, group relations, and open systems theory. His work focuses on uncovering the unconscious dynamics that shape leadership, teams, and organisational culture, enabling businesses to navigate complexity, adapt to change, and unlock their full potential.

With a deep understanding of the psychological undercurrents that influence decision-making, authority, and role dynamics, Calum integrates psychometric assessments, executive coaching, and team development into his consulting practice. His approach is both practical and reflective, equipping organisations to explore the hidden factors that drive performance and interpersonal relationships.

Calum has a strong academic background and extensive facilitation experience. He is a passionate advocate for social dreaming, unconscious group processes, and systemic transformation, fostering deeper insights into how individuals and groups function within broader organisational systems. His ability to combine academic rigor with practical insights makes him a trusted partner for leaders looking to transform their teams and organisations.

Through his writing, consulting, and experiential learning programs, Calum continues to influence the field of organisational psychology. He holds a PhD in Consulting Psychology for the University of South Africa and is a certified Analytic Network Coach. During his free time, he enjoys show jumping his horse.

Aaron J. Nurick, Ph.D.

Aaron is Professor Emeritus of Management and Psychology at Bentley University in Waltham, Massachusetts, USA where he has taught courses in Interpersonal Relations in Management, Emotionally Intelligent Leadership, and Social Psychology. He is the author of *The Good Enough Manager: The Making of a GEM* 2nd edition (Routledge, 2020) and articles in several journals, including *Human Relations, Psychological Bulletin, Human Resource Management*, and the *Journal of Management Education*. He is an editor of the international journal, *Organisational and Social Dynamics,* and is a Board member of the International Society for the Psychoanalytic Study of Organizations. Over his 44-year career at Bentley University, he received numerous awards for teaching, scholarship, and advising, including the Gregory H. Adamian Award for Lifetime Excellence in Teaching in 2019.

Ansie Prinsloo

Ansie is an Improvement Advisor with global experience in healthcare and mining industries. She is comfortable developing and spreading improvement initiatives at scale to foster inclusivity, effectiveness, safety and reliability. Her evidence-based and people-centred approach to improvement incorporates improvement science, systems and inclusivity theory. Ansie holds a PhD, MBA and Improvement Advisor accreditation. She is a qualified business analyst, coach, project manager and Occupational Therapist with specialisation in Vocational Rehabilitation. She has contributed to multiple publications within her area of expertise.

Lynne Rutherford

Lynne grew up in South Africa, where she obtained her B.A. in modern languages from The University of Natal, her Higher Diploma in Education from the University of Stellenbosch and a Post-Graduate Diploma in Tertiary Education from Unisa. After teaching in Amanzimtoti for four years, she moved into the field of learning and development in Johannesburg, working in Retail, and then becoming Head of HR in Merchant Banking and then Insurance. Lynne moved to London in 2001 and headed up the leadership academy for a large global insurer before working in Brussels to head up the Talent Management function in a global banking group. Following the 2008 global financial crisis, she joined a global supply chain solutions group as SVP of Talent and Learning. She was based in London, and worked all over the globe, developing and delivering programmes at all levels, with her main focus on executive and future leader development.

Lynne also has an MSc in Counselling from the University of London, Birkbeck College, and is a trained Co-Active coach.

She retired in June 2020 and now spends her time volunteering in her community, managing various projects. She is fluent in French and Afrikaans, loves to read Dutch literature, and has completed two marathons. Lynne is married with two children and two grandchildren.

Bedelia Theunissen

Bedelia is an Industrial Psychologist, HR Executive, talent strategist, and change leader with a passion for helping organisations thrive in times of transformation. Guided by her belief that "without leadership, no change is possible," she combines deep expertise in organisational culture, leadership development, and the future of work.

She currently leads initiatives that align leadership, culture, and innovation with long-term strategy, and is pursuing a PhD focused on developing a predictive model for leadership and cultural transformation in research-driven organisations. Bedelia believes that the AI era can be a catalyst for growth, inclusion, and purpose – if people are equipped with the right mindset, skills, and support. She writes and speaks about the evolving world of work, ethical leadership, and the human side of digital transformation. Her personal motto is inspired by Mahatma Gandhi: "Be the change you want to see."

Ruan Viljoen

Ruan is a professional oganisational development practitioner. He specialises in Rogerian, Humanistic and psycho-analytical group process facilitation. With over 10 years of consulting and facilitation experience. He currently holds the position of Director of Business Development at his current company – Mandala Consulting. Ruan is personally trained by Dr Don Beck and Dr Loraine Laubscher in Spiral Dynamics and adaptive intelligence and he is an expert on the Change State Indicator and Integral Values Map (IV-Map) instruments that describe adaptive intelligence. His unique contribution to the field of study of multiculturalism lies in generational theory. He is a Type Coach in MBTI and today, he has successfully implemented various transformational processes of which the most recent is in the health care and mining industries within South Africa. And last but not least, Ruan is part of the African team that has started the Jungian Coaching School for Africa, in which he holds the position of lecturer, faculty member & business development.

Chapter 1

The External Environment and Transformations in The World of Work

1.1 Introduction

The global landscape has undergone profound changes over the last 5 years. Rapid advancements in artificial intelligence (AI), shifts in globalisation dynamics, the unprecedented disruptions of the COVID-19 pandemic, emerging geopolitical conflicts and episodes of current volatility are the order of the day. These intersecting forces and their collective impact on the world of work are impacting organisations, leaders and organisational development and change practices for good.

While AI and digitalisation accelerated productivity and reshaped job roles, the external shocks of the pandemic, impacts of both public and covert uprisings and unrest and stagnant economies have introduced significant instability and inequality in global labour markets. Organisations that adjust faster to these changes have an unprecedented competitive advantage to sustain.

We need to lead differently in the face of these challenges and transformations. Old ways do not seem to work in the same way today. Taking a step backwards to reflect on how to intervene in an effective, systemic way to assist to co-create a better, more functional future with long-term benefits for all the shareholders offer a valuable pause in the busy-ness of today's pre-occupation with executing in the never-ending race of surviving and producing. Adjusting to these tectonic shifts in external conditions become crucial for strategists, C-suite executives, business leaders and specialists that deals with organisations.

Our sense of control is eroding in this new volatile and chaotic, fast adjusting, ever changing context. Ways to adjust, to emerge and to create a sense for self and others become important for meaning and significance. Organisations that aim to grow and sustain themselves will need to embrace perpetual transformation and build adaptability into their core organisational DNA.

1

In this chapter, the trends in the outer world are considered. The implications of these disruptions are explored on individual and organisational aspects such as identity, positionality and intersectionality. A view is taken on how the world of work will look like in 2030 and 2040. It is for this world that Organisational Development and Change (ODC) practitioners must prepare organisations. The role of leadership in this changing world and ODC functions and practitioners can embody their role are considered. A chapter layout is presented as the conclusion of the chapter.

1.2 Trends, Disruptions and the World of Work

Organisations must address issues such as job insecurity, the rise of the gig economy, and mental health challenges. Moreover, ensuring inclusivity and diversity in a globalised workforce will be critical, particularly as demographic shifts continue to alter the composition of the labour market. As technological innovation accelerates, regulatory frameworks may struggle to keep pace. Organisations will increasingly need to navigate a complex environment of data governance, privacy laws and ethical considerations surrounding AI and big data. To ensure new ideas follow the rules and are ethical, we need to regularly update our internal rules and work closely with regulators.

The table below presents the implication of various aspects on organisations and predicts what these challenges will present in 2030 and 2040.

Table 1.1 Challenges in the World of Work Today, 2030, and 2040

Aspect	Today	2030	2040
Technological Integration	Rapid digitalisation driven by remote work technologies; initial AI and automation adoption.	AI deeply embedded in routine operations; automation and predictive analytics dominate decision-making.	Advanced AI shaping autonomous enterprises; near seamless human-AI collaboration; quantum computing disrupts industries.
Work Models and Flexibility	Hybrid work arrangements balancing remote and office-based work.	Predominantly hybrid, gig, and project-based work; traditional full-time employment declines.	Fully decentralised, location-agnostic, AI-enhanced work environments; work is task-oriented rather than role-specific.

Aspect	Today	2030	2040
Employment and Job Security	Coexistence of traditional employment and the gig economy; job displacement concerns.	Traditional job security declines - dynamic, adaptive employment models emerge.	Employment becomes continuous learning-based; AI-human hybrid workforces dominate.
Workforce Skills and Reskilling	Growing focus on digital literacy; emerging skills gaps in automation and AI.	Lifelong learning culture becomes essential; AI-driven personalised training predicts and addresses skills gaps.	Real-time AI-adaptive learning integrated into daily work; emphasis shifts from reskilling to intelligence augmentation.
Leadership Styles and Organisational Structure	Predominantly hierarchical leadership with an emerging shift toward collaborative practices.	Decentralised, networked leadership; leaders act as facilitators in AI-enhanced, cross-functional teams.	Post-hierarchical, distributed leadership; decision-making is collective, dynamic, and AI-augmented.
Organisational Change and Development (ODC)	Change management is reactive and episodic.	AI-driven change diagnostics enable proactive adaptation; continuous change management becomes embedded. Human skills like resilience and critical thinking are stimulated by ODC interventions.	Organisations continuously reorganise/ restructure using AI-driven feedback loops; adaptability is a core strategic function. Humans give soul to systems that can otherwise be so optimised that the exponential value is destroyed. Unique value propositions lie in humans and cannot be easily duplicated.

Aspect	Today	2030	2040
Multi-culturally Sensitive Assessments in ODC	Traditional, standardised assessments dominate, often lacking cultural nuance.	Greater focus on culturally sensitive assessments to predict behaviour in diverse teams and global workforces.	AI-driven, culturally adaptive assessments predicting leadership behaviour, team dynamics and organisational fit in real time.
Global Divide and Inclusivity	Significant digital divide - some regions rapidly adopt technology while others lack necessary infrastructure.	Risk of widening digital exclusion; deliberate inclusive policies needed to bridge technological and economic gaps.	Potential for a deeply bifurcated world unless global policies prioritise equitable digital access and economic inclusion.
Work-Life Balance and Well-being	Blurred boundaries due to remote work raising concerns over digital burnout and work-life balance.	Extreme connectivity challenges require structured digital well-being policies and mental health initiatives.	AI-driven personal well-being optimisation; continuous connectivity risks cause new work-life integration strategies.
M&As, Globalisation, and JVs	Globalisation continues with cross-border M&As; geopolitical instability occasionally affects investment patterns.	M&As and JVs increasingly driven by technology, AI and sustainability imperatives; geopolitical tensions force localisation of supply chains.	Global business redefined by AI-driven partnerships and decentralised economic hubs; geopolitical power shifts drive industry realignment.
Political Instability, Wars & Global Trade Impact	Regional conflicts and sporadic wars create trade disruptions and organisational uncertainty, though global systems remain relatively resilient.	Increased frequency and intensity of wars, coupled with heightened political instability, force organisations to diversify supply chains and embed robust risk management practices.	Widespread, enduring political instability- driven by resource scarcity, climate change and geopolitical rivalries- radically transforms global trade patterns, compelling organisations to adopt hyper-agile, decentralised operational models.

Robust responses on all levels to the changes in the outer world are imperative for organisations to grow and sustain. National governments and international bodies must collaborate to craft regulatory frameworks that support technological adoption while mitigating its adverse effects. Policies aimed at reskilling and upskilling the workforce, enhancing digital infrastructure, and ensuring financial stability are crucial to navigate the complexities of the new work environment.[2] International cooperation is essential in managing the spillover effects of geopolitical conflicts and international trade implications. The changing nature of work, accelerated by digital transformation and remote working trends, will probably exacerbate socioeconomic disparities. New solutions are needed for systemic wicked problems that remain largely unsolved. Fast and agile organisational responses to changing external conditions are critical for growth and sustainability.

1.3 Why Another Book on Organisational Change and Development?

With increasingly diverse and dispersed workforces, the need to build inclusive, psychologically safe cultures that support virtual, remote and cross functional collaboration is a business priority as cultural transformation is on the agenda of most organisations. Sustainability is increasingly embodied in business models and treated as a primary concern – ODC practitioners need to inform this agenda directly. The proactive transformation of the workforce is critical to ensure agility and flexibility in the DNA of the organisation.

Companies that fail to anticipate skills for future execution of strategy may later face severe shortages in talent. Internal upskilling ecosystems that continuously equip employees with new competencies are a key differentiating factor in organizations. This plays directly into the domain of ODC. Capacities are not only developed for the current realities in this approach – but also for future challenges. Co-creating a workforce that together concrete the conditions for organisations to grow and sustain becomes crucial. The focus on organisational growth and sustainability that this book brings is a critical shift towards indicating the intrinsic value of ODC. The transformational and lasting effects of this field of study, if planned as a science, facilitated as an art and practiced as a craft may just be the differentiating factor that distinguish companies from each other in this world where unique value propositions erode with alarming speed.

The continuous and multifaceted evolution of the workplace demands a rethinking of how organisations approach change. Traditional ODC models, once central to understanding and managing organisational transformation, are increasingly fragmented. They no longer provide a one-size-fits-all solution; instead, they require a context-sensitive, agile framework that recognises the diversity of organisational cultures, global socio-economic realities, and rapidly evolving technological landscapes. ODC practitioners are challenged with assisting companies and leadership in it to have agility. The decentralisation of corporate structures, the shift from rigid hierarchies into more fluid, team-based organisations will accelerate and allow for a faster response to uncertain external environments. Real-time restructuring, pivoting of strategies, workflows and resource allocation because of the predictive ability that science and AI-driven tools can provide excels the speed of change.

A new book on ODC is essential because it would:

- **Integrate Multidisciplinary Perspectives:** Synthesise insights from digital transformation, human behaviour, cultural sensitivity and risk management to offer a holistic view of change.
- **Address the Fragmentation of ODC Approaches:** Reconcile diverse schools of thought in ODC, offering adaptable models tailored to varied organisational contexts.
- **Reintroduce Core ODC Principles:** Revive fundamental concepts such as organisational culture, human psychology and adaptive systems that have been sidelined in favour of purely technical change models.
- **Equip Leaders for Continuous Transformation:** Provide leaders with tools to harness AI-driven diagnostics, culturally sensitive assessments, and hyper-agile strategies-critical for long-term organisational resilience.
- **Bridge Global Inequalities:** Emphasise inclusive strategies that address the digital divide and geopolitical instabilities, helping organisations navigate a world where technological advancements coexist with deep-rooted socio-economic challenges.

Change can no longer be viewed as a challenge to overcome but rather an inherent state of individual and organisational being. Remembering what ODC all is about, considering new links in knowledge and looking towards what can be, creates significance for an academic, pragmatic and multi-culturally sensitive approach to a book. This book presents an integral, scientific evidence based yet inclusive way of taking up the catalyst leadership role of an ODC leader in an organisation. The time to constellate this function as a strategic key differentiator in the domain of creating organisations that grow and sustain, is now. **ODC as a function is no longer about managing resistance to change but increasingly focuses on how to enable and create systems and ecologies what will thrive on continuous evolution**.

Old ontological views and frames, and epistemological ways of making sense of reality create similar systematic interventions that result in predictable causal dilemmas. ODC, as a field of study, must continue to evolve and keep a keen eye and corresponding reflection on the way in which social systems are considered, and intervened in. One sided frameworks and attempts seem peripheral. Even meta-theories do not offer the depth that was searched for. The following questions arise – must we intervene at all? And for what purpose? Must a book of this nature even be written when AI can be consulted and with the press of a button to create a way to intervene? And how does one tackle a phenomenological topic of this nature that indeed creates touchpoints to reflect and adjust their own practices and tested ways?

Maybe the only way to tackle this predicament is to offer personal experiences of an ODC practitioner and her philosophy. Narratives of how others are viewing and practicing ODC may also be considered. A reflection on how organisations were left more functional after ODC interventions may assist too. An attempt to balance theory with practice to complement own views with other ways of addressing organisational issues; to weave together as many ways of describing the social phenomenon – without describing it with known theory; and a deliberate effort not to be descriptive, provide quick fixes and a myopic view, may be helpful. In this book the position was espoused to take kairos-time, deep time as per the old ways, and consider various domains of exploration such as individual, collective, contextual, theoretical, pragmatic, organic and emergent views clustered together in an original compound of insights, views and experiences on the phenomenon of ODC.

1.4 How The Field of Study of ODC Can Support Organisational Growth and Sustainability

Organisational Development and Change (ODC) is the field of study that attempts to optimise individual, group and organisational dynamics and behaviour in response to changing life conditions. Increasingly, the following aspects become key focus areas for ODC strategists and practitioners. The absence of a single, consistent method for implementing Organisational Development and Change (ODC) is widely acknowledged in both academic and professional circles. However, this very diversity in approaches can serve as a strategic advantage for firms, enabling them to distinguish themselves and ensure long-term sustainability. ODC consultants focus on supporting individuals and organisations to crystallise their identity, explore their positionality and render the intersectionality of roles functional, flexible and optimally. The enablement of leaders to lead in the new world of work, while adjusting to the external conditions presented to them; are a key consideration for an ODC practitioner.

ODC initiatives equip organisations with the tools to remain agile in volatile environments. The rapid integration of artificial intelligence (AI) and digital technologies has forced many organisations to rethink their structures and processes. By adopting

ODC strategies, companies can redesign workflows, reallocate resources, and upskill employees to harness the potential of new technologies. Such adaptability is critical in responding to the dual challenges of automation and the shifting demands of global markets.[3] External shocks-ranging from the COVID-19 pandemic to regional conflicts and economic instability-have underscored the necessity for continual organisational change and adaptation. The pandemic sped up remote working and digital transformation, interesting organisations to revise connection, collaboration and operational strategies – all aspects in the sandbox of ODC.

ODC provides a framework for managing these transitions smoothly by promoting change readiness and resilience within the workforce. External changes forces organisation to adopt more flexible and responsive business models in order to stay relevant, to ensure continuity and competitiveness and therefore sustainability, in uncertain times. A key aspect of ODC is its focus on culture-building, an environment where continuous adaptation is the norm. This innate capability to adjust also encourages innovation, enhances employee engagement, and supports knowledge sharing. Organisations that embed a culture of continuous adaptation are better prepared for rapid shifts in the external environment, enabling them to respond to opportunities while ensuring the functionality of the organisation.

ODC initiatives also play a pivotal role in managing workforce diversity and inclusion. As organisations become more globalised, cultural differences and varying national contexts influence work practices and employee expectations. Structured ODC processes help in aligning diverse teams with strategic objectives, ensuring that change is inclusive and that all employees are prepared for new ways of working. This approach is significant when considering the varied impacts of external events across different regions, with the changing interest of multiple, diverse shareholders and the rising level of knowledge and publicity that access to technology enables.

Ultimately, the impact of ODC extends to the strategic realignment of organisational goals with environmental realities. By fostering an adaptive and innovative mindset, ODC not only improves operational efficiency but also positions organisations to sustain long-term growth and sustainability. Leaders who effectively implement change management models such as Scharmer's U-curve,[4] can steer their organisations through turbulent periods and emerge more robust and agile – as long as they acknowledge systems have a mind of their own and without a very clear understanding of the complex nature of social system phenomena, change efforts in itself are senseless. There is a stark realisation that not one model alone gives us a grip on the multi-faceted, emerging and self-organising nature of social systems. A dynamic, meta-frame approach and integral philosophy is probably more congruent with the complex nature of the dynamics at hand. Inclusivity, as the underpinning philosophy to ODC as offered in this book, offers a way to deal with these complexities in a dynamic, conscious and consistent manner – forever changing its angle to the conditions at hands while weaving collective alignment and therefore collective energy to be wired around the task at hand.

1.5 The Role of ODC in Organisations

Customisation and Flexibility

Given that organisations differ in culture, structure, strategic intent and aims, and external pressures, a one-size-fits-all approach to ODC is impractical and, in fact, illogical. Instead, successful organisations tailor their change initiatives to reflect internal realities and industry-specific challenges. Leaders who sensitively adjust change processes to the unique cultural context tend to achieve smoother transitions and greater employee engagement.

Distinguishing Organisations Through ODC

Organisations that continuously adapt through ODC are more likely to foster a culture of innovation. This agility enables them to react to environmental changes and proactively shapes market trends. The ability to manage change effectively serves as a buffer against external shocks-be it economic downturns, geopolitical conflicts, or technological disruptions-thus reinforcing the firm's competitive position.[5, 6] Well-managed change processes can bolster employee morale and engagement, reducing turnover and ensuring the retention of critical knowledge and skills.

Ensuring Organisational Growth and Sustainability

A wise CEO once shared with me that if there is not continuous organisational growth – there is decline. This reminds the second law of thermodynamics that energy in a system will wind down without external intervention. Organisational growth is thus critical for organisational sustainability.

Sustainability in this context extends beyond environmental concerns to encompass economic and social dimensions. By embedding mechanisms for ongoing learning and skills development, organisations can keep pace with evolving market demands and technological innovations. A robust ODC framework enables organisations to anticipate and respond to emerging challenges, ensuring that strategic initiatives remain relevant over time. Organisations that integrate sustainability into their change processes also address social responsibility and environmental stewardship with positive effects on organisational sustainability.

1.6 Lay Of The Land Of The Book

What follows in this book is a journey through the deep and intricate world of ODC, where inclusivity, leadership and transformation are not just concepts but living, breathing forces that shape the organisations of the future. As we move into the next chapters, we begin by laying the foundation, exploring what ODC truly means in a post-post-modern, ever-evolving world. The reflection starts in **Chapter 2: A good story begins somewhere**. The complexity of change, the interconnectedness of systems, and the organic nature of transformation become clear. **Chapter 3: ODC Conceptualised** introduces the conceptual grounding of ODC, defining its nature and its role as a discipline that navigates complexity through natural design principles and adaptive systems thinking, and explains the link to the title of the book, namely **Organisational Growth and Sustainability.**

From here, we inquire into one of the most critical aspects of ODC- the inclusivity process. **Chapter 4: The Inclusivity Process of ODC** focuses on the enablement of individual presence, emotional containment and an organisational gestalt of inclusivity. At its heart, this is about creating spaces where individuals, groups and entire organisations can thrive. It is about presence, emotional containment and the establishment of an organisational identity that is not only sustainable but deeply human. This section challenges us to reflect on the prerequisites of true inclusivity and the non-negotiables that must be in place for transformation to occur.

But change itself is a process- one that requires understanding, patience and an awareness of the conditions necessary for true evolution. We explore the intricate phases of change, from laying a new foundation to rewiring and cementing the future. Alongside these practical steps, we draw inspiration from the alchemical journey of transformation, where the chaos of the unknown, the burning away of the old, and the courage to step into the new become essential rites of passage for any organisation seeking true growth. **Chapter 5: The C in ODC - change presents a structured perspective on** change within ODC, exploring transformational phases, large-scale change processes, and metaphors from alchemy that illuminate organisational transformation. Through a deep dive into the principles of natural design and complex adaptive systems, we begin to understand that change is not a linear process but a radical and often unpredictable unfolding of innate potential – or destruction.

In the second part of the book, the journey continues. We immerse ourselves in **The Science, Art and Craft of ODC - Chapter 6**. Transformation is not merely about frameworks and methodologies; it is about people. It is about diagnosing, designing, and delivering change in a way that honours both the tangible and the intangible- the numbers and the narratives, the strategy and the soul. Through real-world insights, we uncover lessons learned from large-scale change initiatives, exploring both the successes and the inevitable struggles that come with transformation.

As we enter the third part of the book, we shift our focus to the people at the heart of ODC. We begin with a reflection on emotional intelligence and the essential qualities of the 'Good Enough' manager- one who leads with capacity, competence, character and commitment. Prof Aaron Nurick guides us in **Chapter 7: Emotional Intelligence and the Good Enough Manager – A Pragmatic Approach to Organisational Development and Change** through an exploration of the role of leadership today. Leadership is not about perfection; it is about authenticity, about stepping into the uncertainty of change with wisdom and adaptability. All work is self-work and a team cannot be strong if the individual members are not. Personal transformation begins internally; Alice Coelho explains in **Chapter 8: How the Alchemy Began – The Call.** This call offers an initiation into something sacred. This journey is personal and collective, an unfolding that leads us to deeper ways of seeing and being.

Chapter 9: The Dance of Facilitation explores facilitation methods, including psychological and emotional frameworks that enhance group effectiveness and functionality. In **Chapter 10: How Groups/Systems Can Become Functional, Mature, and Optimal,** Dr Calum McColm offers how groups come together, how systems mature, and how psychological and emotional defences can either hinder or accelerate progress.

The book transitions into the pragmatic and multi-disciplinary practice of ODC in organisations. Here, Dr Ansie Prinsloo, in Chapter 11: ODC in Practice offers real-world application, linking it ODC to Quality Improvement Science and presents the Inclusivity Quality Improvement Framework. Integrating these "doing" methodologies with inclusivity – the manner in which we can practise it – becomes a central theme, reinforcing the idea that true transformation does not happen in isolation but through intentional, collaborative efforts.

Finally, we arrive at a call to action – Chapter 12: Crafting Inclusive Organisations that take up their role in society, with Dr Annarosa le Roux. This is more than just a theoretical exercise; it is a responsibility – she claims. Contextual intelligence, the ability to truly see and work within complex environments, becomes key. Through case studies and lived experiences, we reflect on what it means to practise and to move beyond rhetoric and into real, lasting ODC strategies with lasting impact.

In the last part of the book offers a smorgasbord of interventions - practical approaches that can be applied across industries and organisational cultures - Chapter 13: Smorgasbord of Interventions. In the final content chapter, Chapter 14: The Evolving World of Work, Standards of Good People Practices, and ODC, Dr Ajay Jivan from the South African Board of People Practices (SABPP) discusses the intersection of strategic HRM, organisational development standards and governance in the changing workplace. The world is shifting, and organisations must not only adapt but also lead with integrity, inclusivity and vision.

Chapter 15: Final Thoughts offers a consolidation of the book. This book is not just about organisations. It is about the people who make them, the leaders who shape them, and the cultures that sustain them. It is about a future where work is not just a function but a space for meaning, connection and continuous evolution. The journey ahead is one of discovery, of challenge, and of profound transformation.

Hopefully, thoughts and inspiration are stirred in the reader. Maybe it solicits more stories of what has worked in other context and memories of effective and ineffective system interventions may resurface. And maybe, some ODC practitioners are motivated to try what they believe in their bones will move a system through the challenges of the today's absurdity and non-function. As there is nothing new under the sun – maybe the invitation is just to breathe, consider and renew insights already hold. And maybe my quest to do human better drives the publication of this book and is the invitation merely that - to further the imperative for social and global systemic agility in the spaces we touch.

The invitation is clear: step in, engage deeply, and be part of the unfolding story of Organisational Development and Change and its lingering effect, if practice with heart.

PART 1

Setting the Scene

Chapter 2

A Good Story Begins Somewhere

A little magic can take you a long way.

—James and the Giant Peach

2.1 Background

The lingering idea of revisiting my second book, *Organisational Change and Development: An African Perspective*[7] that was published by Knowledge Resources in 2015 has been simmering in my mind for years. Its abbreviation, OCD, has regularly initiated light-hearted teasing - "If you were truly OCD, wouldn't you prefer CDO?" – highlighting the ironic alphabetical priority of the human condition. Bion[8] warned us that when a group is formed, there is always pathology. Silently, this just made me smile as this field of study thrives on paradox and fluidity and it is hard to pin down.

OD and Change are contextually different each time they come into play

Over the years, the nomenclature of this field emphasises the very nature of it – it is dynamic and contextual. And it is practised differently by different specialists informed by different fields of study. And should it be any different?

> It happens in the spaces in between – focussing on the
> functionality of a system rather than the content itself

I became aware that I no longer think in the same rigid terms and frames that I once knew. In 2015, I was preoccupied with some basic assumptions:

> "There is nothing new under the sun."

> "Why do we get fixated on bespoke methods of the
> day and forget the human element?"

> "What happened to the field of study, that I love so much?"

> "Why can the MAGIC that real Organisational Development
> (OD) in action create not be duplicated?

> "What is sustainability, after all?"

At first, this insight left me cynical. As humans, organisations and social systems, we repeat the sins of the forefathers. We also do not learn from experience. And when we, in fact do, we have an inability to convince a system to think and therefore behave afresh.

Over the last decade, increasingly, the reflection shifted to: What will it take for us to evolve – as geopolitical regions, organisations and the humans in them? How can the soul in our organisations be rekindled? And what does sustainability really mean when applied to our ecology that we inhabit? It is no longer referred to in the same rigid terms I once knew.

In 2024, I repeated the desktop research to study how 18 listed companies on the JSE practice OD and again, like in 2014, I find no real similarities. Sometimes the function is clustered under Human Resources, sometimes under strategy. There are cases where it reports on finance. Or services. And it often disappears into the DOING component thereof, namely Organisational Effectiveness or a reductionist version under communication.

There is not, and should not be, a single ODC way

Although I am heavily informed through my journey with the development of theory in individual, group and the development of nations; the pragmatic experiential experiences that I was exposed to early in my career in the field of Organisational Development and the wonderful journey of applying the theories and approaches gathered over three decades in 52 countries across the boundaries of industries such as mining, banking, financial services, defence health and retail.

The ethical considerations of the field of study became important too – not to do harm. In such I started to play an active role in Professional bodies such as the International Society for the Psychoanalytic Studies in Organisations, the Don Beck Spiral Dynamics Integral Foundation, the Clare Graves Foundation and the South African Board of People Practices. Giving back became more than writing, lecturing and coaching. It was an honour to be invited to join the Club of Rome to contribute to creating better conditions for humanity.

In my practice, I may have shifted significantly from the ways I was taught. The need to leave a pragmatic frame to the next generation of practitioners became less important. A quiet realisation started to form. It is a craft and a science and an art that is deeply shaped by context, creativity and the unique needs of the moment.

Sometimes incidents stop you in your tracks and make you consider the way you view the world. After a lovely relaxing day at a spa; my I-phone was grabbed from my hands during an armed robbery. I was on the phone with a corporate connection in the DRC. He must have felt so helpless. How he searched for me left a huge impact on me. Things started to move in slow motion. It was a real drama to replace the phone and create connectivity again. I missed important strategic conversations. Earth angels crossed my path. My sons were very concerned and empathetic. I also realised who will be there for me when I am in real distress and where my angst will create an inability to connect.

A few days after the traumatic event, a very humane yet strong, strategic and integrated executive gifted me with three sessions with Helga. I did not really know what to expect. I still contemplate that everything happens for a reason. I saw the soul of that female executive and was reminded that soul in organisations is critical to create a compassionate culture. The journey with Helga was arguably one of the most significant and sacred interventions in my life. My own dynamic became quite visible. Childhood traumas surfaced again. I became quite aware of repetitive patterns and was reminded of the old saying that we breath death. I realised that we were all just waking each other home. Life is short... Maybe Jung was right in saying that we all must live our myth.[9] And that the purpose of my life is to support (wo)man leader(s) and humans to find their voice. It also reminded me of the willingness to explore in my 20s with the interplay between kinesiology and emotional intelligence; bio-danza, holotopical breathwork and vision quests – the real OD interventions I enjoy and the things we forget as we are seduced to do the task at hand – life.

Finding my voice, yet again, also became important in this book. I did not want to write academically in the same way I did before - yet not lose the very important anchoring. I did not want to describe the measurements of behaviour anymore- yet not lost the scientific nature of my work. I did not want to share auto-ethnographic voices in the same way I did before, as I had such a need to move to a more collective co-created space. *My way is indeed not the way.*

...it is the only way I know...

It was during a breakfast with Wilhelm Crouse from Knowledge Resources that the realisation struck. I cannot just revise the book on OD. It needs to be rewritten. The adaptation of the abbreviation Organisational Change and Development came from an adjustment of ODC to OCD from the Academy of Management. Until there is a better name for this strategic practice, that is the domain where this work is anchored.

In a conversation with a friend on the beautiful Rooi Els in the South African Western Cape province, we contemplated about the importance for finding a right title for a book and how to make sure that the degree of narratives incorporated in a textbook are just enough. That recalled a story that was told to me by a Montana cowboy just outside Billings. I wanted to connect by inquiring about the number of cattle he kept. In a very distinct American tone, he responded, "just enough for my land." I then changed my approach and inquire "how big is your land?" The response was "just enough for my cattle". The response made me contemplative.

May this book be "just enough"-a-blend-of anchoring in solid and credible theory, case studies where the field of study included snippets of pragmatic insight, questions to crystallise our view on ODC and the conditions and in effect the prerequisites for it and the lived experiences of facilitators, strategists, coaches, consultants and leaders that entered this field of consciousness.

An executive that became a friend, Dimitri Giannakis that refers to himself as the reluctant CEO, said the following in terms of this approach: "A qualified statement and quote from me: It may not apply to all, but it will apply to many that have somehow become CEOs."

May this book, in a way, apply to you too.

2.2 The Journey of a Witness to The Field of ODC

After a very meaningful 16 years as the managing director for Consulting, a niche Organisational Development (OD) house, I wanted to explore my belief that "we teach best what we need to learn most." My career path circled through diverse terrains – after years of academic work, I returned to corporate life, leading OD functions in a multinational mining house and navigating the complexities of post-merger cultural integration in the largest SADC distribution channel tied to a Saudi Arabian mining entity. The unprecedented challenges of the COVID-19 pandemic presented itself. For me, it was an exciting, challenging yet meaningful and sometimes scary laboratory to test psychodynamic theory about how systems adjust when no one knows what to do or how to adjust to changing life conditions.

The almost two decades at Mandala taught me a lot:

- That human dynamics have the same archetypal ways – the context is different.
- How not to do things.
- That you are as respected in a place as the size of your feet[i].
- The importance of translating between contexts and use the language of the system – that is, if the large-scale transformational effort is not to renarrative the culture.
- Then still the old stories are important.

---

i   A Ghanaian wisdom

- To meet the system where the system is at.
- Not to superimpose your views on others.
- To keep true to ODC nature – to diagnose, to develop, to deliver and to delineate.
- To quantify the return of OD investments on the system.
- That sometimes you need to walk away.
- That you are like Nanny McFee often – called to help when the "children are out of control."[ii]

All the above lead to the insight that OCD is like the stock exchange or property market – it has most impact when it is practiced in a counterintuitive way. By being faster in intervening strategically when others are paralysed; and by making the unconscious aware in individuals, groups and organisations, vicissitude is dealt with more functionally. The view that the global crises can be seen as having the nature of a psychoanalytical process helped to make sense of the collective confrontation with uncertainty, grief and adaptation. The quicker the unconscious trauma is dealt with; the more energy can be unleashed on the task at hand that manifests in safe production in mining; patient care in nursing; customer centricity in banks and other outcomes, such as innovation and agility in systems.

Within three months of joining an international mining house, the pandemic impacted us all. All hands were on deck, helping that gold and platinum production do not totally come to a hold, while minimising the risk of the spread of the unknown virus. This context provided fertile ground to explore OD principles and with a CEO that was totally supportive and a real solid leader, the value of this way of working became clear.

Within a week of the pandemic, a large-scale OD initiative was launched in the company. We provided a container for the 300 execute and high-level management and higher in the organisation in the form of individual growth in partnering with a local university. The collective leadership went through daily sessions – focusing very purposively on adaptive intelligence (Beck, Viljoen, Scharmer, 5th industrial revolution, systems thinking, African philosophy) and emotional intelligence constructs (Bar-On). Soon we extended these strategic conversations to the D-bands and created a great collective sense of being and leading. I am beyond thankful that I had the opportunity to test the assumptions of industrial psychology and adult development theory to a real-life situation. ODC for me became like fluid that filters through sand. Finally, the residue remains in the sand, allowing pure collective intent to percolate. For a while, that is.

---

ii   Reference to a 2005 movie where a kind widower and his seven rambunctious children, facing financial ruin, turn to a witchcraft-wielding nanny to help get their household in order. The children here refer more to the leaders than the employees.

After the initial strategic response to the pandemic, my focus calibrated inward. The need in the system became human resource leadership rather than the facilitative, hands-on interventions that had always been my calling. The senior role in the organisation was surely challenging and exciting. I however, divorced from facilitating and intervening myself. I was strangely untethered. Deeper questions into my own assumptions surfaced.

For 20 years worked in the health industry, and after a tragic helicopter crash where 5 key doctors lost their life, I was asked to support with the trauma debriefing of the accident. Suddenly, it became clear that although I love to strategise; I also want to do THE WORK. To apply limited life energy to real people in real settings with the accompanying ripple effects to the people they serve; reminded me of what I long know – that I want to contribute towards "doing human better". I could no longer escape the questions:

- Am I too theoretically stuck in my construction about individuals, groups, organisations and social systems?
- How can I unsee my seeing?
- What if the theories in which I anchored are so reductionist that it defeats the purpose of making things more?
- Could these assumptions about the way that humans react still hold true in a world so irrevocably different?
- Or is it really that different?

> *ODC practitioners all study the same phenomenon in different ways*
> *I will not pretend I wasn't petrified. I was. But mixed in with the awful*
> *fear was a glorious feeling of excitement. Most of the exciting things we*
> *do in our lives scare us to death. They wouldn't be exciting if they didn't.*
>
> *Danny the Champion of the World*

2.3 Rebalancing Into My Science, Art and Craft

It was hard to transcend from corporate back to an OD entrepreneurial and consulting practice. Maybe it was a rather traumatic transition. I became unstuck. I wanted to honour my decision to leave the Mandala practice to my boys. Mandala became a known brand with international distribution rights of the Integral Values Map, the Change State Indicator, the Benchmark of Engagement and a method towards Inclusivity that stood the test of time. It was very fulfilling when Dr Shannon Nell's PhD thesis was published in 2022 that critically analysed this ontology, methodology and approach over a decade. With her publicly stating that the graduation ceremony that without this work nursing in that organisation would not have been able to withstand the impact of Covid, a tremendous sense of appreciation was felt. If they just know how much I have gained from working in that system and how it informed my very assumptions about the work.

My thinking has evolved significantly since 2016. I really loved the strategic challenge of being around an executive boardroom. Being a consultant leaves you with the complexity challenge but strips you of the responsibility and the mandate. What if I want both? Torn between the need for complexity and belonging to an exec team and the practice of OD where time stands still for me, I was reminded of a conversation with a senior manager in the banking sector that passed away. On sharing the same dilemma, she smiled and said, "as if you do not in the role of consultant have the complexity of more corporate worlds and are in fact still in corporate." Maybe it is indeed functional to blend in an integral practice, the science of the field of study, the art of leading and the craft of practice.

2.4 ODC an Individual Practice, Through Others

It was over a glass of wine and soup for breakfast at our favourite hide away, Paputsis in Linden, where my friend Dr Jan Bosman said: "Griet, you must facilitate. That is how you gather your stories. You are sad because you, as a gatherer of stories, are not doing that."

What became clear is that:

- I will have to remember by own myth and align again to my own life's purpose – conooiouoly. The price of not doing it is too big. Developmental theorist such as Jung[10] and Erikson[11] were right after call. That will result in becoming fulfilled or cynical. In a life of despair and not a life of integrity.
- The wise words of Dr George Lindeque, in his attempt to finish well, also struck a chord.
- I need to work towards unleashing human energy to be wired around organisational intent.
- That I love to be held accountable and will stand by the value of interventions of this nature.
- That I would rather walk away if all the building blocks and conditions of building functional systems cannot be sustained over a set period in a setting.
- That I am still looking for that executive that would allow profit share rather than rewarding me on a daily/monthly fee – I so believe in the worth of ODC...

Recently, after securing a tender on culture optimisation, I shared with the CEO that indeed I would not tackle it the way that the tender specifications insist on. I was contractually obligated. What really make me believed again that one should speak one's truth was his response: "you are allowed". By that he meant that there was a self-authorisation to share your view. This openness to hear, and the mandate that came from that was a reminder of the importance of sharing what you see, from your angle and your experience and not be too concerned about the positional power and authority in systems.

This reminded me that I often retold the story of Pinocchio in MBA class settings. The cynical version is that he was a wooden boy that lies – and then his nose grew. In the adapted version, he was a puppet dancing to the wishes of the puppet master Geppetto. He had to cut the strings, experience terrible ordeals like growing donkey ears (listening) and spending an extended period in the belly of a whale (with the dark unconscious) to go back home as a REAL boy. Geppetto was happy. He always wanted a real child – even if naughty.

My original purpose of trying to enable voice in organisations became crystal clear again: How can we enable our humans in systems to have voice towards a better future?

In 2024 I met a solid salt of the earth miner in the DRC with an amazing interplay of humanity yet strict, fair, loyal and task orientated - a leader with head and heart. Analysing the outcome of the different leadership profiling assessments he completed resulted in the conclusion that this leader can be described as an emotional, intelligent, integral, second tier leader. Previously, he managed a Zambian mine that was fully localised and outperformed the other comparative operations in the same mining house, employing a significant number of expatriates. In an understated way, he embodied all the different theories that I believe an ODC practitioner must tie together to make sense of leadership behaviour in complex systems. His clever, calm, value-driven logic pragmatically confirmed my theoretical assumptions. A renewed interest in the field of study and realisation of the impact of this way of leading in diverse systems on business growth and sustainability was kindled. I was encouraged to take up my craft again; remember my science and practise my art. He inspired me to start writing again and document the untold stories of working in rural spaces to ensure that there are more African and recent case studies published presenting examples of where the needs of multiple stakeholders are blended into a more functional way of being and doing - achieving both individual and organisational aims with sustainable results.

One more corporate sprint is in the cards for me – with the right amount of international complexity and the mandate to effect real change for the good. Until then, I gather lived experiences in the laboratory of organisational settings and document the untold stories. Maybe one can do both.

It is hard to write a book of this nature in isolation. Not only is my specialised field of study Inclusivity; ODC, in its purest form, is always working through leaders and never wants to be seen as the driving force behind organisational renewal. There is no bigger compliment for an ODC practitioner if a business leader takes ownership of a transformational effort. Meaning arises if, in the words of Frank Sinatra – if both the leader and the ODC practitioner can simultaneously say "I did it my way!"

This is illustrated by the case below:

> Christo Viljoen was an engineering manager at Damang Gold Mine in 2009. His assessments were promising. Not only were his levels of work (which indicates his complexity handling ability was high; he also had an interesting worldview for an engineer- a worldview that can be described as humanitarian. An OD process was introduced by Dawie Strydom, the HR Executive, that enabled the OD to work in the case study in Ghana. As Dawie is a seasoned business leader that optimally functioned on a strategic level in the expat world; he enabled a large-scale transformational effort based on multi-culturally sensitive diagnostics. The BeQ culture study was introduced in that system.
>
> Christo called me in and explained that he cannot support an effort of this nature. He illustrated a clear understanding of what goes wrong with OD that is not principled and systemic. He distanced himself from the effort.
>
> He was, however, loyal to Dawie and respected him greatly.
>
> Before the intervention started in mining operations, Dawie asked Christo to enable conversations with the union to get the buy-in of this important stakeholder. Christo complied with five Sessions with union reps and leaders were scheduled.
>
> Day one Christo introduced me as the consultant that wants to do some work there. Day two, he introduced me as an expert that understands "these things". Day three he said, "As leader, I would like to do this. Help me, please?".
>
> Dawie and I just smiled that evening.
>
> This was the beginning of one of the most satisfying and sustainable OD journeys I ever embarked on. A journey of this nature is never successful if one attempt it individually. As HR executive, Dawie provided the strategic insight, mandate and oversight. Christo became a key role player in the organisational play - that of a steadfast father; leader; "owner of the farm"". In that space, I hold the role of catalyst. I could be extracted, and the system was different after our collective interventions, of course. I was not the only role player on the OD side. The full story is told it the book Inclusive organisational transformation and acknowledgement was given to all key role players.
>
> The people of Ghana should, however, be mentioned here. The leadership challenge was truly embodied. Earlier this year (2024) the mine became fully nationalised. It was such an honour to work with professionals, inflicting sustained systemic growth.

I can rationalise it and argue that on stratified systems level 5 and higher, where efforts move into a more collective space that it is seldom the effort of an OD practitioner alone that enables sustainable large-scale change. To be honest: I also think the approach followed here highlight a personal preference too. As social scientist and academic, it makes me happy to acknowledge the primary source of data/thinking and contributions.

Towards the end of writing the book, I invited Ansie Prinsloo to support with sections as editor. I was blessed to journey as coach with Ansie before I became her academic supervisor. Although we hardly had the space to work together in corporate; I know that she contributed a lens that I do not spontaneously consider, although the underlying DNA of our values is similar. Ansie asks Doing questions; through integrating Being knowing. I ask Being questions through integrating the Doing ways. Our various fields of study create an integral approach to organisational transformation that results in a positive reflection on business indicators and results. (Ansie, may we work together in a system one day and see if my hypothesis can be accepted).

Although I am seen as a leading scholar in the field, with a specialisation of the adaptation of social systems to change and multi-culturalism, I feel that the more I experience, the less I know. I have invited the authors, practitioners and social scientists – mostly as witnesses of interventions; but also as actors on the stage of transformation. They are acknowledged as co-authors in the various chapters.

2.5 The Nature of The Field of ODC

*Meanings are not important," said the BFG. "I cannot be
right all the time. Quite often I am left instead of right.*

The Big Friendly Giant (BFG)

An attempt to describe the field of ODC the following delimitations came to mind:

- OD is not HR nor is strategic HR necessarily HR.
- Organisational Development and Organisational Design are symbiotic fields - but distinctly different.
- Change management is not communication.
- Any field can be "dumbed down" to meaningless activities.
- OD interventions are not Learning and Development.

It is a field of its own. In the next chapter the field will be conceptualised.

An attempt to describe the field of ODC, the following came to mind:

ODC is an ancient yet recent view on humanity

As a scholar I relied heavily on a primary source in my previous publications. Most of these ideas remained over centuries. Authors like Jung[12], Freud[13], Bion[14], Graves[15], Beck[16], Senge[17], Jaques[18] and others remain my academic ancestry. No cosmetic attempt will be made to find a new theory – but rather a contemporary exploration of evolution of the field and contextual application are of importance.

ODC is messy

The practice of the field of study is not static. Nor is it formulaic. The very essence of it is endlessly adaptive and uniquely crafted in every iteration. It is deeply contextual.

ODC needs courage

> Nature loves courage. You make the commitment, and nature will respond to that commitment by removing impossible obstacles. Dream of the impossible dream and the world will not grind you under, it will lift you up.
>
> Terence McKenna (1946-2000)

As ODC practitioner or leader, you speak to what is missing rather to what is known. It is not necessarily the popular believe. The question of "what do we not see?" or "what do we not know from our knowing" renders these conversations and dialogues in the domain of the personal and collective unconscious. It is uncomfortable and not known. Without courage, we will not be able to do things in a different, more functional way.

You cannot be before you are

Graves[19] reminded us about the inability to see before the questions are asked. In a world that is so polarised politically, economically, technologically wise, and socially, the forces that can pull in various directions often leave systems of any form in survival mode and are paralysed. ODC provides a holding space for knowing – archetypical parenthesis that contains a system for a while and balancing it towards a please of knowing and being more while the doing happens. It helps us to have a chance at not repeating the same unconscious patterns with the same results in a more disturbed external reality to ensure individual and collective longevity.

It's a science, art and craft

The integrity of good ODC practice resides in the interplay of valid, multicultural diagnostics that acknowledge multi-culturalism and different ways of forming identity and ontological stances; the art of designing context applicable solutions with a twist to move a system through the stuck-ness and the craft to take people with you on the journey. Without this ability and the underlying assumption you intervene simultaneously on individual, group, collective and contextual domains – change is not sustainable.[20]

You start anywhere in the system

In the ideal world, the executive will mandate an ODC function to support the organisation to achieve a culture change, to make the company future ready or to prepare leaders for a different reality. Alternatively, a task like a post-merger and acquisition attempt or the optimisation of JV dynamics is presented. A change like creating a behaviour-based safety culture can present. Some will say the doing comes first – the strategy. But that strategy in its very nature is informed by current thinking – and indeed often aspirational. At the end, for me at least, it does not matter anymore. You should just start. As consciousness through awareness, alignment and growth happen on any of domains of ODC (individual, group, organisational, contextual) it will have an impact on other domains. The magic happens when leadership – on D-bands and higher in and organisation – collectively tackle a superordinate goal; and blow human energy and intent into those systems with a hopeful disposition. More about this follow later.

Old ways must be remembered

Humans have an innate ability to understand change – if it is meaningful to them personally. Some old sayings that can be considered and used to translate meaning though the organisation. The local context and language can be used with significant effect. Myths and stories are universal and can be used to create shared meaning. Cultural intelligence is important to ensure that diverse employees follow the strategic intent of an organisation in a harmonious manner.

2.6 About My Seeing (Philosophical Stance)

In putting the metaphorical pen to paper (this manuscript was typed), I realised that in a way my identity cannot be defined anymore through the descriptive words I used before. Being called an entrepreneur, an academic, an executive all leaves an unfulfilling taste. I find being called a spiral wizard very egocentric. Indeed, it makes me a bit rebellious. I am also not an author. I just also write too.

In a way, it was important before to share my view, my story. That has faded. It was important to anchor my thinking in primary theory. ChatGPT or Grok AI can help with that (albeit not always accurate). From an integral way, one should look at – your inner I, the outer I, the inner WE and the outer WE.

From an ontological perspective, my inner self recognises that I collect stories. As part of the collective I, together with others we are inquirers into the human condition. In the inner we, I believe my stance is a quiet onlooker to social interplays. In the outer We, I believe I am an impact player towards functionality and sustainability, intending to leave things better.

I guess this makes my philosophical stance a blend of post qualitative[21], ethnographic[22] and phenomenological[23] assumptions about and epistemological way of integral[24] and holism.[25] Methodologically, a hermeneutic phenomenology[26] blended with social constructivism[27] underpins the book.

I believe that we tell our stories to ourselves and to order to life. By listening attentively, we look for the social, moral or ethical lesson in our attempt to make sense of the meaning of the tale. We interpret what we see and experience through the most workable lens. This results in a kaleidoscope of different interpretations of the same narrative - a phantasmagoria of perceived realities. Though a shared story, like a vision or mission of an organisation- for a while that is, we impose shared narrative upon disparate beliefs and may achieve something magical. In this book, my lived experience as an ODC practitioner, in relation to others, is shared.

2.7 ODC Defined for The Context of This Book

In this book, ODC is defined as:

> "a science, art and craft positioned on a strategic level that unleash human energy in a social system by diagnosing, designing, developing and delineating assumptions and behaviours on individual, group, organisational and societal level in a collaborative attempt to make the system more functional and sustainable."

More about this anchoring can be found in chapter 3. ODC through inclusivity, is a multidimensional concept which is determined by behavioural constructs on individual, group/team and organisational domains. The national culture has huge implications on the dynamics in the social system. It is not a quick fix. It is hard work – and some individuals will be lost during the process and disengage. It is not just merely a few mechanistic interventions, but a journey – a new way of behaving is introduced in the social system. In designing a radical transformational strategy, careful consideration must be given to all the behavioural constructs on all the domains as a simplistic, mechanistic and unintegrated approach cannot result in sustainable transformation.

2.8 Final Thoughts

Only a skilful and systemic ODC approach and design that acknowledges the causal interrelations that determine the willingness of employees to engage will have a significant impact. An intelligence, nuanced Inclusivity process, that interweaves carefully designed and executed Doing- and Being-interventions is crucial. These interventions must address dynamics on individual, collective and systemic level at the same time. It must be contextually smart – it must be designed for that specific system and rely heavily on both where the system finds itself and the tension of to where to the system must shift to be functional. The interplay between individual, group/team and organisational dynamics in the over-culture results in human energy in the social system to perform. It is the task of leadership to wire the energy around the task at hand in a conducive way that protects the integrity and identity of the organisation.

Re - ca she whispers

A deep penetrating reminder of three previous visits to the oldest Turkish hammam[iii] in Istanbul. The building from the 17th century retained its original magic. Entering through the green door, that made me bent down and transcending down the ancient steps through the underlit passage can even be described as omnipotent.

A very sacred few hours followed…

Over the years, I somehow ended up here, every time with Nenna. Nenna is much shorter than I remembered her. I think she lost more teeth, and her hair thinned significantly. The welcome was genuine and intimate.

The hammam was empty except for the two of us.

Lying in the heated marble slab, under 32 circles in the domed cement ceiling, I started to relax. The smell of spices from the outside and soap in the round cement room filled the air. I had a fleeting thought of vulnerability as my passport was locked in the small safe that is probably accessible and not really that private. This emotion drifted to a recognition of the recent board meeting in this city of chaos - a city with

---

iii A hammam, is an old Turkish Bath. It is a traditional steam bath and bathing ritual, often with a focus on cleansing, exfoliation, and relaxation. It involves a series of rooms with different temperatures and environments.

halls between walls. My mind drifted to a conversation the morning with Wilhelm Crous from KR – I need to focus on the ODC book – and how I would like to write differently than before.

What changed for me since me first attempt as author is the unwavering belief that I am here to try to do human better… That there is freedom in hope… That all old and new ways lead us to understand better…That we are all witnesses to our shared journeys.

Thoughts and reflections that drifted in my consciousness in that reflective state centred on the very nature of the next chapter – there is nothing new under the sun. And humans as a species can create theories for ever – but it is in a deep systemic nature that we know how to adjust and survive. We all have dealt with the traumas associated with change. We are forced to adjust – or not. As a species, we change to survive. That is what evolution and adaptation are all about. The process of change is indeed a well-known but often fought against human condition. Metamorphosis.

I must have fallen asleep when I heard:

Re…. Re…. Re-ca.

I filed the synthesis of the scholarly literature exploration about changing away with a word association and relax into an old intimacy that resides in human connection across boundaries of continents, language, gender and age. The dance of change echoes in my heart – as we move forward and backwards in a seemingly chaotic pattern while navigating our way through adaptation…

reJECT

rePLAY and reVIEW

reCYCLE or reSTART

reSURFACE and reAPPLY

reIMAGINE and
reCONSIDER

reTURN

reMEMBER/reJOICE

The archetypal dance
of the change process
was reIMAGINENED.

Chapter 3

ODC Conceptualised

This is the trick.

FigureThis is what all these teachers and philosophers who really counted, who really touched the alchemic gold, this is what they understood. This is the shamanic dance in the waterfall. This is how magic is done. By hurling yourself into the abyss and discovering its feather bed

—Terence McKenna (1946-2000)

3.1 Introduction

Over the years, I realised the practice of ODC is underpinned by changes in the life conditions that are met with corresponding changes in the world of work. As organisations are the interface of business indicators in response to the changes in the external environment; it is in this domain that the calibration really happens. It all boils down to the adaptive capabilities of individuals and the systems they operate within.

The more we know about the way that social systems function, the more we adjust to the very being of organisations. I guess, that is, if we are conscious about these changes and conditions. Systems thinking, quantum physics and our understanding of living systems play a significant role in how we adjust collectively as organisations. This applies to all types of organisations, from families that organise around creating a better future to all – to how profit driven organisations, NPOs; local governments and even geo-political spaces interact between multiple stakeholders.

As stated in paragraph 2.6 the ODC is viewed as

"a science, art and craft positioned on strategic level in an organisation, that unleash human energy in a social system by diagnosing, designing, developing and delineating assumptions and behaviours on individual, group, organisational and societal level in a collaborative attempt to make the system more functional and sustainable"

The title of the book: Organisational growth and sustainability is directly tied to the practice of this definition and viewed as the outcome of this approach – even if it means that the function of the organisation is transformed to something else or the form of the entity morphs into another configuration.

As one part of a system becomes more functional or in other terms, conscious, it has an unconscious and often unintended implication on the collective. It **is widely believed that in a family dynamic, the system organises around the most dysfunctional individual. This is sadly the case with organisations too.** Employees often collude to keep the unconscious patterns in place and respond to the influence/reactions of strong leaders to maintain equilibrium or mitigate the impact thereof on self and others. Rising levels of awareness or consciousness in an individual in a system systemically result in a new reality to be faced by the rest of the system. This leads to change.

In conducting an extensive literature review as preparation for this book; it became clear to me that the Inclusivity Framework that emerged as an outcome of my doctorate, can still be accepted as an organisational development and change frame.[28]Initially, this framework describes Inclusivity as an ODC philosophy what can be adapted to create radical transformation. It became clear that it also can be viewed as a methodology to drive radical individual, group, organisational and societal transformation. This chapter relies heavily on this framework; that later became an empirically tested model and was acknowledged internationally as such.

In short, the following figure explains why organisations adopt the essence of this adaptation and the importance of the rising level of consciousness, that creates awareness of adaptation.

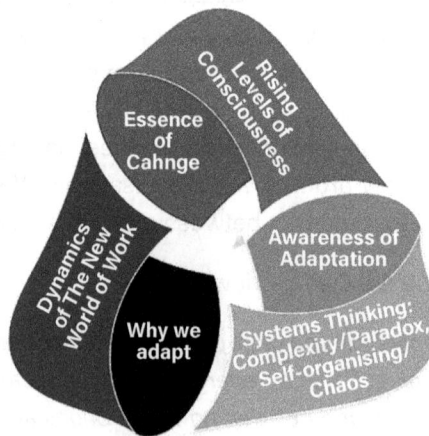

Figure 3.1: Why we need to adjust

The organisation or social system that will respond soonest and more congruent to the changes in life conditions have the biggest proclivity to survive.[29, 30] Effective change processes do exactly that – it shortens the period of adaptation to changes in individual, group, organisational and contextual domains.

ODC is defined in this chapter. The nature of ODC is carefully explored. Inclusivity is adapted as the way in which ODC is optimally performed in organisations. The chapter concludes with a plea to ODC practitioners to see themselves as leaders in social systems, rather than cool onlookers in solving a mechanistic problem. In fact, ODC practitioners can be viewed as catalysts or even alchemists.

3.2 Definitions of ODC

Organisational Development (OD) and Change is a multidisciplinary field that seeks to enhance organisational effectiveness and adaptability through scientific, planned interventions. It integrates theories from behavioural sciences, management and systems thinking to improve processes, culture and human interactions within organisations. The essence of OD lies in its emphasis on integral, systemic and living systems values, co-operative approaches, and long-term, sustainable change.

Beckhard[31] provided a foundational definition of OD as:

> *A planned, organisation-wide effort, managed from the top, to increase organisational effectiveness and health through planned interventions in the organisation's processes, using behavioural science knowledge.*

Organisational change refers to the structured and strategic alteration of an organisation's structure, culture or processes to adapt to internal and external pressures. Lewin's[32] *Force Field Analysis* and his three-stage model of change-unfreezing, changing, and refreezing-remain foundational in understanding how organisations transition through change. Today, we know that the phenomenon of change is not so linear. The one change result in multiple self-organising new unintended consequences and can hardly be isolated. However, what can be accepted is that successful change requires a deliberate process of dismantling old thinking patterns before new behaviours can manifest – acknowledging that new behaviours result in new systemic implications to continuously become aware of, acknowledged and respond to.

Integrating organisational development, change and inclusivity

The integration of inclusivity into OD and Change emphasises that transformational efforts should not only aim at structural and process efficiencies but also prioritise cultural dimensions. Inclusivity ensures that change initiatives are equitable and that diverse voices contribute to the co-creation of new norms and practices.

Burke and Litwin's[33] *Model of Organisational Performance and Change* further underscores the interdependence between cultural factors and change. Inclusivity as a radical transformational methodology as defined by Viljoen[34], leads to increasing change capacity in a system to adjust to changing life conditions while acknowledging the very nature of the phenomenon of change and social adaptation AND the appreciation that rising levels of awareness as an outcome of ODC work manifest in create new predicaments, impasses and opportunities to be dealt with by leaders in an attempt to sustain their organisations. By embedding inclusivity into this model[35] – as well as other mechanistic and on the surface simplistic frames to change, organisations can ensure that the transformational processes align with humanistic and systemic principles, and render it more transferable, authentic, modifiable and thus sustainable.

Organisational Development and Change, as a discipline, serves as both a science and an art, blending empirical methodologies with a profound respect for human values. Integrating inclusivity into OD and Change ensures that interventions are not only effective but also equitable, fostering sustainable transformation that respects and uplifts all organisational stakeholders.

It is accepted in this book that an ODC process leads to inclusivity as defined by Viljoen[36]:

> A radical organisational transformational methodology which aligns the doing and the being aspects of the organisation around commonly defined principles and values, co-created by all. It is a systemic approach that focuses on underlying beliefs and assumptions and challenges patterns within the individual, group and organisational psyche to engage in an inclusive manner with the aim of achieving a shared consciousness that will manifest in sustainable business results within the context of the specific industry and national culture in which the company operates.

Inclusivity is adopted as the overarching approach to sustainable individual and organisational change in social systems of any nature or of any configuration. It is the ontological stance adopted to describe the philosophy of ODC. This is as on archetypal or structural level, there are similarities in the factors that impact the dynamic at hand. The content of each configuration is different, though.

Inclusivity, through ODC, enables a diversity of thought

Inclusivity does not mean that there is a similarity in terms of the group dynamics of the sub-groups within the system. If a culture is inclusive, then the leader's natural style will emerge, and his or her personality typology preferences will have a direct impact on the sub-culture that is created. Inclusivity relies heavily on the leadership depth within the organisation.

Functionality of the leader(s)

The maturity level functioning of the leaders within an organisation is of critical importance in the success of this approach. If the personal strength of the leader is not highly developed, then the leadership will not be shared as willingly within the group. In this book, the concepts of individuation [37]the extended definition of emotional and social intelligence [38] and the bio-psycho-socio adjustment to changing life conditions[39, 40] are utilised to illustrate that conscious and unconscious ways in self and others can be integrated to enhance functionality. At the end, all work is self-work.

Inclusivity on individual level implies that a person can integrate the various parts of the psyche – from the ego, the shadow, the masculine and feminine parts thereof and the deep unconscious individual and collective archetypes at play. On group level, it implies that all voices in the group are heard; and unconscious patters in the dynamic are addressed purposefully. Archetypes can be made aware, gamesmanship acknowledged, and group awareness created. The organisation and the contextual domain/society can also be seen as a group. Inclusivity therefor applies to these domains too. By not considering the containing system or over culture of a social system like an individual or a group in a change process; change can hardly be sustainable.

ODC has a focus to optimise individual behaviour – in the context of other systemic interplays as can be seen in the figure 3.2 below. The context can be described as the over culture – the social systemic dynamics in the containing system of the system we study.

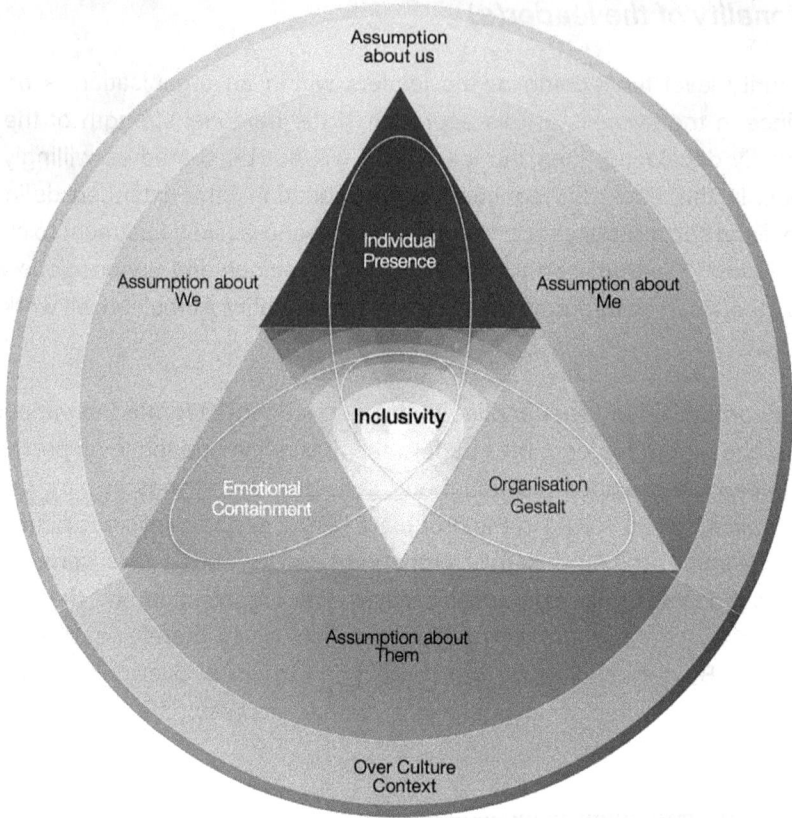

Figure 3.2: Inclusivity in the context of assumptions

The question of how individual voice can be unleased becomes critical. Taking away the constraints that prevent individuals from sharing their views verbally or through action, allowing the leader to remember their own unique essence and ensuring conditions for voices to be unleased in an inclusive, conducive manner.

The ability of leadership to deal with differences, adversity and complexity and to build inclusivity in the turbulent times during transformation or ambiguity are critical for organisational and societal sustainability in the future. Leadership must create a culture of inclusivity in their organisations to ensure that the human energy in the system to perform is unleashed, and available to wire around organisational doing and being – unleashing human energy to perform.

Inclusivity is hard

Inclusivity is underpinned by the following paradoxes:

- To achieve voice, the voices of others must be heard.
- To lead the empowered, the empowered must be allowed to lead.
- The creation of inclusivity means that leadership must voice less, yet not lose its own voice.
- It is simultaneously more difficult, and yet easier, to become real (or conscious).
- Power must be delegated to gain power.

Paradoxically, inclusivity is easy too. It is what we all aspire to – where we are heard, understood, respected; where we have a voice, and our voice is heard. We innately know the human way and understand the dance between doing and being on a cellular level. Consciousness is creating on a DNA level, where knowing arises from this dance. Just as dancing – we go shuffle. Sometimes rhythmically and other times more haphazardly. The African saying "as the music changes, so does the dance". If we move forward, together, even if our styles are different, there is progress. Soul comes when we enjoy the dance. It is contagious.

Inclusivity has unintended implications. A theme of exclusion may evolve. Groups that can be described as inclusive sometimes form such strong identities that, by the very nature of their identity they become exclusive. Non- performance, non-adherence to values and principles and unethical behaviour are then not acceptable to the total system and are, therefore, excluded.

3.3 Nature of ODC

Natural design principles

Natural design principles as initially explained by Orr[41] apply psychological and biological insights to social systems and consider concepts such as the internal feeling, motivation, adaptation and development of a system, rather than reductionist explanations of how we can take things apart. Principles to consider are:

- One-size-fit-all solutions are never helpful
- A natural design process that searches for the DNA-like archetypes in the core of the social system is critical
- The unique nature of the rhythms and interconnections that flow through it should be described
- An awareness of the energy flow is critical

- One must be able to understand how the total entity responds and what the needs are for shifts

It is important to early detect the ebb and flow of the social system, the unique patterns within the dispersal of information and the energy that is unique to diverse functions and sub-functions. Leaders should be able to detect the deepest questions of existence and motivations in their systems and wire it together around a task at hand.

Complex adaptive systems

Freeman[42] warns that leaders in systems are conditioned by the prevailing culture. Organisations are often to have a mechanistic manner and humans in them are reduced to objects with which are engaged with from the outside in. This view restrained us from truly embracing the implications of organisations as living systems with ecological properties.[43] The adaptation of a frame that organisations have the properties of intelligent Complex Adaptive System, are helpful. Through the conscious seeking of its intelligence, its complexity and its adaptability, the nature of the organisation can be acknowledged and made known.

A myriad of intricacies present itself when looking into what is considered this nature. The ever moving, seemingly isolated and fragmented series of events, activities and entities collectively adjust to changing life conditions. Without considering the following complications, the nature of the ecology can be misunderstood – with dire consequences:

- Those seeing and understanding the system
- Additional information that they are seeing and attempting to understand as well as the insights gained in the process of interpretation and understanding, and
- In the judgement, which results in the choice of action
- The organisation in the mind of its members, as well as
- How the system connects across boundaries and how that effect the parts and the collective

Maybe the premises is that ignorance is bliss, can also be helpful. But arguably with a negative implication on sustainability and adaptation. Freeman[44] holds the view that complexity is not the problem – but what is unknown and is found in people who exist in the system. These are people whose actions, thoughts and perceptions are influenced by their worldview, personality types, context, emotional state, value statements, spiral dynamics codes/or value systems, the place they occupy in the intelligent system and many other possibilities discern an individual at one point in time.[45]

Integral and not polarised

Different archetypes of value systems that create diversity of thought and different ways of organising were identified by Graves[46] and Beck[47]. Different questions of existence are considered by mature functional adults. Eight archetypes of value systems that oscillate between individualism and collectivism are identified can be categorised by a colour code as allocated by Beck and Cowan.[48]

- **BEIGE:** How can I survive?
- **PURPLE:** How can we sacrifice for the tribe and traditions?
- **RED:**   How can I get power – away from the tribe?
- **BLUE:**   How can we sacrifice for the future?
- **ORANGE:** How can I achieve success?
- **GREEN:** How can we sacrifice for the planet and humanity?

A big realisation sometimes happens – what if none of these value systems (also called codes or worldviews) work to solve our problems? A new way of making sense of the world may be needed – one where all the different worldviews can be wired in a way that makes sense for their own reasons of existence, while the collective conditions are also considered. ODC practitioners that understand how people and systems adjust to changing life conditions can consult and intervene a bit more purposively and functionally. The following pre-occupations then arise:

- **YELLOW:** How can both you and I survive? And become more functional? How can we be in flow? And flexible?
- **TURQUOISE:** How can we create a tribe for humanity that is truly integral and pluralistic?

An overall superordinate goal that can be described as a YELLOW goal can integrally tie all the value systems in a social system together so that polarisation is minimised. This integral way of considering adult development is sometimes referred as spiral dynamics. The colour codes are used throughout the book to refer to the bio-psycho-socio way in which different people make sense of reality.

Non-linear and radical

In the book, *Organisational Change and Development*[49] change models were compared on organisational and systemic level with change models on individual levels. The purpose here is not to do a literature review of how the field developed, but where we land today with insights about radical transformation on all domains. Radical change is archetypal in its very nature. The individual or the organisation embarks on a hero(ine) journey into the dark unknown, to resurface in a way that is more mature, integrated or functional.

Behavioural change is always radical

As profound transformations are reshaping systems at every level, behavioural change is required. Behavioural change always results in emotional reactions. The following change curve describes the process on all domains quite well and integrates human reactions to change too.

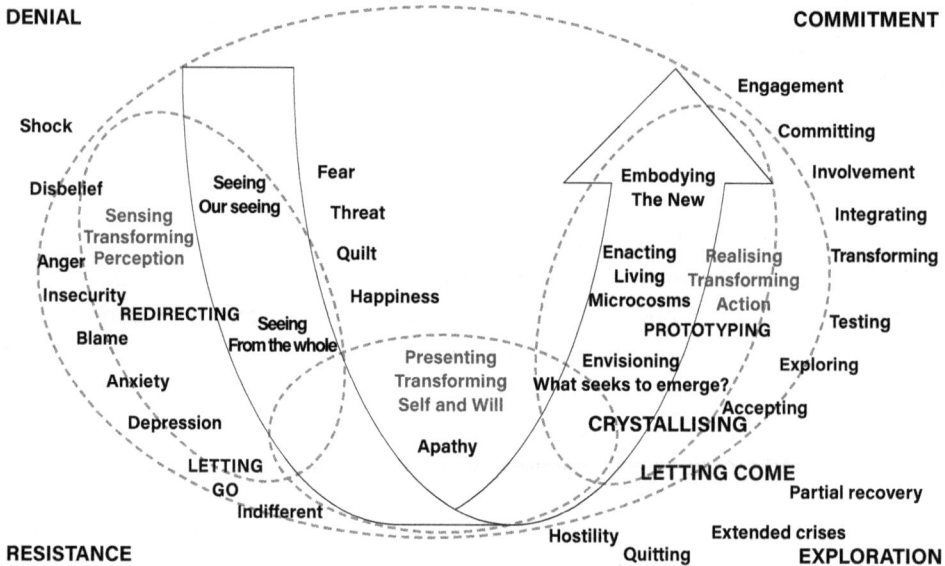

DENIAL   COMMITMENT

Shock   Engagement
                                                                       Committing
Disbelief   Seeing   Fear   Embodying   Involvement
        Sensing   Our seeing   Threat   The New   Integrating
        Transforming
Anger   Perception   Quilt   Enacting Realising Transforming
Insecurity   Happiness   Living   Transforming
        REDIRECTING Seeing   Microcosms Action   Testing
Blame   From the whole   PROTOTYPING
        Anxiety   Presenting   Envisioning   Exploring
                                   Transforming   What seeks to emerge?
        Depression   Self and Will   Accepting
                                   Apathy   CRYSTALLISING
        LETTING   LETTING COME
        GO   Partial recovery
        Indifferent   Extended crises
                                   Hostility
RESISTANCE   Quitting   EXPLORATION

Figure 3.3: Human reactions to change. Adapted from Viljoen[50]

The reflection of stated in the autoethnographic note above has a similar insight.

Beck and Cowan[51] and Beck, et al.[52] described five change states namely alpha, beta, gamma, delta, new alpha. The Change State Indicator (CSI)[iv] describe how an individual's energy is dispersed around these five states.

---

iv   Based on the work of Beck (1994) and distributed by Mandala Consulting

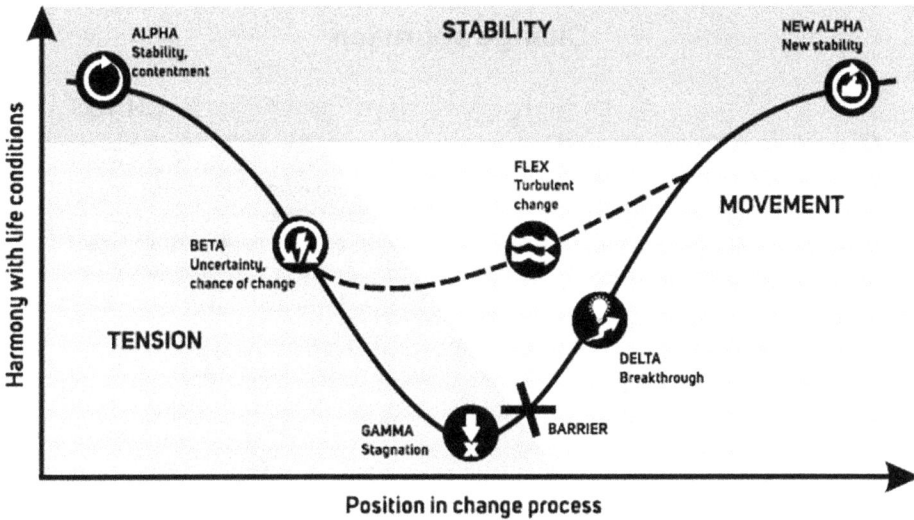

Figure 3.4: Change State Indicator adapted from Beck, et al.[53]

The vertical axis indicates the extent to which a person is in harmony with his or her life conditions; the higher the score in the top indicators (alpha and new alpha), the more a person perceives his or her life conditions as harmonious. Higher scores in the bottom indicators are a sign of friction concerning current conditions. The horizontal axis shows the flow of a change process. Major changes often go through this entire dynamic process, showed by the blue lines, from harmony to friction and back to harmony.

A good metaphor might be flying through a complex weather system. There are safe passages with clear, stable conditions (Alpha). However, there can also be turbulence (Beta) and even wind shears (Gamma). At the transitional areas are tipping points (Delta) that can either cause us to turn back or move on to clear skies once again (New Alpha).

The "Prefers Order" and "Thrives on Chaos" scales indicate where the person sees their personal pendulum to be. It's also important to recognise that the human behaviour itself is essentially an open system. The ability to deal with change within us ebb and flow, brighten and dim as conditions - both internal and external -change. Thus, the world-in-motion and the brain-in-motion are constantly moving through stages, in and out of steady states (Alpha and New Alpha) through transitional phases (Beta, Gamma, Delta).

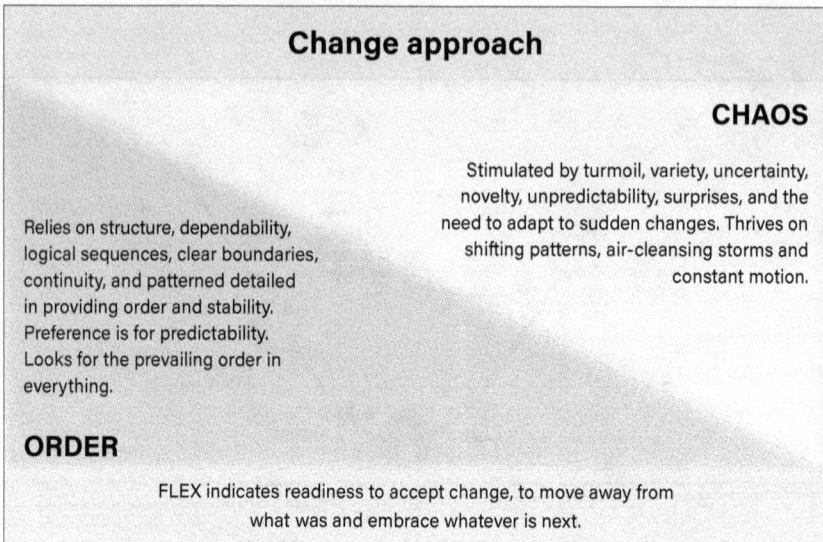

Change approach	
	CHAOS
Relies on structure, dependability, logical sequences, clear boundaries, continuity, and patterned detailed in providing order and stability. Preference is for predictability. Looks for the prevailing order in everything.	Stimulated by turmoil, variety, uncertainty, novelty, unpredictability, surprises, and the need to adapt to sudden changes. Thrives on shifting patterns, air-cleansing storms and constant motion.
ORDER	
FLEX indicates readiness to accept change, to move away from what was and embrace whatever is next.	

Figure 3.5: Chance Approach. Adapted from Viljoen[54]

The "Flex" scale indicates the relative ease with which these changes occur. For some people, shifts are rather easy. For others, they are crisis points that consume vast energy.

Two very different approaches to change are described namely a PREFERENCE FOR CHANGE versus a THRIVING ON CHAOS. In table 3.6 below, these two approaches are described. The CSI also gives an indication of the individual, the groups, the organisational or the societal change paradigm. Two change paradigms are identified, which can be described by to themes namely: MORE OF THE SAME or REFRAMING.

Table 3.6: Change Paradigm adopted from Viljoen[55]

Change paradigm	
First order change	Second order change
Change occurs within a system which, itself, remains unchanged. ▪ Restore balance. ▪ Improve within givens. ▪ Rooted in past decisions. ▪ Renew, Refurbish, Reform. ▪ Work harder and Smarter.	Mega-systems shift to new paradigms, new assumptions and new consolations. ▪ Generated by outside events/influences. ▪ Driven by perceived future. ▪ Puzzling, Unexpected, Paradoxical. ▪ New wine; new wineskins.
Basic theme: MORE OF THE SAME	Basic theme: REFRAMING

A systemic interplay of ways to adjust and sensemaking, questions of existence and coping mechanisms are available to different individuals to deal with the multiple combinations external and internal challenges posed to the individual, the group, the organisation or the society, will lead to the CHANGE OPTION that emerges. This change option can be described either as evolutionary or revolutionary. These options are described in table 3.7 below.

Table 3.7: Change Options Adapted from Viljoen[56]

Change options	
Evolutionary option	**Revolutionary option**
Previous problems solved	Demands fundamental change in structures/systems
Potential in the brain	Unrelenting "All or Nothing" assault on barriers/obstacles
Access to new systems	Defends actions by finding noble purpose for "the cause"
New models and patterns	Prototyping the new
Available resources	New realities emerging
Consolidation and support	Insitutionalising

3.4 Final Thoughts

*And once the storm is over, you won't remember how you made
it through, how you managed to survive. You won't even be
sure, whether the storm is really over. But one thing is certain.
When you come out of the storm, you won't be the same
person who walked in. That's what this storm's all about.*

Haruki Murakami

ODC results in transformational processes that introduce all the typical emotions that are characteristic of a radical change effort. This could be a challenging process, especially in the initial phase during which the decision-making is translated throughout the organisation, and all voices are invited. Leadership should be willing to sit and listen carefully to conflicting and even negative voices, guarding against keeping grouches, victimising or becoming negative towards the individual. This 'storming' phase of change should be viewed as a normal phase for successful transformation. Often here, leaders get scared and incorrectly identify resistance to a proof that the proposed strategy does not work – often with devastating effects on those that are early adopters and what to make things more functional. Through all the phases of change, ODC practitioners can make the process more aware – and through the interweaving of science, art and craft; shorten the process of adaptation.

Chapter 4

The Inclusivity Process of ODC

---

*Never do anything by halves if you want to get away with
it. Be outrageous. Go the whole hog. Make sure everything
you do is so completely crazy it's unbelievable.'*

said Matilda.

'You'll never get anywhere if you go about what-iffing like that.'

– added Charlie (and the Great Glass Elevator).

Somewhere inside all of us is the power to change the world.

4.1 The Domains of ODC and What it Enables

ODC simultaneously considers, diagnose, plan for and delivers on the Individual and collective domains. The collective domain can be divided into the group/team domain, the organisational domain and the contextual domain. The contextual domain has a component that considers the national culture of the society and the country in which the organisation operates. Further industry dynamics play a role here.

Ultimately, through DOING (strategy and task functions such as team mechanics sessions) and BEING (values and behavioural functions such as team dynamics), leaders in OD and change and other leaders (formal and informal) must wire the human energy around the DOING and through the BEING to unleash human energy to perform. This energy can cause engagement and commitment with the corresponding positive result in business indicators. It also can cause apathy where there is not enough human energy in the system to sustain and **entropy** will kick in. Human energy that is disconnected results reflects in negative performance as mirrored by business indicators.

On considering a change on an individual level, it is important to consider how individuals adjust to change. This domain results in individual presence. Groups must also continuously adjust to changes. Here, emotional containment is provided. As organisations collectively make conscious adjustments and changes to changing conditions in the political, socio-economic, technological, environmental, national and international factors and dynamics; and organisational gestalt is forming.

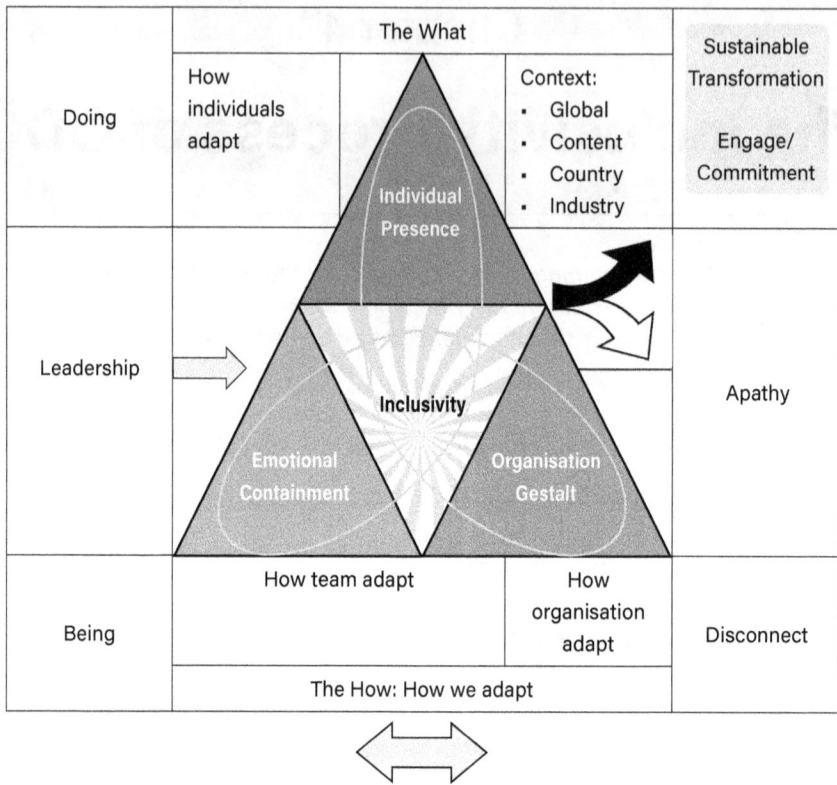

Figure 4.1: Inclusivity through leadership Doing and Being. Adapted from Viljoen[57]

Each of these domains are described below. Human adaptation is layered and complex and is influenced by forces above and below the level of the conscious mind to move through these adjustments or radical interruptions and even traumatic events. ODC consultants play a significant role in all these domains through embodying their leadership role on the stage of the psychodrama of organisational life.

Enabling individual presence

The adaptive ability of the individual in the diverse new world of work plays a critical role. A combination of perceptions about the self, the group and the organisation, together with the capabilities of the individual, will determine whether the outcome is positive or negative. This will lead to either engagement or disengagement. The key role of ODC practitioners in the years to come will be to construct organisational cultures that are conducive to diverse thinking systems. Inclusivity strategies should be implemented proactively to ensure engagement at individual, group and organisational level.

Individual presence is influenced by self-view and the individual's appraisals of the others with whom he/she interacts. Therefore, interaction between individual group members will take place smoothly as long as there is a mutual understanding of differences. This interpersonal understanding has its origin in the need for certainty, coherence and predictability. In facilitating the harmonious interaction between individuals between whom there are considerable differences, congruence will liberate diverse members and enable them to contribute fully to their group. As a result, interpersonal congruence becomes a mechanism through which groups can leverage fully in terms of diversity.

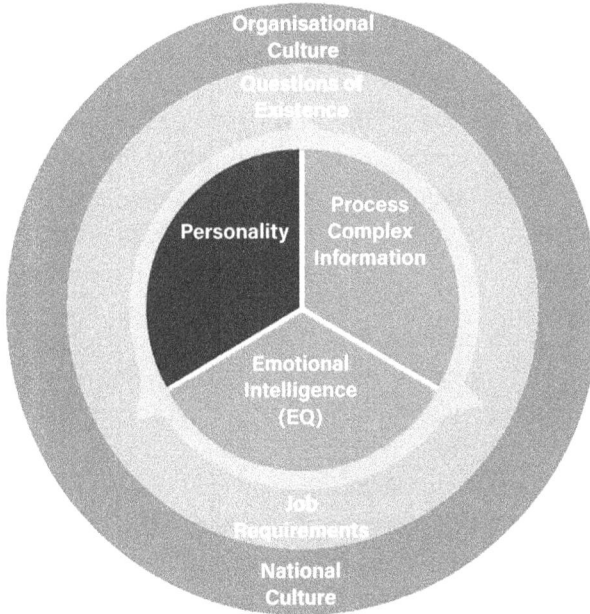

Figure 4.2: Interplay of psychological constructs to create congruence – Adapted from Viljoen58

An interplay of personality (MBTI), complexity handling ability (CPA), emotional intelligence (BarOn EQi) and the individual's question of existence (CSI and IVMap) and the congruence thereof with the role, the company, the culture and the national culture determine the ego strength of which the individual can present themselves in the workplace. This, together with the human energy in the system (BeQ) described in paragraph 4.2 the I-engage, determines the proclivity of an individual having functional presence – having a voice.

Leadership development through ODC and other interventions is critical as In *"Reinventing Organizations"*, Laloux[59] writes that *"[a]n organization cannot evolve beyond its leadership's stage of [consciousness]."* Collective leadership development across functional boundaries through ODC interventions becomes an important aspect for D-band and higher /N-3 and higher in organisations.

Providing emotional containment

> *The question is not how you can make better rules, but how you*
> *can support teams in finding the best solution. How can you*
> *strengthen the possibilities of the team members so that they*
> *need the least amount of direction-setting from above?*

Jos de Blok

Cohesion is seen to help create the strong teams that are needed to move organisations forward. However, over time, flexibility is needed to adapt to changes. This flexibility could, in fact, arise from a diverse work group force of which the unique backgrounds and perceptions are valued rather than suppressed or silenced. Leaders must encourage minority group members to be true to their own backgrounds and heritages. It is their very uniqueness that provides organisational benefits. Leadership is thus presented with a paradox – how to ensure that individual voices are heard whilst simultaneously facilitating a sense of consensus and alignment amongst diverse team members, as emotional containment must be provided. In the next chapter, more detail will follow on how to decode this complexity of diversity.

Group dynamics can be optimised by team development interventions, psycho-analytical events such as Tavistock events that focus on understanding unconscious group processes and defence mechanisms. It is important to take the phase of group formation and maturity into account, and not to underestimate the political gamesmanship and pecking order challenges that unconscious group dynamics present to the individual group members. The purpose of a group is to be synergetic. One plus one must equal three. Often, employees are stronger on their own and there is process loss when operating in teams. ODC practitioners should be able to consult to group dynamics as it manifests in the here and the now, in the daily life in the organisational ecosystem.

Creating an organisational gestalt of inclusivity

The concept of inclusivity is far more comprehensive and more systemic as is currently the case with the definition of inclusivity as presented in literature. The author considers the concept in terms of a radical 'organisational transformational methodology' in terms of which both the doing and the being are aligned to ensure inclusion, significance and agreement. Organisational strategy should be underpinned by inclusive organisational policies and procedures and a structure congruent with organisational intent.

ODC practitioners should adapt the resource perspective on an integral performance management way as their unique contribution to business and work towards an organisational gestalt that is conducive to inclusivity. Here, both strategic alignment and value congruence should be considered – with the question of how to assist through the individual development process. Only in such a behavioural framework can organisational behaviour be optimised. An organisational gestalt of inclusivity, that antonyms congruence with the societal gestalt, is a non-negotiable for sustainable organisational adaptation.

Inclusivity unleashes conducive human energy in a system that can then be used for the executing of organisational strategy. It gives life to people that inhibits organisational systems. Leaders wire this energy around organisational tasks in a way that aligns with the values of the organisation.

Emotions may also be described as forms of energy, says Jane Middelton-Moz (2). According to scientific laws, energy has three positions as positive, neutral or negative. Einstein taught us that it is not possible to destroy energy, although friction may cause energy to decrease – the principle of entropy. Energy may, however, be transformed from one form to another. Leaders in organisations should wire the human energy around organisational strategies to achieve sustainable business results. Energy has a virtuous nature or a vicious nature – to very different archetypes with corresponding implications on business results.

The various systemic energy archetypes can be clustered into four categories namely engaged, involved, apathetic and disconnected. Each archetype has unique dynamics that are visible in the day-to-day operation in the organisational ecology.

In a culture of inclusivity, the energy in the system is perceived as conducive. This category is called **engaged**. Everybody is involved and shares his or her singular viewpoint; non-performance is not tolerated, and everyone assumes personal authority. There are high levels of support, trust and respect. Leadership tends to be humane and vulnerable, as mistakes may be shared and speedily resolved. The energy in the system is in a virtuous cycle, and all the emotions mentioned in this context once again reinforce the culture of inclusivity. In an engaged system, employees do not act elegantly. In the differences between ideas and voices, tension is created that manifests in creativity, innovation and growth. When irritation creeps into the human energy in the system declines, but is still virtuous. Now the narratives in the organisation are characterised by frustration, gossip and complaints – but individuals still want to be there. This category is called **involved.**

In a system in which the energy to perform is negative, a vicious cycle will be formed. People will not feel that they are trusted, supported and respected. Therefore, individual defence mechanisms will come into play and group dynamics will become destructive. Employees cannot be present in the here and the now and do not take up personal authority. In-fighting will take place, people will withdraw, and power play and political gamesmanship will be commonplace. It will not be possible to share personal emotions without penalties being exacted, and nobody will admit to mistakes to protect themselves. People will tend to blame others for whatever goes wrong. Such a system can be described as **disengaged.**

If a system is neutral, the system will be indifferent or **apathetic** – either do not care anymore, could not care less or have tried too often with no reaction to implement change. Voices are not brought to the organisational table, and people do just enough to survive. In such a system, there is not enough energy to perform the task at hand. The strategy plan of year one stay unexecuted and is still on the agenda to be implemented the next year. According to principles of entropy, such a system will deteriorate significantly without intervention.

Jung[60] (4) reminded us that a person might fight either the internal or the external world at anyone time, but not both worlds simultaneously. Thus, if a person focuses internally to cope with that, the external work will be neglected. This will manifest in lower levels of customer service and deterioration in the quality of work. Leaders should do everything possible to shorten the period during which an individual spends energy on self-preservation or adaptation. Focussing on enhancement of emotional resilience, improving reality testing and influencing current mental models may accelerate this individual change process.

4.2 Prerequisites of Human Energy to Perform

The prerequisites of human energy to perform can be described as a synthesis of the following constructs:

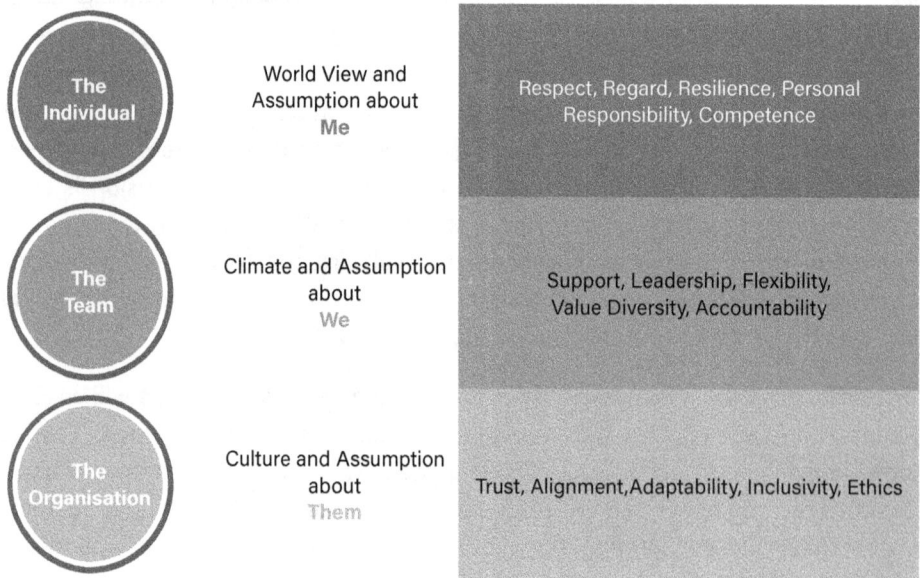

The Individual	World View and Assumption about Me	Respect, Regard, Resilience, Personal Responsibility, Competence
The Team	Climate and Assumption about We	Support, Leadership, Flexibility, Value Diversity, Accountability
The Organisation	Culture and Assumption about Them	Trust, Alignment, Adaptability, Inclusivity, Ethics

Figure 4.3: Prerequisites of Human Energy to Perform

Individual domain

- *Respect* refers to an assumption or indication of good faith and value
- towards another person.
- *Resilience* refers to the adaptive capability that individuals must continue disregarding difficulty in doing the task at hand.
- *Regard* refers to having a positive self-view and self-awareness. It further refers to both the perceived weak and strong points of an individual and how he or she deals with it.
- *Corporate citizenship behaviour* refers to the willingness of individuals to do more than what is expected of them, in other words, goodwill towards the organisation.
- *In Flow* refers to the degree to which the individual's potential is matched with the complexity and challenge at hand.

Emotional intelligence development, OD interventions such as Personal Purpose, Self Mastery, Authentic Leadership interventions, coaching, and alternative modalities workshops can enhance this domain. Leadership profiling instruments such as the Bar-On EQi and the Hogan suite of assessments. Can support participants in understanding their dynamics in this domain well. Schein's[61] career anchors also contribute to better understanding.

Chapters 7 and 8 deal with this domain.

Group/team domain

- *Support* refers to the extent that individuals feel encouraged, cared for
- and assisted by others.
- *Teamwork* refers to the functionality of the team dynamics resulting in synergy.
- *Diversity* refers to the degree to which diversity of thought, race, gender, age, language and nationalities are valued.
- *Accountability* refers to the degree to which an individual is held responsible for his or her contribution and behaviour by their team.
- *Supervision* refers to the direct line leadership capability that is needed by managers to effectively manage and lead employees. It also specifically applies to the depth of leadership at the supervisory level, as effectiveness at this level has a direct impact on the achievement of organisational goals.

Team establishment sessions can unleash positive group outcomes. Team mechanics workshops refer to how roles work, how group make decisions and focus on the WHAT of a team. Team dynamics workshops deal with the patterns in a group – the dynamics and HOW the team works together. Personality type assessments like the MBTI and Belbin team roles can help significantly to understand differences in teams. Organisational storytelling works well in this domain – especially to translate strategy through the organisation. Appreciative Inquiry is an invaluable methodology to apply here – finding what is right in a situation, rather than what is not that functional.

Chapters 9 and 10 speak to how unconscious dynamics in groups can be made conscious to increase functionality.

Organisational domain

- *Trust* refers to the degree to which the intent of others is believed to be authentic and pure.
- *Ethics* refers to the sense of the individual that the right things are done in the organisation.
- *Alignment* refers to the degree to which teams have shared understanding 75 of the values of the organisation and the strategy of the organisation.
- *Inclusivity* refers to the degree to which individuals feel that they are being made part of the organisation. The practice of co-creating plans and strategies is utilised.
- *Sustainability* refers to the ability of the organisation and individuals to adapt to changes in external life conditions and respond congruently internally.

In the organisational domain, strategic vision, mission and values can be derived and translated through the system in natural team and tetra functional domains. It can be wired into performance indicators and individual development plans. The Benchmark of Engagement provides invaluable insights into pre- and post-diagnostics and what leadership collectively can focus on. The Benchmark of Engagement, described in chapter (Chapter 12), was designed to measure constructs with high consistency and reliability in multicultural settings and is diagnostic. It provides a plan for ODC practitioners to identify where to intervene and how to ensure that human energy is unleashed; in a systemic manner that can describe shifts in the underlying assumptions in an organisation that describes organisational culture. Skills like dialoguing serve leaders well. Other techniques like world café methodology bring groups of people together and linger in the minds of participants in a sense of co-creation and inclusion.

Often, ODC practitioners ensure that the organisational structure is designed in a way that ensures optimal functioning in embodying identity, adaptation to positionality and conscious intersectionality in systems.

Clouds form and then go away because atmospheric conditions, temperatures, and humidity cause molecules of water to either condense or vaporise. Organisations should be the same; structures need to appear and disappear based on the forces that are acting in the organisation. When people are free to act, they're able to sense those forces and act in ways that fit best with reality.

From Laloux,[62]

It is important to ensure that the organisational array follows operating model principles that ensure that the identity of the system is protected, yet the structure allows for the agile adaptation to life conditions through the organisation's vision, mission, values and governance.

In Chapter 11, organisational applications of ODC are discussed.

Societal contextual domain

The external social environmental dynamics are best described by Spiral Dynamics. Although, Hofstede[63], Trompenaars[64] and the Globe studies[v] can also inform the context effectively, from an ODC angle, the adaptation of the colourful application of Spiral Dynamic insights, may normalise different, often opposing worldviews and describe the dynamics of a social system on a simplistic yet accurate manner. It is important to note that the above prerequisites describe constructs that are important to unleash human potential to perform across the boundaries of nationalities – and are therefore universal to humanity. Although the structure of different nationalities and tribes organisations and industries can be compared; the meaning that is assigned to these constructs by diverse stakeholders is different and unique.

Cultures, as well as countries, are formed by the emergence of value systems in response to life conditions. Complex adaptive intelligences form the glue that bonds a group together, defines who they are as people and reflects the place on the planet they inhibit. While they are all legitimate expressions of the human experience, they are not "equal" in their capacities to deal with complex problems in society.

As Graves[65] has stated, the question to ask is not how to motivate people, but instead, how you relate what you are doing to their natural motivational flow. In this chapter, the nature of natural design was discussed as a key component of understanding the complex dynamics of social, emerging systems. Different methods and tools of natural designs have been discussed. The leadership equation of Beck[66] should be asked, namely:

---

v   Globe Studies: A unique large-scale study of cultural practices, leadership ideals, and generalized and interpersonal trust in 150 countries in collaboration with nearly 500 researchers. A unique large-scale study of cultural practices, leadership ideals, and generalized and interpersonal trust in 150 countries in collaboration with nearly 500 researchers. Alipour, A. (2019).

HOW should *Who* lead **WHOM** to do **What** for **WHICH** people living **WHERE** and Why?

The Integral Values Map (IvMap) and Change State indicator support largely with describing multicultural dynamics and social systems. By understanding the ontological and epistemological stance of members in stakeholder groups, adaptation can be considered in a conscious manner. Diversity and Inclusion work gets a depth that is undeniable. These instruments can add real value to the individual and all collective domains and provide a psychological exchange rate to enable diverse groups to hear each other without judgement.

Chapter 12 describes a case where understanding the societal dynamics was critical. Although the organisational case presented had a focus on employees, the impact on the society was undeniable.

The human energy to perform must be optimised on individual, group/team, organisational and societal domain to result in organisational growth and sustainability. ODC is the field of study that focuses on enhancing these dynamics on the various domains.

4.3 The Benefits of ODC

The The Benefits of ODC are far-reaching as seen in the figure below. By adopting a complex systems psychodynamic lens to the different domains in which the ODC expert consults to, an assortment of organisational treasures is materialised.

4.4 The Non-Negotiables for ODC Processes

The following might be classified as prerequisites for sustainable ODC interventions:

- Strong, committed top leadership
- Co-creation of strategies and action plans
- Translation of both the doing and the being
- Individual accountability through clearly contracted performance measures linked to strategy and rigorous performance management
- Building the emotional intelligence of leadership (leadership development)
- Allowing and encouraging diversity of thought
- The realisation that inclusivity is a radical organisational transformational process
- Functional and Ethical behaviour on the part of leaders

- Whole system approach
- Interventions in individual, group, organisational and contextual domains AT THE SAME TIME

Individual domain:	Personal growth, enhanced EQ, personal effectiveness
	Higher levels of consciousness
	Allowing of differences
	Hope, pride
Group domain:	Enhanced group dynamics
	Less unconscious group dynamics
	Innovation, creativity
Organisational domain:	Trust, conducive climate and growth
	Sense of belonging, commitment
	Retention of talent
Societal context:	Community building
	Localisation of skill
	Reputable employer

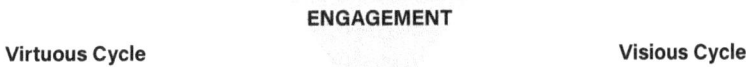

ENGAGEMENT

Virtuous Cycle   **Visious Cycle**

Correlates directly to:	
+	-
Unleashing voice	Disengage
Productivity	Absenteeism
Staff retention	Staff turnover
Employee satisfaction	Apathy
Innovation	Stagnation
Value based behaviour	Negligent behaviour
Customer experience	Poor service delivery
Flexibility	Rigidity

Figure 4.4: How Engagement Results in Business Indicators, adapted from Viljoen[67]

Specific, focused organisational development methodologies and techniques may build adaptive intelligence, change resilience and inclusivity. The contents of an organisational development intervention are not as important as the way in which the intervention is implemented and facilitated. To create inclusivity, leaders may use methods such as world-café methodology, storytelling, appreciative inquiry and dialoguing to allow for involvement, to stimulate participation and to create ownership. These methods are elaborated on later in chapter 9.

4.5 ODC Practitioners as Leaders

One leads, one must follow

Lau Tzu

The Ghanaians reminds us that the person with the sickle cannot see that they do not walk straight. ODC practitioners often provide spaces for this reflection. Jung reminds us that as within so without; and that archetypes help us understand us to deal with this bipolarity. ODC practitioners also need to reflect.[68]

The ability of leadership to deal with differences, adversity and complexity and to build inclusivity in the turbulent times during transformation or ambiguity are critical for organisational and societal sustainability in the future. Leadership must create a culture of inclusivity in their organisations to ensure that the human energy in the system to perform is unleashed, and available to wire around organisational doing and being. This interaction between hard stuff and soft stuff leads to KNOWING or consciousness. That again, results in change.

ODC practitioners assist organisational leaders in the below areas. Quantum physics explains that the observed change the outcome of the reality that manifest. This fact of science ontologically implies that ODC practitioners – disregarding claims of the opposite – impact reality. With the right intent, and because of the strategic positioning thereof, it is logical to derive that in fact an ODC partitioner is a leader.

In this book, when specifically referred to organisational managers with performance measures and official mandate, the term leadership is used.

Leaders provide strategic vision

Your vision will become clear only when you can look into your own heart. Who looks outside, dreams; he who looks inside, awakes.

Jung[69]

A well-articulated vision mobilised employees around the organisational long-term goals, provides boundary conditions that reduce uncertainty and aligns decision making. It provides clarity and focus. Further, a compelling vision not only inspires stakeholders (employees are a stakeholder too), but it also creates belonging and a shared purpose that enhances engagement and ultimately performance. A clearly defined strategic framework that includes the vision, values and mission of an organisation together with a catchy tagline, provides clear direction and helps to differentiate the organisation in the market as it reminds the ecology of the identity thereof. ODC practitioners play an integral part in ensuring that there are shared strategic vision through the facilitation of processes, the consultation to the future requirements of leadership and from the organisation and the actual support in constructing the architecture of the firm.

Through ODC processes, leaders can create a personal vision. When personal values align with organisational values, goodwill and corporate citizenship are unleashed. Human energy to perform is created that can be directed towards initiatives that drive growth. Vision quests can help leaders in organisations to find meaning in life and sustain their energy to perform.

Leaders have courage

There will never again be a time when we will not be 'Collapse-ABLE'.

A little.

Or a lot.

According not to how courageously we meet the challenges ahead, but how deeply we embrace the practices of community, agency, partnership, and equanimity.

Anon

Leadership must display courage. Courage is needed to allow different voices and reap benefits of diversity of thought. In the next chapter, the argument will be made that this aspect, namely the strength and courage of leadership to continue with the transformational process, may just be the leveraging point to future organisational sustainability. Organisational development initiatives lead to emotional intelligence development. Not only can organisational development initiatives lead to reported personal growth that manifests itself, but it also impact on other relationships outside the organisation.

It is courageous to speak from the self, and to not be swayed by political gamesmanship. ODC processes help to become authentic.

Leaders are functional

This strategy creates a need for strong leadership, as there could be a significant degree of *angst* and insecurity within the system and a business case for training and coaching to ensure that the change initiative is successful. The method focuses on ethical and principle-based behaviour, which could possibly lead to unhappiness, and even resignations of employees who have different work ethics or values. The feeling of vulnerability that this might create could influence the initial commitment of top leadership to the change initiative. Self-awareness is a critical emotion to be allowed and valued. Furthermore, the process will create a sense of personal responsibility and accountability. No hiding spaces exist anymore for non- performance or organisational saboteurs. Official forums are used for exactly the purpose they were formed for initially. Gossip declines. Inclusivity rewires the dynamic in an organisation to be functional.

Spiral dynamics indicate a thinking structure that can be described as functional, flexible and in flow – namely second tier leadership. In this system, radical openness, lack of ego, and the taking back of projections that one place on others becomes integral and indeed functional. Viljoen[70] stated that organisations must design strategy from YELLOW[vi] they would like to become functional and agile. This inclusive way weaves together the questions of existence of diverse groups in the organisation into a superordinate goal that incorporates individual and collective systems and unleashes wisdom.

Leaders are alchemists

The old alchemists made gold from primary material. By a complex oscillating way of applying heat and cold in a chemical process the belief was that gold can be derived. At the same time the alchemist follows this process, his psyche is transformed into a substance that was not in existence before – human gold or consciousness. Inner healing can take place. As base metals are transmuted into precious material through this ancient art, an inspirational metaphor for leadership is offered. A parallel can be drawn between an alchemist's ability to identify "talent" in every substance and the ability of leaders to see possibility in the latent potential in individuals and organisations. In this way organisational soul can be (re)surfaced.

Leaders inspire change by modelling behaviour that channels wisdom and ignites inspiration. Established norms must be broken down to uncover hidden possibilities – very much a mining or alchemical process in the underworld (the unconscious of the individual or the organisation). Through fostering a culture of inclusivity, creating trust and a learning space with a focus on growth, teams and the individuals in them reimagine what is possible and transform adversity into opportunity with "precious" outcomes.

The unlocking of unseen potential and the elevation of potential forms an integral part of the function of leaders. Each base material, as does each team member, contains seeds of greatness. Through doing (vision), being (care and compassion) and leading (strategic guidance), the seeds of potential are transformed into thriving talents. It is the role of the leader to magnify the interest and aspirations of their followers with a corresponding dynamic synergy that propels the organisation forward.

---

vi   Spiral Dynamics value systems described by colours are described in paragraph 3.3.

Leaders that are alchemists realise that transformation is not instantaneous. They have an innate knowing that the process is gradual and sometimes tumultuous and that it demands perseverance, will create resistance and objection – but they embrace the uncertainty as part of the process. They continue to redefine challenges as opportunity for growth. Setbacks are framed as the necessary solvent that dissolves old limitation and in the worlds of Senge[71] wet the stage for breakthroughs that enrich not only their own lives but also those of their teams. Every obstacle has potential as a for innovation or improvement. The mundane is transformed through leaders into the extraordinary.

4.6 Final Thoughts

The inclusivity process of ODC is a critical enabler of sustainable organisational performance. By aligning individual, group, organisational, and societal/contextual domains, ODC fosters a culture of engagement, trust, and shared purpose. The interplay of doing and being within organisations determines the energy flow that either drives success or leads to entropy. Leaders play a pivotal role in shaping this dynamic by creating spaces for diverse voices, ensuring alignment between values and strategy, and fostering an environment of accountability and inclusivity.

The systemic nature of ODC requires a multifaceted approach that integrates leadership development, emotional intelligence, and adaptive intelligence. It is not a predefined module or a singular intervention but a transformational methodology that shapes the identity and resilience of an organisation. The ability to navigate complexity, embrace diversity, and sustain high-performance cultures is essential for long-term success of organisations.

Ultimately, ODC practitioners serve as both strategists and catalysts for change, guiding organisations toward a future where inclusivity is not just an aspiration, but a lived reality. By harnessing human energy effectively, organisations can achieve alignment, engagement, and innovation, ensuring they remain agile and competitive in an evolving world. ODC practitioners thus act as catalysts and alchemists in organisational development and change.

Chapter 5

The C in ODC - change

5.1 Introduction

Organisational transformation is an intricate journey marked by resistance, adaptation, and renewal. Change is not merely a procedural shift but a systemic recalibration, influencing leadership, culture, and performance at every level. This chapter delves into the Organisational Development and Change (ODC) process, unfolding its phased evolution and the psychological, structural, and strategic dimensions that define its success.

Drawing from models of transformation, including alchemy, Spiral Dynamics, and systemic change theory, we explore how organisations navigate disruption, rewire behaviours, and cement inclusive, adaptive cultures. The interplay between leadership capacity, strategic alignment, and employee engagement emerges as a critical theme, highlighting the need for intentional, sustained interventions to embed new ways of thinking and working.

As resistance gives way to empowerment and innovation, a transformed organisation does not simply adjust to change – it embraces and internalises it as a continuous state. This chapter provides a roadmap for achieving such an evolution, offering insights into the dynamics, dilemmas, and systemic shifts that underpin large-scale transformation.

5.2 Phases of a Typical ODC Process

In practice, an ODC process is a journey with four phases. Each phase has specific characteristic dynamics and systemic dilemmas. It reminds us of the theory of change described above.

Phase 1: New Foundation

This phase is characterised by vulnerability in terms of individual leadership and in terms of the fragile group relationships. Resistance to change is experienced throughout the system. Employees refer to 'the good old days'. The value of psychometrical testing in identifying development areas for leadership development and optimisation of group dynamics is identified as a critical part of this phase.

Phase 2: The Filtering-through Process

During this phase, everybody participates in training and development. The creative minority participates eagerly during this process. Plans are co-created and contracted at all levels of the organisation. Translation of strategy (doing) and values (being) are characteristic of this phase. Organisational development and change initiatives are implemented and focused on identified development areas. Individuals feel empowered. However, leaders rarely felt comfortable with the way in which some employees speak up – it can be viewed as a leadership challenge. Individuals struggle through different organisational development events, sharing different thought processes and ideas and work towards shared understanding.

Phase 3: Rewiring Around the New

New strategies, new organisational development theory, or a transformational journey are implemented. New behaviours are visible. Employees are surprised by the wisdom of others. More employees are attempting to do things the new way, to speak up and to co-create. The content of conversations changes away from how things were in the old days to how things can be if the new approach/philosophy or strategy is implemented. A renewed level of energy is experienced in the system.

Phase 4: Cementing the Future

During this phase, employees take personal responsibility for the process of creating the culture of inclusivity with the result that it becomes so strong and respected that it would be difficult to reverse after it has been filtered through to all levels. Leadership capacity is built into the system. Quick wins happen and should be celebrated. Innovation occurs and performance indicators reflect positively. Employees are increasingly confident and proud of the organisation. They trust leadership. Employees act as if things had always been done in an inclusive manner.

A typical inclusivity journey embeds all four phases and is co-created by engaging around conversations that matter on all the organisational levels and by involving leadership from social structures. Typically, this large-scale process lasts least three to five years for a system to embody the new behaviours, and act as though things had always been done in an inclusive manner. Then things can never be the same again as conversations take place on the official forums where they are supposed to happen, employees have voice, and leadership truly listens with open hearts and minds.

Different human reactions to change will manifest in each phase. It is critical for leadership to understand these phases and allow the system not to react but respond to complaints, concerns and even rejections of an ODC process.

5.3 The Big 10 Steps of Large Scale Transformational/Change Processes

As documented in the book Spiral Dynamics in Action[72] the following aspects describe the Big 10 steps of large-scale transformational processes. ODC consultants play an important role in these 10 steps. Through a conscious attempt, the speed of adaptation of the system increases significantly.

Potential in the system, culture, or country

1 ODC consultants can help systems by describing the potential in the various systems in an organisation. Capacities and structures for change must be present to understand and implement new thinking. The Change State Indicator and Benchmark of Engagement together with the IvMap and EQi feedback provide amazing insights into where the system is currently. Further, the CPA can describe the complexity of the members of a system, as well as the potential embodied in these leaders. Potential is often a make-or-break condition for change to occur.

Current and previous problems, threats resolved

2 It is important to differentiate between immediate and short-term challenges versus the long-term repositioning, changes and future realities. BOTH need to be addressed at the same time. More complex thinking and solutions emerge when a zone of comfort emerge has been reached and relative equilibrium achieved. Excess energy then becomes available to explore what's next.

Dissonance in the current system

3 ODC consultants must work to create turbulence in the system – a sense that "something is wrong" This can be described as creating a burning platform to change.[73] By illustrating and bringing to awareness the growing gap between Life Conditions and current ways of coping and what the future organisation or system need to adjust sustainably, it becomes clear that old solutions cannot solve new problems of existence. Dissonance may now unleash energy and stimulate fresh thinking for movement along the change journey.

Insight available into probable causes and viable alternatives

4 ODC processes that can help leadership to understand BOTH what went wrong AND what resources and solutions are now required are important. Insight into how systems form, decline, and reform assist leadership in accepting the possibility and means of change. Facilitating processes that consider other scenarios, new models, and alternatives are important. Recognise the potential in the system and enabling the right person in role with the optimal organisational array ensures best fit and congruence.

Insertion of energy to power up people, systems and resources

5 ODC processes can unleash human energy in systems to perform. Energy can be renewed in people and systems. This energy can be wired towards the expected future, towards adaptation for change. The IGNITION and FLOW THROUGH of compulsions

Mapping change FROM what TO what

6 Mapping creates clarity and direction by outlining possibilities for change. For transformation to be meaningful, individuals must grasp what change entails—whether through shifts in life conditions or the evolution of individuals, groups, and organisations. Embedding the 'why' through relevant values, language, and context strengthens motivation and eases the transition.

Leveraging tipping points

7 Leveraging tipping points, defining moments, and influential cases expands potential, broadens vision, and drives action. ODC can help to set the stage to enlarge on the dynamics and reasons for change. Surprises, wildcards, and unexpected events are opportunities to both clarify the change process and add momentum for the shifts.

Identifying and overcoming barriers

8 Identifying and overcoming both internal and external, which have blocked or frustrated change. Barriers may be actors, people, structures in the constellation of influence: family, the 'system', the establishment, etc. It can be very helpful to identify and expose denials, excuses, and rationalisations for not implementing change. Barriers are external AND internal:

It's their fault! We are oppressed and they
will pay   If only... They started it!

In the good old days...When X was the leader...Before Y came....

ODC practitioners collaborate with marketers, press strategists and communication experts to remove or ignore barriers to change. Perception management principles are critical. It is important to construct a solid foundation before leadership is rebuilding the future.

Consolidation

9   Efforts to support the new thinking and actions must be activated. ODC practitioners can support the system during these stages of change. Support during transition is essential emotionally, structurally and socially. During this period, the following can be expected: confusion, false starts, steep learning curves, awkward assimilation. It may take some time to establish change sufficiently to withstand any attacks from negative forces left behind.

Anticipation of the new problems

10   Leadership should be in anticipation of the next set of problems that will arise from the new solutions. ODC consultants can ask the following question:

> **"What new problems will now arise out of our successful resolution of previous problems?"**

By supporting leadership to understand systemic causality and recognise the essential flow between problems and solutions, new thinking, plans and actions will also carry the deep understanding of more rapid adjustment to change as pressure builds because of successes and failures.

Understanding motives and change, forms of stimulation become important.

5.4 Alchemy and the stages of organisational transformation

Alchemy as described by Jung[74] presents a symbolic roadmap for transformation. During this process of metamorphosis, individuals or organisations move through distinct phases of deconstruction, purification and integration. When applied to organisations, these systems describe how systems evolve, adapt and reach a level of equilibrium that brings sustainability – all to adjust to external and internal forces.

Seven distinct phases are presented in this transformational alchemical journey.

Nigredo (Blackening) – Chaos and Breakdown

Psychological meaning

Nigredo represents the death of the old, a stage of destruction, confusion, and crisis.[75] In individual psychology, it signifies ego dissolution, where unconscious material emerges to confront the conscious mind.

Organisational application

Organisational crises, leadership failures, and cultural dysfunctions often initiate transformation.[76] Leaders must acknowledge outdated structures, cultural misalignments, and systemic failures to pave the way for change.[77] Employees may experience uncertainty, disengagement, and resistance, requiring strong leadership to guide them through transformation.[78]

Calcinatio (Burning) – Confronting Dysfunction

Psychological meaning

Calcinatio is the fire stage, symbolising ego purification and the destruction of false attachments. It involves breaking down illusions and exposing hidden dysfunctions.

Organisational application

Leaders must challenge bureaucratic rigidity, outdated mental models, and cultural inertia.[79] Organisational development (OD) practitioners facilitate critical dialogue and emotional resilience training to prepare for change.[80] The burning away of dysfunctions allows for a more authentic, adaptive, and engaged workforce.

Mortificatio (Dying) – Letting Go of the Past

Psychological meaning

Mortificatio signifies mourning and detachment, where individuals or systems must surrender outdated identities and attachments.

Organisational application

Employees and leaders experience grief and resistance as they relinquish familiar ways of working.[81] ODC interventions must support psychological adaptation through coaching, storytelling, and appreciative inquiry.[82] Failure to navigate this stage leads to cynicism, disengagement, or organisational entropy.[83]

Separatio (Separating) – Distilling Core Values

Psychological meaning

This stage involves clarifying essential truths, differentiating what must be retained versus discarded. It is a phase of self-examination and discernment.

Organisational application

Strategic realignment ensures that core organisational values remain intact while outdated processes are eliminated.[84] Leadership must facilitate inclusive decision-making to ensure that employees co-create the new organisational narrative. Separation is essential to prevent regressive tendencies that reinforce past dysfunctions.[85]

Sublimatio (Elevation) – Higher Perspective

Psychological meaning

Sublimatio represents elevation and transcendence, where the psyche gains a broader vision and a higher perspective.

Organisational application

Leaders and ODC practitioners must shift from operational firefighting to strategic foresight.[86] Organisational storytelling, coaching, and reflective practices help employees reframe challenges as opportunities.[87] This phase fosters big-picture thinking, inclusivity, and a renewed sense of purpose.

Citrinitas (Awakening) – Testing New Paradigms

Psychological meaning

Citrinitas signifies intellectual awakening and creative insight, where clarity emerges after prolonged transformation.

Organisational application

New leadership models, strategic innovations, and cultural shifts begin to take hold.[88] Psychological safety must be prioritised to allow experimentation, learning, and adaptation.[89] Employees engage in higher levels of collaboration, agility, and purpose-driven work.

Rubedo (Wholeness) – Integration and Mastery

Psychological meaning

Rubedo is the final stage of transformation, where all previous changes integrate into a harmonious, self-sustaining system.

Organisational application

Organisational culture solidifies into a self-sustaining ecosystem of trust, engagement, and performance that can be described as conjunctio.[90] Leaders no longer enforce change; instead, they steward continuous evolution.[91] The organisation is now adaptive, innovative, and psychologically resilient, capable of navigating future complexities. Goren-Bar[92] applied Jungian theory in a pragmatic manner through ICF-accredited coaching on individual and collective level.

Applying the principles of alchemy to ODC illustrates the importance of psychological, cultural and strategic integration. Systems thinking supports in this approach. Leaders must realise that transformation is all but linear. Rather, it is cyclical and requires ongoing adaptation and problem solving of outcomes of unintended implications of decisions.[93] Change efforts must include emotional intelligence development, result in psychological resilience and sustain high levels of engagement by deploying sufficient support mechanisms to move the system through the change. Organisational change is most effective when employees participate in the transformation process – inclusivity is thus critical. Long-term sustainability is often the idealised future of change efforts – by integrating Rubedo principles, organisations embody the DNA what enable agile and adaptive cultures that continue to evolve.[94]

To become individualised and therefore integral, leaders must go through an alchemic process that is often very traumatic. Integral leaders steer away from implementing rigid interventions and rather allow for emergence, experimentation, agility and integration to reach a more conscious and high functioning organisational state.[95] The risk of not being understood increases as novice ways are discovered. Leaders, however, have followers, Viljoen warns.[96] This echoes the Jungian insight that inner lessens must be applied in the outer world to be really meaningful. Both the internal world of thoughts and reflections and external world becomes important.

5.5 Understanding of How to Change

To be able to understand how to change, one needs to understand the underlying beliefs in the system. Understanding human value systems//codes, the capability in the system and dynamics of the system; insights are informed about the possibility of transformation. Large organisational transformation needs leadership with courage, leadership that will not stray from the belief in their convictions. A leader is not a leader if he or she does not have followers. ODC processes are needed for individual stories to be woven together to create a sense of shared understanding. This enables followership.

Significance must be created to commit to transformation. This often dawns on people when they participate in an integral inclusivity process. By involving people, energy is unleashed. This energy must be utilised around the task at hand, or else may become disruptive. Systemic leverage points should be identified for maximum impact. A new set of problems, screaming for new solutions, will emerge as old ones are solved.

ODC practitioners can provide processes such as change resilience workshops; construct change leaders' capacity and interventions that deal with human reactions to change. By translating strategy throughout the system, shared understanding is created and buy-in is achieved.

As a rule of thumb, I learned to continue with this translation until 50% of the system is tired/saturated.

The rest will then follow.

5.6 Six Conditions for Change

If all six of these criteria are not met, the change process will not have a successful outcome. It is the role of the ODC practitioner to navigate a system and the people in the ecology through the conditions described below:

1   The first condition is the **Potential** for change. Not every individual is capable of change. Change may not always be possible. Open systems allow the greatest possibility to change. Open **systems on individual and collective level** are open-minded, enjoy new stimuli and are not rigid. They study, travel and explore new things. In an **Arrested** system, people are trapped by internal or external boundaries. They can only change if the boundaries are removed. Fear often that keeps people in the exact position where they are. Change is seen as threating. People in a **Closed** system are blocked by bio-psycho-social capacities and cannot adapt. The cause may be developmental, environmental or psychological and the individuals are essentially incapable of change.

2   If a person is not in a Closed system, he or she then needs **solutions** to solve current and previous problems. The goal in meeting this condition is stabilisation of any current threats, either external or internal. As an example, a sick person is not capable of systemic change (living a more whole and healthy life) until the threat of death by disease is removed. As another example, a person with an anxiety disorder will have a difficult time working through change without first solving the problems with anxiety.

3   There also must be **Dissonance** within the individual or within his or her life conditions. Individuals must be uncomfortable in some way. The individual may even become undone – letting go so that the new may enter.

4   The **Barriers** to change must be identified and overcome. The barriers need to be reframed.

5   The individual must possess **Insight** into what caused the previous thinking structure to fail. He or she must have knowledge of what went wrong with the previous system and why and then must have an awareness of new resources that are available for dealing better with the problem. New models, approaches and ways must be available to the individual. They must have the ability to recognise the emergence of new life conditions.

6   There must be Consolidation and support during the transition. Transitions are often volatile and difficult to stabilise.

The question can be asked – what is the cost of not doing ODC?

5.7 Dis-EASE of Change

You're entirely bonkers. But I'll tell you a secret. All the best people are.

Alice to the Mad Hatter after he asks if he's gone mad.

Lewis Carroll

Change creates deep angst in people. It creates disease. The ease of doing things in a known way is interrupted. The inability to make sense out of non-sense leads to a fear of loss and demoralisation and not be able to structure the best way to address the most probable future. Without co-creating an idealised future, systems and the people in them may become seriously disrupted.

Change in its very nature has the following properties:

- Visceral

  When something is visceral, you feel it in your gut. It may be rational where an imminent threat poses itself. It may be primal, where it is an innate fear programmed into our being. It may even be irrational. Leaders often intuitively know what a change is going to come.

- Velocity

  Velocity refers to the speed of change in each direction. The higher the velocity of change, the more important solid ODC work becomes. Organisations change form, there are diversification, mergers and acquisitions, centralisation and decentralisation and continuous adaptation to changing conditions. Velocity can be positive or negative depending on the nature of change.

- Vector

  There is a vector quality to change. There is direction to change. There is also magnitude. By understanding the direction and magnitude of the change, ODC consultants can help to stretch consciousness about it in a way that identity does not become blurred, but indeed an exponential manifestation of the sum of the parts that formed the system in the first place.

- Vicissitude

  Vicissitude describes an often-unwanted change or variation occurring during an interchange or alteration. The necessity of change is an inherent function of change. Change is often unwanted and unpleasant. There is an alternation of emotions to change – a vicissitude to it. ODC practitioners can use strategies, methodology, theoretical models, and interventions to consult to the vicissitude in systems.

ODC practitioners must be aware of the visceral and vectoral nature of change. Further, the velocity and vicissitude of change must be considered when designing for and intervening in change processes in organisations and its people.

A good ODC strategy creates a need for strong leadership and addresses angst and insecurity within a system by anticipating the properties described above. The feeling of vulnerability that the properties of chance can create may negatively influence the initial commitment of top leadership to the change initiative. Leaders must know this and allow the normal emotions associated with change to manifest. Self-awareness is a critical emotion to be developed in leaders so that they can be aware of human reaction to change and differentiate between their own emotions and those that the system project on them. This is a prerequisite to respond maturely, and not react, to the perceived negative reactions to change, that may indeed be functional to move through accelerated human responses during uncertainty and transformation.

ODC interventions can accelerate adaptation to changes. The real cost implication of ODC work can often be described in a consideration of what would have happened if there was no intervention in the first place.

You never change things by fighting the existing reality. To change something, build a new model that makes the existing model obsolete.

Richard Buckminster Fuller

5.8 Organisational Elegance

For achieving organisational elegance, the connection of functions to be performed, forms of design that enable the functions and the fit of people to the various functions and forms should occur. Further, the arousal and sustainability of focus, the triggering and maintenance of flow and the fulfilment of the visions, needs and aspirations of people become critical systemic leadership conditions. As leadership creates the behavioural framework or culture in the organisation, it is their architectural responsibility to create an atmosphere that facilitates engagement, and ultimately fun, as well as perpetual sensitivity to the needs and demands of the future[97], [98], [99] emphasised the importance of integration in organisations as maturity develops and elegance is visibly felt.

The *9 Fs format* should be followed for organisational elegance.

*Leaders should have foresight, ensure congruence, interrelatedness and integration between **functions** of the business, organisational operating model design forms, **fit** to ensure congruence between humans and their posts, focus and flow of human and systemic energy, **fulfilment** of visions, facilitation of **FUN** and co-creating the super-ordinate goal that ensures the desired **FUTURE**.*

It must be noted that the extended definition of an organisation as described by Viljoen[100] applies here. The unit of study is not a corporation only, but also any other living system in which the function of organising happens such as a family, a community, a society or a geo-political region.

Threats of possibility are weaved together in elegant organisations. Tensions are addressed actively. Pockets of listening create containing spaces. Much like mercury, these pockets of high energy can pull together and result in enhanced functionality. Self-awareness and consciousness are heightened, and the future is co-created in a space that is respectful, and intentions are pure. Aspirations and potential present as the future reality. The future is painted with a hopeful disposition and proclivity. A soulful ecology is the result. **Functionality, flexibility,** and **flow** are aspects of maturity that lead to systemic elegance and nuance.

5.9 Final Thoughts

And above all, watch with glittering eyes the whole world around you because the greatest secrets are always hidden in the most unlikely places. Those who don't believe in magic will never find it.

Billy and the Minpins

This chapter describes the nature of change. The process of alchemy is used as a metaphor for moving through stages of change. During change, old paradigms are dismantled – the Nigredo or dark stage of alchemy. Core values are clarified – the albedo stage). Finaly, the insights manifest in transformative behaviours and actions – the Rubedo stage.

In this, the ODC practitioner is the catalyst – it creates a different set of conditions after intervention. Something that was not there before. As we move through life – personally or as organisations, the skill to adjust functionally to changes in the outer world becomes an increasingly crucial capability.

On my way out, Nena called me back.

With depth and care in her dark eyes, she put up an ancient finger and says, "slowly my baby, slowly."

Hope can be

reEMERGED

Part 2

The Process Framework

Chapter 6

The Science, Art and Craft of ODC as a process

6.1 The Science of ODC

By ensuring that ODC is positioned and executed in a well-developed systemic manner, the following steps should be included.[101] A carefully crafted six s D's-process is the base of any sustainable ODC process. These steps are **Discover/Dilemma**, **Diagnosis, Designing, Delivering, Displaying, Delineating.** Each step is described below. Relevant cases and stories are incorporated to illustrate real live examples of how it happens in practice.

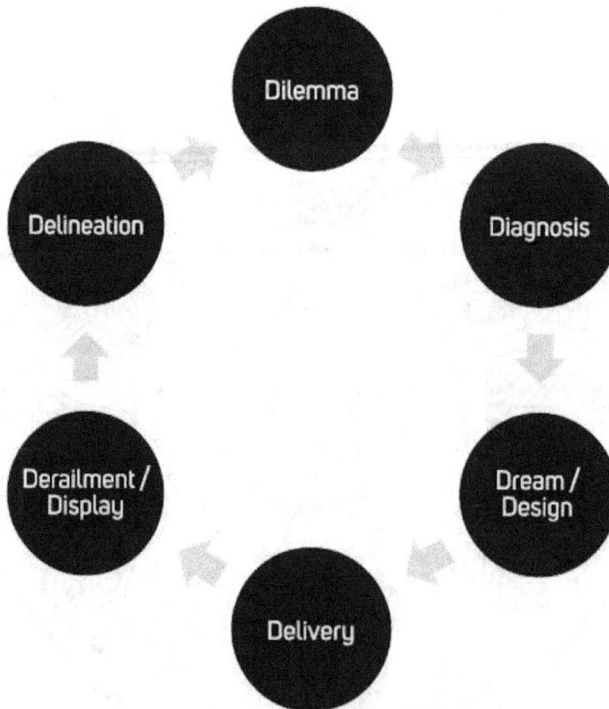

Figure 6.1: The 6 D-process of ODC

6.2 Dilemma

The dilemma present itself in various forms. The case study of Luanda Medical Center below illustrates how a dilemma may may present itself – and when an ODC consultant is asked to get involved.

Case 1: The Luanda Medical Center story

Justin Gavenescu

Background

Luanda Medical Center started as a specialist ambulatory clinic in 2015. The clinic has international specialists and local and is positioned as a top end clinic from the point of view of customer experience, facilities and quality of service. The outpatient department is backed up by a laboratory and radiology department as well as two operating theatres. The clinic was managed by the same general manager from inception in 2015 to 2020 when I was selected to take over from the founding CEO.

The early days

I started in August 2020 at the peak of the Covid pandemic and I immersed myself in a 2-month handover process. My first impression was one of chaos, where no one was in control of processes and basic procedures seemed to be insurmountable challenges. For example, the clinic was unable to meet the demand for Covid testing and deliver results on time as well as invoice for the services offered.

The Covid pandemic was a great opportunity for LMC, as it became the first financial year the clinic turned profitable. My early mandate was obviously to ensure a smooth handover and maintain the profitability of the clinic in a very volatile environment of Angola and post the Covid pandemic.

Angola is an African country very rich in mineral resources. The economy is undiversified and fully dependent on oil and mining. The country has almost no capacity to produce any medical supplies or medication, so everything is basically imported. There is also a severe shortage of specialised and skilled people, including managerial and medical skills.

The triple currency whammy and other 'fun facts'

The Luanda Medical Center is registered in Angola and, of course, we charge for services in the local currency, the Kwanza. Being part of an international Group we report in USD. And because we need to import everything we spend on Euro. Added to this, our business model is based on expatriates (management, doctors and some of the nurses) and their remuneration is pegged to the Euro. The Kwanza is

77

an extremely volatile currency with wide fluctuations mostly downward. The graph below depicts the evolution of the currency over the past five years.

Anyone who managed hospitals knows that hospitals don't or can't grow topline by 65% in one year for example. If you are good and can add new services, you can hope to grow top line by 15-20 % in a financial year. So, in 2023, when the Kz lost 65% of its value in six weeks (the steep line upwards below) we had to introduce drastic contingency measures for six months to maintain the clinic afloat.

In 2024 we managed a 16% top line growth (best one ever in the nearly 10-year history of the clinic) yet the Kwanza lost another 15% of its value, before stabilising. This kind of volatility makes one feel as you are working for nothing when it comes to reporting your financial results in USD or Euro as you are basically working harder for diminishing profits.

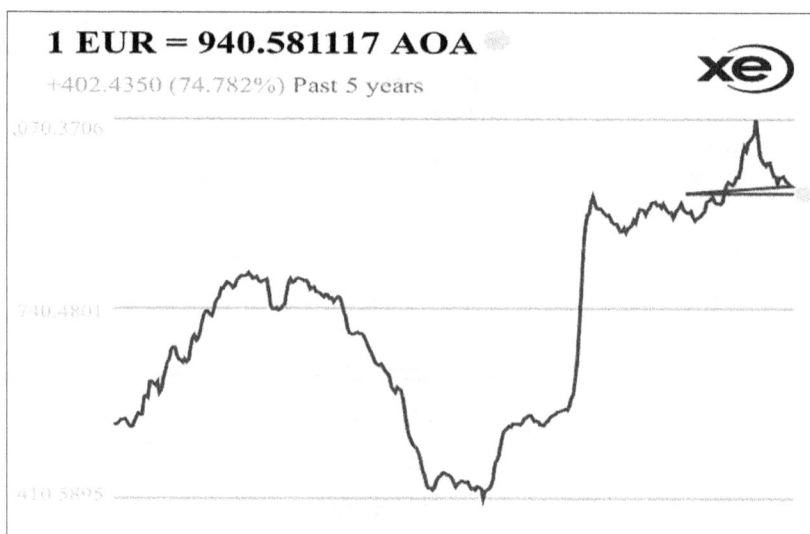

1 EUR = 940.581117 AOA
+402.4350 (74.782%) Past 5 years

Figure 6.2: The volatility of the Angolese Kwanza

The human capital dimension

When I started at LMC in 2020, I was basically the only person with private hospital management experience, except for the outgoing CEO and the CFO at the time. The CFO left one year later. All my senior managers had zero private hospital experience and the key people were in their first managerial jobs. Some managers had previous managerial experience in other industries. Some were medical or nursing professionals and one was completely unfamiliar with healthcare. Reflecting retrospectively, it feels like a trap.

The good times

We emerged from the Covid pandemic and remain profitable. In 2022 Angola had general elections and the Kwanza did the job for us. 2022 was the most profitable year in our history all due to the Kwanza appreciation (the dip in the graph) although in Kwanza terms we shrank by 2%. My team was enjoying the good times and for a short while we all believed we were out of danger.

The wake-up call

Starting in May 2023 until about the end of June, the Kz crashed from 430 Kz to the USD to about 830 Kz to the USD. We were stunned. The only thing we could do in such a short time was introduce austerity measures. We all had to have salary and benefits reductions, and we managed to close the year in the black.

Obviously, such tumultuous times take its toll on people, experienced or not. I felt for a while that my team was lifeless and despondent not really knowing what to do. Very few ideas were coming to the fore, and the execution left a lot to be desired. We knew we had to grow topline and control expenses; it was just not enough or fast enough.

Not being part of a healthcare group, no one could help us with ideas or out of the box thinking about what else we could do. Closed systems cannot continue to grow and innovate on their own forever. I started to collect on the team a return to working in silos, unhealthy rivalry and a lack of synergies.

How to 'keep the fire going'

For me, one of the biggest challenges other than keeping the business afloat was and still is, taking the team with me, creating synergies and getting everyone to contribute to business growth.

In my previous jobs as a Hospital Manager in South Africa, I worked with coaches and organisational development specialists and many times besides being fun and feeling good; it had a significant positive impact on team dynamics and energy as well as team effectiveness.

A hospital management team has about 10-12 members, and if these people work together synergistically, great things can be achieved.

We invited a coaching company to work with the team; we had the individual and team Enneagram, and some of my colleagues chose to have individual coaching sessions. In the short term, it felt like we were making progress, but later on, we returned to our old selves. Organisational interventions need to be continuous and not once off. People under stress revert to their basic functioning mode.

In mid-2024, I contacted an organisational development specialist and invited her to come and work with me and my team. This is the first face to face, in person sessions we had with such organisational specialist.

The sessions were productive, fun, and people could open up and talk to each other, almost self-diagnosing where the issues were. Of course, this is just the beginning of a process and not a once off intervention. And, of course, there are no guarantees of success or certain outcomes. This work, combined with some team member changes because of natural attrition has a chance to inject a new vision and energy into a team that feels exhausted and defeated by the external factors, not in our control.

When is the right time to intervene?

At what point should the leader ask for help? When is it the right moment to add external energy to a closed system that is running out of oxygen and therefore the 'fire' dims? Based on my experience here, the sooner the better. One should not wait and only try external intervention when all else fails. Organisational work and people development is always worth the time, and the money spent in my experience. If I regret anything, is waiting too long.

The next steps

I always say that optimism is a choice. And optimistic people live happier, more rewarding lives.

In 2025 we will continue our work with the organisational development consultancy, and we will focus on building capacity in our people. As Steven Covey says in his famous *'The 7 habits of Highly Effective People'*[102] we will strive to maintain the P-PC balance; one habit being the balance between Production (what we give, offer or produce) and the PC being the Production Capability. Our production capability is the capacity of people to bounce back and continue producing.

It is critical to identify what is required for each client. A good ODC practitioner suspends own judgement and meets the system where the system is at. It is also important to contract on the outcome, while carefully stretching the system to the degree where transformation can happen. The variance between the need of the multiple stakeholders, the responsible line manager and the future stretch to be weaved in should be carefully understood. I found myself saying something of this nature often during this stage:

Like a fine golden chain that gets knots in when you don't wear it – that is how culture and interventions of this nature are. It does not really matter whether you try to unknot from the left or the right. Each knot that gets untangled creates a new challenge. It is important not to pull – it may break. One needs to continue diligently until the chain hangs elegantly around your neck. Be mindful though – by taking of attention and leave it too long in a jewel case, it surely will get knots again,

6.3 Diagnosis

One day Alice came to a fork in the road
and saw a Cheshire cat in a tree.

'Which road do I take?' she asked. 'Where do
you want to go?' was his response.

'I don't know,' Alice answered.

'Then,' said the cat, 'it doesn't matter."

Lewis Carroll, Alice in Wonderland

A scientific, diagnostic pre-measure is critical to understand exactly where the dynamics are on individual, group, collective and contextual levels. This diagnostic should be multi-culturally sensitive and illustrate the driving forces/ constructs of a behavioural manifestation. A deep anchoring in behavioural science, organisational psychology, individual psychology, group psychology and multicultural psychology is important. Good diagnostic capability helps us scientifically understand the current reality and development spaces in individuals, teams, organisations and societies. This approach saves a lot of time and money.

Without the tools to do scientific, multi-culturally valid and reliable diagnostics, and ODC practitioners are like a doctor that tries to guess what disease a patient present without blood tests and X-rays/scans. Indeed - over time - the dynamics may lead the consultant/leader in the same direction. The risk of misdiagnosis and the waste of time is expensive and ineffective. The unintended costs associated with less effective systemic choices, is profound. It is even more escalated higher when less informed systemic choices are made on the executive level. The impact on culture can be detrimental.

Diagnostics: Doing

Various organisational diagnosing doing tools and methods to determine ways of intervening include:

The Organisational Effectiveness Model, as outlined by Weisbord[103] decades ago, focuses on assessing the efficiency and effectiveness of an organisation by examining its six key components: purposes, structure, relationships, rewards, leadership, and helpful mechanisms. This model still provides a holistic view of the organisation and offers practitioners a comprehensive approach to diagnosing areas of strength and areas needing improvement.

The Benchmark of Engagement (BeQ) as described in paragraph 4.2 offers a diagnostic on individual, group, organisational and contextual level – on both the Being and the Doing level. Although the reliability and validity of the assessment is high in multicultural settings.[104] It stays a perception study and should be supported with other methodologies such as working through solicited data – documents and process mapping.

Another critical framework that has proven valuable in the field of ODC is systems thinking. One of the most widely recognised contributors to systems thinking in organisational contexts is Peter Senge.[105] Senge's work, particularly in his book The Fifth Discipline, has revolutionised how organisations understand and approach change, offering a dynamic perspective that integrates feedback loops, patterns of behaviour, and systems archetypes. Systems thinking allows ODC practitioners to diagnose the complex and often hidden interrelationships within an organisation. By applying this lens, practitioners can identify recurring problems that arise from system-wide dynamics, which may not be immediately obvious through more conventional diagnostic methods. Kim[106] identified several systems archetypes, or recurring patterns of behaviour/dramas, which can be used to diagnose the underlying causes of common organisational issues. These archetypes help to expose the structures that perpetuate ineffective behaviours and responses.

Diagnostics: Being

As a behavioural scientist with a scholarly background, and through study leading of over 100 master's dissertations and doctoral theses; I strive to be at the forefront of development in my field of study. Time and time again, I tried a different set of diagnostics and explore widely and with every adaptation and approach that I am aware of. However, over and over my hypotheses were confirmed that in diagnosing individual, group and organisational dynamics with integrating a contextual lens, the following approach offers face validity and reliability in transnational, developing and developed contexts.

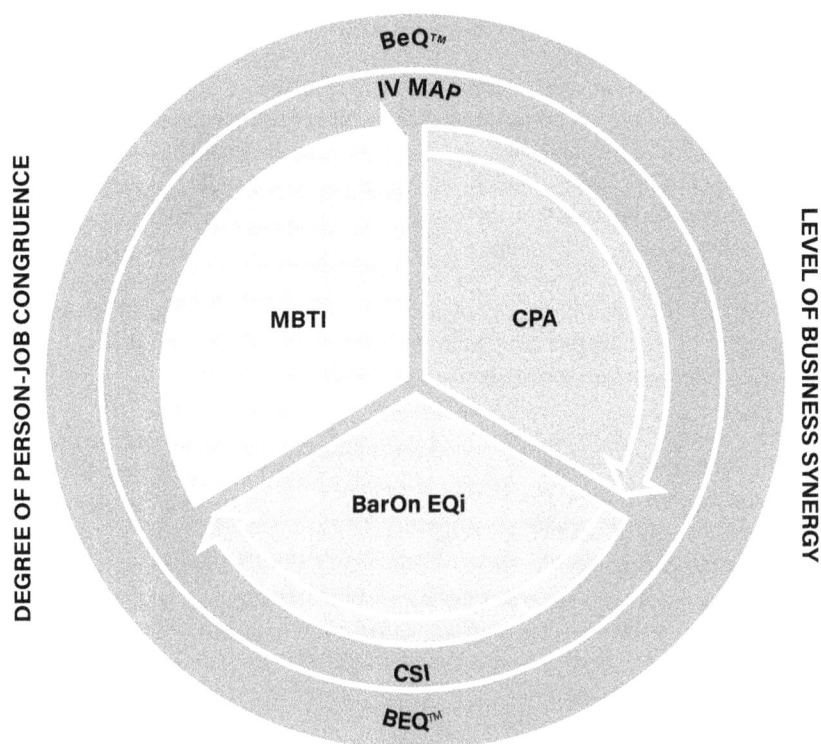

Figure 6.3: Assessments to use

It is not the purpose of this book to go in too much depth in nature and validity of the battery assessments that I prefer to use. That is important is that from an ODC perspective, I use assessments as a process and not only diagnostic. I also interweave the theory into the organisational development journey that is designed and facilitated. Post-intervention analysis is also informed by the post-measures provided in the approach. To showcase the ROI is critical for the legitimacy of an ODC process. A dashboard is presented to leadership during a feedback session with a trained and accredited psychologist under the ethical code and legislation of the specific environment. Confidential information is translated into leadership competencies and managed through the execution of IDPS in the organisation.

It is important that the diagnostic tools impact business decision-making as seen in the case below. It can provide intelligence to pro-actively remove constrains and pre-empt risks. In industries like mining, uninformed decisions may have devastating effects. The line between ODC, training and development and HR is not always clear. Neither is it always important. In various parts and pieces of the system ODC practices can work together to unleash human potential. Some cases are presented in the Appendix X that is not pure L&D but not pure ODC either. This diagnostic approach is used in most of the case studies presented in this book.

Case 2(a): Diagnosing the Situation in Ghana

Various interviews with a phenomenological nature were conducted with key decision makers to understand clearly what the dynamic is. Initially, the case organisation a mining house in Ghana engaged in a (BeQ) engagement study to understand a decline in business indicators such as low production outputs and a general perception that the people in were lazy. The question was also asked whether a third-world country could really comply with international safety and quality standards. Little did the executive management team expect the workers to shift from apathetic to engaged in nine months, for the international safety prize to be won by this mine (and for eight consecutive years after that) and for all expectations to be exceeded in less than a year.

Further, the Change State Indicator (CSI) and IVMap were conducted to understand the multicultural dynamics well. It became clear that Leadership largely holds a value system of ORANGE[vii], while workers had a centre of gravity of PURPLE and could therefor described as collective with the overarching need to belong and serve the community/the tribe. Leadership and the workforce could not hear each other. The pre-diagnostic helped to inform systemic mapping and gave invaluable insights into the weaving together of the diverse groups – ensuring that different questions of existence were understood and diverse needs were met while business outcomes were achieved.

The results of the BeQ research showed a very different picture than the original assumptions of the executive management team. Workers did not feel respected. This mostly happened for the following reasons:

From where they lived to where they worked was 22 km. It took an hour and a half to drive on the deteriorating road that was often washed away by the tropical rains.

The food was not cooked properly during lunch times.

There was no water in the pits of the mines. There were not enough showers, so miners could not go home clean.

The leaders did not speak to the workers.

By the time the research team became involved, the management was not willing to invest more money in an asset that did not produce an outcome. Innovative ways had to be found to make sense of the situation.

This phase carefully considers the business culture and climate, develop pre- and post-measures, conduct ethnographic studies, do quantitative and qualitative assessments, apply psychometric tests and indicators and create a diagnostic capability that renders invaluable information that can be transformed into business intelligence.

---

vii   Spiral Dynamics value systems described by colours are described in paragraph 3.3.

Effectively diagnosing and describing organisational, group/team, and individual dynamics with construct-based, multi-culturally sensitive tools can help us optimally identify the systemic leverage point. Rather than giving a whole system metaphoric vitamins or over-the-counter medicine, the right substance (interventions) can be provided exactly where it is needed. Different systems can be dealt with in different ways.

6.4 Dream/Designing

After the dilemma was presented and the diagnostic state was conducted, the ODC practitioner must design the intervention(s).

ODC practitioners can support line partners and groups to dream about the future – to envision it. Design Thinking processes, as per Ackoff[107] can help to identify the gap between the most probable future and the idealised future. Systems Thinking understanding is also crucial.[108, 109] Scenario planning can also indicate the ideal future – in a large group event of this nature the future trends are compared with internal challenges and aspirations and the most probable and ideal scenario is identified.[110] As part of the strategic framework, ODC practitioners can support line to construct a vision, mission and values statement. These statements can be underpinned by a strategic tagline. Various facilitation techniques, such as dialoguing, Appreciative inquiry and world café methodology can be applied.

A stratified systems theory lens[111] is adjusted for designing an ODC philosophy and journey. Strategic ODC choices are impacted by the time frame of the ODC approach and how it is sustained by translating it through the organisation. Adapted from Jaques[112] and informed by the consulting practice of BIOSS,[113] the following strata must be considered and designed for offering an integral sustainable ODC approach:

Table 6.1: Applying Stratified Systems Theory to ODC

Strata	Time Frame of Discretion	Theme	ODC Approach	Focus Area
6	10 – 20 years	Environmental Scanning/ Shaping Context	ODC Philosophy/ Contextual Influence	Shaping the future
5	5 – 10 years	Strategic Intent	ODC Philosophy/ ODC Strategy	Shaping the future
4	2 – 5 years	Strategic Development/ Modelling	ODC Strategic and Operating Model	Planning for the future

Strata	Time Frame of Discretion	Theme	ODC Approach	Focus Area
3	1 – 2 years	Best Practice/ Optimisation	OD Plan per year	Planning for the future
2	3 months to 1 year	Diagnostic Judgement/ Specialisation	Interpreting diagnostics/ Specialised facilitation	Managing the present
1	1 day to 3 months	Quality	Doing assessments/ Facilitating	Managing the present

A good ODC strategy aligns with the organisational strategy on the same strata of strategic positioning. In a large corporate, and ODC approach must follow for all the different strata to render the ODC strategy stratified.

The following activities must be embarked on:

- Design of an ODC strategy to enhance individuals, groups and organisations in relation to systemic dynamics.
- Joint-action planning to design the way to move forward.
- A typical ODC strategy can have this nature:

Table 6.2: A typical ODC journey

Organisational Level	Key Strategies/Interventions
LEADERSHIP	F-bands, E-uppers, E-lowers, D-uppers, D-lovers
SUP ERVISOR	Middle Manager, Supervisor
WORKERS	Team Leader, Workers

Column interventions (across): Strategic Alignment · Collective Leadership · Values alignment and behaviours · The Organisational Way · Benchmark of Engagement · Engaging with the workforce · Aligning Services with Operations · Teaming · Operating Model · Technical Rewiring · Team Sessions with Workers · Leadership and Behaviours competencies · Talent Bench · Technical Competencies · Training and Development · Diversity and Inclusion/Employee Wellness · IDPs · Performance Management · Remuneration Choices · Psychometric Assessments · Culture Measure

❶ Leadership ❷ Purpose ❸ Doing ❹ Being ❺ Measurement

ODC practitioners often consult on organisational arrays and structural choices in contemporary organisational strategy and interface with other strategic HR or Organisational Effectiveness/Design experts. Organisational design plays a pivotal role in shaping an organisation's strategic direction, operational efficiency, and competitive advantage. The selection of an organisational structure determines the flow of communication, decision-making efficacy, and the ability to adapt to external complexities. Contemporary organisations face increasing pressure to navigate dynamic markets, technological advancements, and evolving workforce expectations. As such, the structural choices and organisational arrays adopted by businesses must be both strategically aligned and adaptable. An integral approach is needed to ensure that the formal blueprint created by an organisational structure ensures human adaptation necessary for sustained performance – and the other way around.

A holacracy is as an alternative and more holistic organisational array that can be explored at the top of the organisation. This is a decentralised management system that replaces traditional hierarchies with self-organising teams, known as circles, which have defined roles and responsibilities.[114] Unlike hierarchical models, holacracy promotes autonomy, agility, and rapid decision-making, fostering a more adaptive and innovative organisational culture. Organisations that implement holacracy in Africa, such as the Meridian Group of Companies and Jet Education Services Zappos, have reported increased employee engagement and operational efficiency. This is aligned with the insights on holacracies derived from Laloux.[115] However, challenges such as role ambiguity, resistance to change, and the need for a strong cultural shift must be addressed for successful implementation.[116]

In part 4 of the book, different approaches are mentioned to indicate the type of interventions that are available to the ODC practitioner. Different providers can be chosen to deliver the interventions. What is important in the choice of providers is that the underlying philosophy should be similar and that the approach must further the overarching strategy.

Case 2(b): Designing ODC Strategy in Ghana

Ghana is a country with 78 tribes. It is close to the equator, with an average temperature of 39 Celsius and humidity mostly around 98. There are two seasons – summer and the rainy season. Three months a year the harmattan wind blows from the Sahara, and everything is red with dust. It became very clear during initial conversations that Ghanaians who worked in the case organisation showed a PURPLE[viii] thinking system, as described by Laubscher.[117] The design of the engagement transformational strategy relied heavily on this diagnosis as described in case 2 (a) above. First, before the engagement study began, the local nannas

---

viii Spiral Dynamics value systems described by colours are described in paragraph 3.3.

(chiefs) were consulted. The research team explained they were there to listen and asked permission to speak to the people. This was a very helpful move. Everyone was willing to share their views. Employees initially reported not feeling consulted. Initially, they did not trust the engagement process and although more and more people (who had not necessarily been invited to the specific session) attended, initially little was said. However, soon, the allocated room was too small to contain everyone that attended the sessions. A lovely positive and contagious vibe/energy was unleashed – everyone wanted to share their story and participate in the group conversation that focused on what was important to them. If not, everyone could speak to the researchers. Notes were written on whatever material could be found, often in the local language, Twi. Every script was translated to consider that every story was considered.

The inquiry approach had two phases: first the research was conducted and then feedback was given. This formed part of the larger process of organisational development and change. During the feedback sessions, some hilarious moments occurred. When the researcher said something with which everyone agreed, the group would shout "EXACTLY" with one voice. Although the request was that the questionnaires would be completed anonymously, in Ghana, people insist on writing their names on their forms – they feel their voice must be heard. After the presentation of the BeQ, a Ghanaian leader asked why foreigners make this so difficult. "If you want guests, you need to make our house warm and are our organisations not our employees' houses" This seemed to be a fair question to our leaders. Do we spend energy in creating a sense of belonging, in a culture that can be described as warm and in a workplace that creates psychological safety for its employees' The management team tried for years to sort out the situation with the deteriorating road. Government would not allow only 20 km of a 600 km road to be repaired. If they wanted that strip to be improved, the whole road had to be improved. This was simply not profitable. The EXCO team decided to drive the bus for a week. After one ride, the HR director reported he had a terrible headache. To help with his headache, all the windows were opened (but the dust from the bad road blew in). The general manager removed one of the big scrapers from the pit and used it on the road in a daily attempt to improve the part of the road used by the mine. Of course, not having a scraper in the pit led to a loss in production. During a joint action-planning session on how to solve the issue, a group member came up with the idea of changing the service-level agreements with the contractors of the buses. It was agreed that over the next six years all buses had to be equipped with air conditioners. In that way, the windows could be closed, and people would not arrive at work or at home red from the dust. This was the core of the issue of feeling disrespected.

The HR executive immediately implemented this approach, and over years the fleet of buses was equipped with air conditioners – but slowly: by the fifth year, 40 of buses were still without air conditioners. As a researcher, I felt very humiliated that what we had promised did not happen within the time constraints. I explained to the group that we were running late with our plan. The most humane response ever embraced me. The group ensured me that if things were improving, they were happy. I learned something about being African that day. Employees reported they did not feel respected because the food that was provided was not cooked properly. This problem was relatively easy to sort out. Ghanaian food is stew-like and takes a long time to prepare properly (The Ghanaians only say "proper"). Because of ineffective scheduling the cooks did not have enough time to prepare food the proper way. This was sorted out quickly by implementing a new schedule.

Case 3: Africa is Not For Sissies

Doing research in Africa is often not for the faint-hearted. Some of the Ghanaian mines are situated just above the equator. In summer, the temperature reaches 48 degrees Celsius and humidity levels measure 98%. This is malaria world. Doing research in such a setting requires the researcher to be available at shift changes, which are often early in the morning and very late at night. Mali and the DRC have similar weather conditions. During one such a session under African skies, with just a damaged grass roof between them and a massive African storm in Mali, the author's co- researcher continuously pushed her around. The author was totally invested in the group dynamics and became slightly irritated with her colleague. She did not realise that the minute she stood still spiders dropped from the roof. Her co-researcher was gently moving her out of the way of the approaching spiders.

In PURPLE[ix] cultures, it is important to first ask the permission from the local chief or elders in the village before one physically starts with the work. In that way, the social structure supports the research efforts. In these cultures, it is considered rude not to eat what is served. The author ended up reluctantly eating snakes, spiders, raw fish and guinea pigs. It is important for ethnographical researchers to emerge themselves in the culture that they study, and to request support for the research from the local chiefs or elders in the social system.

Malaria mosquitos are most active during the early morning and at dawn. It is also the time of the day when most shifts change. The author once asked a 32-year-old Ghanaian if he ever had malaria. He burst out in uncontrollable laughter. Later, he explained that he probably had malaria the same number of times that she had flu. She had made a wrong assumption based on her own living truth and sounded quite foolish. She ended up by getting malaria four times.

Case 2(c): Culture Study Research in Ghana

Three o'clock one morning, before a shift started in a big mine group in Ghana, the research team left the camp to meet with the participants of a study on behaviour-based safety for the first focus group. There were 15 participants in the group. To the team's dismay no one responded to any of the questions asked, and all were very with-holding. Even our Twi-speaking translator could not manage to get the group to participate in the focus group. I felt totally disillusioned. Following the session, a participant asked to speak with me privately. He apologised for the perceived failure

---

ix   Spiral Dynamics value systems described by colours are described in paragraph 3.3.

of the session and advised that I ask permission from the local nanna (the elder in the village) to do the work there. He also explained that I greeted people from the left to the right, and in Ghana it was done the other way round. He further explained that by only speaking to 15 people that day, I excluded others and that it was important to them that everyone should be included.

We made a lot of cultural mistakes that day.

We spoke to the nanna straightaway. The next morning, over two hundred and twenty participants arrived in time for the focus group. They explained that the nanna told them that if you pushed a good man up a tree, he would bring fruit for everyone, and this was a good initiative. We explained that we really would like to hear all the voices, divided the group into small groups each with a researcher, and conducted a mass focus group in the chop shop (the cafeteria). The results were deep and meaningful. We also distributed blank sheets of paper at the end of the session, inviting people to anonymously express their thoughts on the inquiry question. To our surprise we got all the forms back from the empty box provided for this purpose. All the forms had names on. On trying to find out why people would respond so honestly and then still add their names to it, when the invitation was to do so anonymously, I was told that if a person wanted to say something, he must not be scared to add his name to it. Although our research design targeted only 30 percent of the population, we ended up by speaking at 98 per cent. It became very clear that in Ghana it is important to speak up respectfully about things that were important to you.

An array of ODC approaches and processes are tied together in a plan that can support the execution of a well-designed ODC strategy. Interventions on individual, group, organisational and contextual level are developed and project scoped. Interventions such as individual leadership development workshops, coaching, diversity interventions, emotional intelligence development, personality type analysis, Spiral Dynamics interventions and change resilience capacity building can be offered.

6.5 Delivery

This phase uses top consultants, facilitators, and subject matter experts to deliver ODC interventions. The specific regulatory environment in which the organisation operates dictates the compliance to follow. Registered individual and organisational psychologists/ licenced professionals typically conduct the diagnostic phase. The design phase is done by ODC subject matter experts in partnership with the business. The delivery phase relies heavily on the diagnostic phase.

The following roles are played by the ODC practitioner:

- A change consultant guiding an organisation through a disruptive restructuring, helping employees process fear and uncertainty.

- A leadership coach assisting executives in shifting from command-and-control leadership to a more adaptive and emergent style.
- An ODC practitioner using different techniques and questions to help leaders and teams reframe challenges and find new meaning in their work.
- A facilitator of large-scale interventions where employees collectively engage in reflecting on the past and co-creating the future.

Facilitator

The term psychopomp organises from mythology. It is a figure that guides souls from one state to another. In ODC this concept can apply to the process of assisting organisations to navigate transitions, uncertainty and deep systemic change. In the delivery phase of ODC the practitioner can be a facilitator or a consultant. The ODC practitioner acts as coach and subject matter export, too. Some roles during delivery of interventions that the practitioner can embody are:

- Facilitator of Transition: Just as a psychopomp helps souls cross from one realm to another, an ODC practitioner guides an organisation from its current state to a future transformed state. This role is critical in culture shifts, leadership transitions, and deep systemic changes where organisations must "let go" of old ways of working to embrace the new.
- Guardian of Psychological Safety: The psychopomp ensures that individuals and teams feel psychologically safe as they navigate uncertainty. This means creating spaces for open dialogue, emotional processing, and acknowledging the losses and resistance that accompanying change.
- Interpreter of the Unconscious Dynamics: In psychoanalytic and depth psychology approaches to ODC, the psychopomp helps surface unconscious resistance, shadow elements of organisational culture, and unspoken fears that hinder transformation. This can involve narrative work, storytelling, or deep reflection processes that uncover the real drivers of organisational behaviour.
- Bridge Between Worlds: A psychopomp in ODC acts as a translator between different levels of an organisation-between leadership and employees, strategy and execution, past and future. This is especially relevant in mergers, restructuring, and culture integration efforts, where different organisational identities and logics must be reconciled.
- Symbolic Holder of Change: Sometimes, organisations need a symbolic figure who represents the journey of transformation. The ODC practitioner, coach, or leader plays this role by embodying resilience, adaptability, and vision, showing others how to navigate the unknown.

Many change processes fail because they do not address the emotional, psychological, and cultural dimensions of transformation. The psychopomp role in ODC reminds us that beyond strategy and structure, change is a deeply human process that requires guidance, meaning-making, and psychological containment.

Consultant

As consultant the ODC practitioner can bring any content to the table such as strategic processes, systems thinking processes, group mechanics processes. It is helpful if the consultant is psychoanalytically informed. Such a consultant applies depth psychology, unconscious dynamics, and systemic thinking to help organisations navigate transformation. Unlike traditional OD consultants who focus primarily on strategy, structure, and behavioural interventions, a psychoanalytical consultant explores the hidden emotional, symbolic, and unconscious processes that shape organisational life. Some functions during delivery of interventions that the consultant can embody are:

- Surfacing Unconscious Organisational Dynamics: Organisations, like individuals, have unconscious drives, defences, and patterns **that** shape decision-making, resistance to change, and leadership behaviour. The consultant helps leaders and teams recognise these patterns, such as repeating crises, groupthink, authority projections, or cultural myths that hinder transformation.

- Holding the Emotional Container for Change: Large-scale change often triggers anxiety, resistance, and grief as employees and leaders navigate uncertainty. A psychoanalytical consultant provides a safe space for dialogue, where hidden fears and tensions can be acknowledged and worked through. They ensure that the emotional side of change is integrated into ODC interventions rather than ignored or suppressed.

- Exploring Leadership Archetypes and Power Dynamics: Leadership roles often evoke archetypal projections (e.g., the hero, the parent, the scapegoat), which influence how leaders are perceived and how they act. A psychoanalytical consultant helps leaders understand these unconscious identifications and how they affect decision-making, authority, and group relations. They also explore power, hierarchy, and authority dynamics, helping organisations develop more functional cultures.

- Working with Organisational Shadow and Resistance to Change: Every organisation has a shadow side-the parts of its culture that are denied, repressed, or unspoken (e.g., toxic behaviours, unacknowledged conflicts, hidden biases). The consultant helps organisations confront and integrate these aspects rather than allowing them to undermine change efforts. Resistance to change is often not just about the content of change but about deep-seated fears, identity shifts, and past traumas that need to be processed.

- Psychoanalytic Interpretation of Organisational Culture and Narratives: Organisations tell stories about themselves (e.g., "We are a family," "We are innovative," "We always survive crises"). These narratives shape identity and behaviour. The consultant deconstructs these narratives and helps organisations reflect on whether they support or hinder growth. This is useful in mergers and acquisitions, cultural transformations, or legacy issues, where conflicting identities may emerge.

- Facilitating Deep-Dialogue Interventions: Psychoanalytical consultants use reflective spaces, group dynamics analysis, and Tavistock-inspired systems interventions to explore what is happening beneath the surface. They help teams engage in honest conversations about trust, authority, belonging, and organisational purpose. This is especially powerful in executive coaching, leadership development, and crisis interventions.

This approach prevents surface-level interventions that ignore deeper systemic issues and dysfunctional patterns. It enhances resilience and adaptability in individuals and systems and integrates individual, group and organisational psychology into change processes,

The context in which these ODC roles and functions are fulfilled is critical to consider as the two cases below illustrate.

Case 4: Doing Business in Tanzania

In the gold mines of an international mining house just south of Lake Victoria, Tanzania, the precious yellow metals are mined each day. The sound of heavy machinery and the movement of vehicles are the norm at the mine, which produced around half a million ounces of gold and increased this figure by nearly double in two years. Prior to the mine's opening, the population of the local village was under 30 000; today it is home to around 120 000 people, roughly 80% of whom are dependent in one way or another on the mine. The mine reached a significant achievement by producing three million ounces of gold in 2005, contributing significantly to the gold production of Tanzania.

During 2005, the mine owners, who up until that point had been making extensive use of contractors to fulfil several of their mining functions, decided to go owner-mining whereby they would purchase the contractors, their staff and their equipment and mine as a single, united entity. Logistically this had huge implications in terms of the increase in staff size, increased use of facilities on the mine, maintenance and operation of equipment, integration of a wide variety of skilled and unskilled staff into an existing workforce and the emotional and diversity components of integrating people (and their mind-sets) from just about every corner of the globe. The workforce at the time had expanded from 481 full-time employees with an additional 1 685 employees provided by 14 contractors to 2166 workers. An integration effort was needed, not only with employees but also in terms of processes, structures and operations. Most important was the cultural integration. An engagement study was conducted to understand the mind-set of the workforce and the contractors.

The BeQ research suggested that the workforce valued practical guidelines on conducting tasks, had realistic expectations, and needed concrete and specific step- by-step instructions and specific outcomes. The workforce was described as trusting, kind and considerate, sensitive and gentle and extremely observant of the behaviour of their superiors. The workforce described the management as aloof, private, reserved and hard to get to know. The results were surprising to management, as they expected the workforce to request better remuneration. The results of the climate study indicated clearly that rather than simply undertaking a monetary intervention, supervisory development, soft-skills training and strategy alignment also needed attention.

A transformational strategy was drafted and proposed interventions were suggested. An emotional intelligence journey based on the theory of Bar-On was implemented in the organisation. As the entire management system (Exco, Mancom, HODs and supervisors) had been influenced by this restructuring effort, a specific organisational development intervention, namely, a self-mastery process based on emotional intelligence theory, was implemented. All those leaders who were involved participated in this three- day humanistic facilitated intervention that focused on systems thinking principles, the new world of work and the way in which personal values relate to organisational values. During the interventions, specific emphasis was placed on developing emotional intelligence, the ability to function well in multi-cultural settings and how to enhance engagement.

The Exco and Mancom teams participated in a facilitated team-building session in an external venue. Personality-type differences were used as the basis of this humanistic organisational development process. During this session the emphasis was on understanding the similarities and differences between individuals, deciding on roles and responsibilities and sharing each other's expectations. The value statement of the organisation was revisited, and the group co-created a purpose for the team. Two weeks after this session, the 26 most senior employees in the organisation engaged in a psychoanalytical Tavistock event, which focuses on dealing with the unconscious dynamics within the group.69 Issues such as political gamesmanship, power plays and splits within the organisation were explored. The reasons for trust issues in the organisation were explored in a facilitated context. Individuals were given the opportunity to feedback on the impact of their behaviour on others, and they agreed on behaviour and actions that should be initiated, continued or terminated. Direct feedback was given and all the "unspeakable(s)" – such as the dynamics of expatriates versus locals – were addressed. It was decided that all the natural teams (teams that worked together in their day-to-day operations) should engage in team development sessions to optimise group dynamics. The decision was also made to adopt a humanistic facilitation approach as described by Rogers, 70, which is based on emotional intelligence theory, during these team development sessions. In this way behaviour would be normalised at the same time as the unintended impact of behaviour would also surface. The total workforce was involved through the application of industrial theatre focusing on diversity dynamics, stereotypes in the system and shared understanding of organisational challenges. During big systems events and through storytelling, facilitators assisted employees to focus on their own emotional intelligence skills and to co-create action plans to improve dynamics back in the workplace. These interventions focused on influencing the mind-set of staff and enhancing empathy, self-regard and reality testing.

The metaphor of climbing Mount Kilimanjaro together was used to create a shared understanding of the task at hand at the mine – namely working together respectfully towards organisational success.

Results of intervention

No follow-up climate study was done to determine changes in the inter-organisational dynamics, as the management team changed significantly. However, eight of the 13 group members in top management in the organisations were promoted within the two years after the interventions. A post-measure EQi was done to determine individual growth on selected members of the Mancom team. The group that participated in the re-measure consisted of five expatriates and eight locals. The total emotional intelligence score increased from 104 to 110. In the sample group of 13 leaders who participated in the post-measure, the total emotional intelligence scores of only three leaders did not improve. As two individuals whose scores decreased had gone through personal trauma, it can be deduced that only one score decreased with no specific reason.

It may be concluded with statistical certainty that the emotional intelligence journey delivered the desired results in improving the emotional intelligence i-scores on the Assertiveness, Self-regard, Interpersonal Relationship and Assertiveness subscales. Although not statistically significant, the other two subscales that were targeted for development during the design of the emotional intelligence journey, namely Problem-solving and Optimism, also improved by over five points each. It was the goal of management to integrate the two workforces without losing production time. In the end production was stopped only for a one-hour celebration.

No production time was lost, and no lost-time injuries occurred. In addition, external international auditors documented the success of the integration and identified the organisational transformation journey as the best they have discovered in all their years.

Case 5: The DOING Part of Systems Can Help to Wire Organisational Change into Being

Hugo Coetzee

A few years ago, working for a big mining organisation, the top line management (General managers) was asked to conduct a survey of their belief on how the various service departments are proving they required service to them (their perception and not necessarily based on facts and figures). The results of this survey were that HR was one of the worst functions in delivering what the line managers expected and or needed from them. Key to this was the fact that HR did not focus on "manning" of the operations – having the right person, with the right knowledge, skill, ability, experience, and mindset, at the right time, in the right position or role, doing the right work, the right way.

From this was born a program to promote and drive manning of the operations. It was a system driven process, starting as all system work should, from the mapping of the process, first the "as-is" and then the "to-be", after identifying the constraints on the "as-is" process using the theory of constraint and then optimise the process – to ensure improved effectiveness and efficiency. This then became the "to-be" process, we then followed a methodology of first determine if we do not have an existing system that can execute the "to-be" process, if not, can we buy one off the shelve, that can be used as is (vanilla implementation) or can be configured that can execute the "to-be" process, if not we need to develop one using the "to-be" process as the map to do so.

Critical here is that this is where the change management journey starts, the organisation, especially the line manager (client) and the end-users (service delivery department employees) must be made aware, understand, and believe that the new process (not the system) will make their work life's better. The system is the tool to assist with the execution of the new "to-be" process. Next critical step is to ensure that all parties know and understand the end goal and that they thus are consulted during the writing of the Business Requirement Specification (BRS) and ideally should co-sign off on the Scope of Works (SoW).

Next is to ensure that the development is done with the operations for the operations, not somewhere in isolation or at head office. Take the end-users and line management with, do agile development with sprints, and do Unit Testing (UT) at the operation, involving the end-users and line management as much as you can after each sprint. If it is possible, identify during this process a strong leader from line management (as high as possible in the organisation) that is the natural leader (that person who everyone listens too when he/she speaks) and make him/her the system champion.

In this case it was a senior General Manager. Listen closely to the ideas and remarks from this person and incorporate as many of it as you can into the system and or process (even if it means another revision of the" to-be" process flow). What you want to achieve here is that the person starts to first feel and then believe that this new system or a lot of the functionality in it was his idea. This helped us tremendously later when we started to implement and roll-out the system. I then also ensured that this person is the first adopter of the systems and encourage him to become an advocate of the system (it is his belief that it is in a big way, based on his ideas after all, and in this case the truth in many ways – one of the modules was for example built step by step exactly as he described it to function). User Acceptance Testing (UAT) was also now much easier and faster as many were involved in the design and UT during the sprints.

During and after roll-out we made sure that, where possible, our system champion was involved, and that excitement was created for the new improved process and the tool (the system) take to make it even easier to execute the process. We developed metrics to measure the improvements to enable us to communicate the whole time all the various improvements on effectiveness and efficiency, many times reminding the organisation what the metrics were before the new process was implemented. Next, we negotiated and succeeded in adding some of these metrics to the performance contracts of the end-users, driving the adoption of the new process, utilising the system as the tool, even better. We also arranged for events where good stories were shared, wins were celebrated and rewarded and more ambassadors of the process and associated system as a tool, was trained and announced.

This led to organisational level of adoption and a change of focus within HR to manning, so much so that two years later when another round of surveys were done with the senior line managers, not only did HR came out tops, but the General Managers requested that some of the other lower performing service departments adopt the same strategy that HR had followed, to ensure their service delivery improve and are more relevant to what is important for them as senior line managers.

6.6 Derailment/Display

In any transformation process, a space exists where the system tests leaders' commitment to the proposed change. A large scale behavioural based change process in a mine can fail if after focused interventions and hope and alignment is created an executive visit an underground site without wearing the prescribed protective equipment. It can also manifest in surprising behaviour throughout the system as the case below illustrates.

Case 6: Wisdom From the Cleaner

Charmain Viljoen

When evaluating factors that drive an organisation's bottom line, elements such as sales, marketing, and cost management are often highlighted. However, a critical component that is frequently overlooked is leadership. Effective leadership not only sets the vision and strategy but also establishes the organisational culture and operating model (OM) that facilitates successful strategy execution.

Research indicates that leadership has a significant impact on organisational performance. A study published in the Journal of Management found that transformational leadership positively influences both employee satisfaction and organisational effectiveness.[118]

Leadership sets the vision and strategy, creating an environment that either fosters or hinders the successful execution of these plans. Organisational culture shapes the operating model, which in turn provides the structure, processes, and governance that enable leaders to implement their strategies effectively. Leaders define the purpose and goals that support the OM and drive the behaviours and mindsets needed for it to function successfully. A mismatch between leadership style and the OM can lead to inefficiencies and resistance, whereas effective leadership can inspire, empower, and enhance performance.

In the early stages of my career as a young HR professional within a division of a multinational oil and gas company, I witnessed firsthand the profound impact of leadership on organisational culture and the operating model (OM). Our Managing Director (MD) at the time exemplified inclusive leadership by integrating HR (me, as a newly graduated HR professional) into the senior management team alongside operations and finance, fostering a holistic approach to decision-making.

During a significant market downturn, our division faced substantial challenges threatening its survival. Recognising the gravity of the situation, the management team, with the MD's full support, initiated bi-weekly communication sessions open to all employees. The goal was to share the company's challenges transparently and engage the entire workforce in problem-solving. To ensure clarity across a diverse audience-from semi-literate general workers to highly qualified engineers-we employed a simple analogy: comparing our operations to a bakery. We explained financial concepts by likening raw materials to ingredients like flour and eggs, overheads to the bakery's building and equipment, production costs to utilities such as electricity and water, and the final products to cakes. This analogy made it easier for everyone to grasp how increased input costs could erode profits.

At the conclusion of each session, employees were encouraged to share insights, propose solutions, and ask questions, all of which the MD addressed candidly. This approach cultivated trust and empowered employees to take ownership of the company's challenges.

In one memorable session, a general worker raised his hand and highlighted an issue: despite smoking being prohibited on-site, he had noticed cigarette butts on the floors he cleaned. He expressed concern that if inspectors observed these violations, the factory's insurance premiums might increase due to the perceived higher risk, thereby elevating input costs and further diminishing profits-something the company could ill afford at that time.

This incident was a profound testament to effective leadership and employee empowerment. A semi-literate general worker not only comprehended the company's financial situation but also recognised his role within the larger operating model. He performed his duties with purpose and actively engaged in addressing the company's challenges, taking ownership to help resolve them.

This experience underscored the critical importance of transparent communication and inclusive leadership in fostering a culture where every employee feels valued and responsible for the organisation's success. By demystifying complex financial concepts and openly discussing challenges, leadership enabled employees at all levels to understand the operating model and contribute meaningfully to organisational development and change.

This approach not only strengthened the operating model by aligning all employees with the company's objectives but also facilitated organisational development by building a cohesive, informed, and proactive workforce ready and engaged to navigate and drive change.

This case study illustrates the intricate relationship between leadership, culture, and the operating model within an organisation.

6.7 Delineating

Evaluating the solution progress through quantitative and qualitative re-measuring assessments and delineating next steps. Using valid, construct-based assessment tools that are multi- culturally sensitive for pre- and post-intervention analysis and for the quantification of the return on investment of ODC strategies and interventions. The results and ROI of ODC interventions must be quantified. It is helpful if shifts in underlying beliefs in systems that result in culture are reported on.

Case 7: Health Care Case Study

Dr Shannon Nell

The BeQ can used as post-measure for culture growth. Nell[119] conducted a PhD study that documented the shifts in culture on individual and collective level over a decade. She studied how capacity of nursing leaders can be developed. Here are the findings of one year on the collective level as described by the BeQ.

Table 6.3 Company 'A' consolidated BeQ September 2015.[120]

Consolidated BeQ™ Results	September 2015	N = 292	Variance Oct 2014 to Sept 2015
Construct	Domain	Percentage	Percentage %
Respect		86.92%	13.89%
Resilience	Emotional Presence (perceptions of self) **92.04%**	94.68%	8.66%
Regard		97.57%	3.51%
Corporate citizenship		91.01%	9.47%
In-flow		89.69%	11.40%
Support		87.32%	16.10%
Teamwork	Emotional Containment (climate) **88.71%**	93.24%	9.56%
Diversity		93.16%	7.82%
Accountability		87.14%	18.18%
Supervision		86.36%	15.78%
Trust		76.33%	21.69%
Ethics		81.00%	19.69%
Alignment	Organisational Gestalt (culture) **86.53%**	95.12%	6.49%
Inclusion		88.33%	13.71%
Adaptability		87.04%	16.84%
Caring orientation		84.96%	18.75%
Total BeQ™		**88.99%**	**13.15%**

A 13.15% increase in culture as scored by 192 nursing leaders and as indicated by the BeQ is viewed as highly significant.

Growth on individual level was quantified by changes in the collective BarOn EQi scores, as seen in the table below (204-unit managers):

Table 6.4 Leading the Company 'A' Way: Company 'A' summary of EQI of Unit managers pre,- post and post-post measures[121]

Company A - Unit Manager (UM) EQ-i Pre- and Post- measures	Avg Cluster 1 measure UM	Avg Cluster 1 Post-measure UM	Avg Cluster 1 Post-Post-measure UM	Avg Cluster 2 measure UM	Avg Cluster 2 Post-measure UM	Avg Cluster 3 measure UM	Avg Cluster 3 Post-measure UM	Avg All Clusters measure UM	Avg All Clusters Post-measure UM
Inconsistency	2	0	0	0	0	1	0	1	0
Positive impression	1	1	1	1	0	1	0	1	0
Negative impression	1	0	0	2	0	1	0	1	0
Total EQ-i	99	109	108	97	109	95	108	97	109
Self-perception composite	98	109	109	92	109	94	110	95	109
Self-regard	102	110	109	92	100	101	110	98	107
Self-actualisation	100	109	110	90	115	87	110	92	111
Emotional self-awareness	98	108	108	94	112	93	109	95	110
Self-expression composite	101	108	108	96	104	91	105	96	106
Emotional expression	99	107	105	96	111	98	105	98	108
Assertiveness	101	108	107	95	101	91	106	96	105
Independence	103	108	108	96	100	84	103	94	104

When interpreting the results it is important to note that the post-assessment score must be over three points below or three points above the original pre-assessment score to indicate a statistically significant five and ten points is considered highly significant.[122] The EQ-I average score of 99 points that was the initial measure also incorporated EQ-i results as low as 64 points. The lowest measure in the post-measure was 94 points. Higher than 85 points and lower than 115 points are viewed as part of the normal distribution. The shift from 99 points to 109 points also indicated a shift from unit managers who often struggled with the challenges of daily work to unit managers who can now cope better than the average person with day- to-day challenges from a leadership perspective. Nell[123] found that because of the process of enhancing the capacity of nursing leaders in the system, the onslaught of COVID could be buffered. In her own words:

"Early in 2020, the COVID-19 pandemic struck.

It is exactly the fact that the capacitation and development of nursing leaders from this facilitated intervention had extended to include all leaders in all divisions, that inclusivity has become entrenched throughout Company 'A.' This has contributed to Company 'A' being able to respond, cope, assist and support staff, patients, communities, doctors and allied health professionals during the massive and uncompromising influence and effect of the COVID-19 pandemic. No-one in the world, in all sectors of South Africa and in Company 'A' has escaped being impacted.

The ability to respond collectively was an imperative within Company 'A' to adapt rapidly, pivot and change everything that was known to meet the demands and requirements of the never-before-seen type of severely ill patients. The nursing leaders consciously applied the constructs of inclusivity and diversity of thought in the radically changed world of work. What has been observed reflects that nursing leaders have led from the front; they have relied on their emotional intelligence, resilience, trust, decision making, personal authority and professional autonomy to manage the complexity of the situation in which they have found themselves.

Exponential learning and development occurred every day. Knowledge and co-operative leadership with behaviours reflecting care and caring have risen to new heights. The personal insights of the leaders supported their ability to nurture close working relationships with every department to become an interdependent partner in the care of patients. Conflict management, co-operation and support for, and of, others consolidated cohesion across silos and power distances that had previously existed. Consistency and standardisation of practices materialised alongside innovation, problem-solving and solution-focused approaches to ensure patient care is operationalised successfully.

From the early days of the pandemic in March and April 2020, the nursing leaders were quickly able to recognise that a negative reaction from colleagues, patients or communities could reflect underlying fear and uncertainty surrounding the pandemic. The nursing leaders' strong coping skills, adaptability, empathy, the emergence of new information and the flexibility to co-create and co-design solutions, was imperative to ensure real-time relevance and application without compromising systems, processes and, ultimately, patient care. The nursing leaders have selflessly put themselves at risk in this time of dire need. The tragic loss of many lives is deeply mourned. However, within this, a renewed sense of worth, value and purpose in the service of humanity is evident and continues. The development of inclusivity has contributed to making this possible."[24]

Case 2(d): Delineating Results of the Ghana Case

In eight months, the mine in the study won the international safety shield of its multi-national company – a wonderful performance, considering that only a few months earlier they were last in line for this award. The BeQ was re-measured for five years. In the consecutive BeQ measure the local Ghanaians reported that they were respected and indicated higher levels of engagement. A complete case study, which also reports on the impact on productivity and other business indicators, can be found in the book Inclusive Organisational Transformation.[125]

ODC practitioners that keep personal journals and make field notes can contribute significantly to case studies that are lectured on at university by publishing their insights. Further, self-reflection can be taught in ODC interventions. Through personal reflection emotional self-awareness is increased. The ability to realise what is yours to handle and what you contain on behalf of others is also an important skill. Reflection helps us in this regard too. It is a way to make sense from non-sense. Organisationally, it helps us to translate Doing and Being interventions and experience into measurable ways of describing trends on individual and collective domains. As one problem is solved, new ones are created. The post-measure and reflections around it also enables a new cycle of diagnostics. Repeating this pattern can overtime result in optimising both individual and collective behaviour.

6.8 Lessons Learned from Large Scale ODC Processes

In the many conversations over more than a decade with Dr George Lindeque that was the Head of HR of Eskom in the 1980s and responsible for a co-determination effort and radical organisational transformation the following lessons for managing large-scale transformation were shared. George had a way of using the few carefully chosen words that hit home. Less was more with him. The role that he played in the South African landscape during that time is still a story that needs to be told. We planned on writing a book on Finishing Well by applying the academic rigour of Plummer's[126] approach to life histories – a reflection of how an executive can transcend meaningfully after a corporate career into the next phase of life. For this journey and to prepare for the weekly 90-conversations to follow over tea and biscuits George listed the following lessons for managing last scale transformation:

- Leadership must come from the top.
- Leadership should understand what change and organisational development all is about.
- They must have the courage and conviction to do it and then DO IT.
- Leadership needs to ask the people, they know the answer, get the people on your side.
- It takes much longer that originally predicted or wished for...
- There are no quick fixes or magical formulae – it should be carefully planned and supported by integrated processes.
- The following is critical: the vision, excitement, energy, urgency and passion.
- Keep focussed, keep your head down and your eye on the ball – know what you are doing and why you are doing it.
- Intervene – things do not happen by themselves. Get on with it and stay on the front foot.
- Measure and keep your finger on the pulse.
- Think BIG but see SMALL (Small jackals destroy the vineyard).
- Hard work and more hard work – keep on keeping on and do not despair.

- Know your world. Understand the basics and move through the chaos.
- It will be messy.
- Operate on instinct – anticipate.
- Communicate in a structured way (tell them what you are going to tell them, tell them and tell them what you have told them).
- Transparency and honesty.
- Deal with the concrete throwers and watch the boundaries.
- Timing is important– but know that there is never a right time.

What will linger in my mind forever is that every time I joined a new organisation as HR exec he would ask, "and who is your aircover?" He believed that Organisational Development can only be successful with the mandate and support from leadership. As leaders do not always want to adjust to change, often there is resistance when an ODC practitioner consults about what must shift to get to the idealised future. Leadership must understand human reactions to change and the nature of the ODC process well enough to allow the normal reactions that a large-scale process of this nature unleash.

6.9 Final Thoughts

The process of ODC is both a science and an art – woven together in a craft, requiring a balance between structured methodologies and human-centred adaptability. This chapter has explored the six-phase framework of ODC, from diagnosing dilemmas to designing and delivering interventions, while also considering the risks of derailment and the importance of delineation.

Case studies have illustrated the complexity of real-world ODC applications, reinforcing that successful change efforts depend on understanding systemic dynamics, cultural contexts, and the interplay between leadership and employees. The importance of continuous learning, iterative interventions, and strategic alignment cannot be overstated.

Ultimately, ODC is not a onetime event but an ongoing journey. Organisations that embrace both the analytical rigour and the human elements of change are better positioned to navigate uncertainty and build resilient, adaptive systems. The lessons learned from large-scale ODC initiatives reinforce the necessity of leadership commitment, clear vision, and sustained effort in fostering transformation. By integrating scientific insights with practical wisdom, ODC practitioners can drive meaningful, long-term change that benefits both individuals and organisations.

Part 3

The Human
System

PLEASE, FORGIVE ME, IT'S MY FIRST TIME ON EARTH

-

I am still learning how to be alive-
how to allow my heart to leave my sight,
to attend school, to grow up.
I cannot comprehend the arguments
used to bomb the lungs of children,
to leach the Earth of her marrow,
to ban books about love.
Some days, I am paralyzed by grief.
There appear to be pages missing
from my manual. Perhaps I was
improperly configured when
they installed my software.
I do what I can. I am asking the experts.
I am Googling for answers.
I am trying my best. Please forgive me,
it's my first time on Earth.
—Danielle Coffyn

Chapter 7

Emotional Intelligence and the Good Enough Manager: A pragmatic Approach to Organisational Development and Change

Aaron J. Nurick, Ph.D.

7.1 Introduction: How I Came to This Work

My interest in organisational development and change dates back over fifty years to my undergraduate experience at the University of North Carolina – Chapel Hill. Having grown up in a long-standing family business, I thought it wise to study business administration, perhaps with an eye towards law school. I discovered that the functioning of business through accounting, finance, operations management and the like did not interest me, that I did not have a "head for business" as such, and my average grades reflected this ambivalence. What I did not expect was that my business major would introduce me to the field of organisational behaviour through a required course of that title in my junior (third) year. I did not know that this field of study existed.

On the first meeting of that team-taught course, the lead professor, a well-known scholar, introduced the class to the idea that an organisation is an open system, a dynamic exchange between a bounded organic entity with its environment, and that people were at the heart of this continuously adapting system. I was fascinated, little knowing that this was my entry into the field that would become my profession. I embraced the theories, took more courses (including psychology courses), performed well, and professors encouraged me to go to graduate school to pursue my growing interest. I was fortunate that despite my mediocre academic record; I showed promise and was conditionally accepted into a master's program in organisational psychology at the University of Tennessee.

I excelled throughout my graduate studies, and early on I was moved to the doctoral program, where I focused on the growing field of organisational change and development. This was during the mid-1970s when such aspects as job enrichment, group relations, and the "quality of work life" were of growing concern and influence in both theory and practice. I had a wonderful opportunity while at Tennessee to be hired as a research assistant under the auspices of the Institute for Social Research at the University of Michigan, as of their Quality of Work Life Program, a long-term national research project with several study sites. My action research work with the change program, originating at an engineering branch of the Tennessee Valley Authority (TVA) the largest producer of electricity in the southeastern United States, enabled me to collect quantitative and qualitative data; develop skills in organisational observation, interviewing, assessment, and statistical analysis; and complete my dissertation on participation in organisational change. I became a scholar and practitioner in organisational change and development with an emphasis on individual psychological well-being.

I brought this portfolio of interests, passion, and skills to my first (and only) academic position at Bentley University near Boston, Massachusetts, where I pursued a path in teaching and research for the next 44 years. My central focus became the area of interpersonal relations in management and emotionally intelligent leadership, as I taught signature courses in a variety of forms for all those years. During this time, I also deepened my thinking to include psychoanalytic theory, particularly the systems' psychodynamic approach to the study of human beings in organisational settings. This orientation brought me full circle with the systems introduction of my first undergraduate course.

This chapter shines a light on these interwoven themes that I have been developing for half a century. Effective human functioning in organisations is a complex interplay of conscious and unconscious forces combined with organisational structures and systems in relation to an ever-changing environment and eco-system. I will focus on a concept that I developed known as the "good enough manager", or GEM, based on a qualitative research study of the most effective managers in a variety of organisational settings. How do we create and nurture the GEMs that thrive in a turbulent and emotionally challenging environment? The following paragraphs document the evolution of my thinking, teaching, and practice.

7.2 Emotional Intelligence in a Fragmented and Polarised World

While browsing one of Boston's many bookstores in early 1995, I came upon a display of a new book with the title *Emotional Intelligence*. I was immediately intrigued, bought the book and started reading it while seated on a bench in the Boston Common. Daniel Goleman, a science journalist for the New York Times with a Ph.D. in psychology, summarised a growing body of work by various scholars exploring this dimension of human intelligence.[127] One of the originators of this line of thought was Harvard Education Professor Howard Gardner, who expanded the main theories of intelligence beyond the cognitive to include several other forms, such as mathematical, kinaesthetic, musical, and what he termed the "personal" intelligences that comprised social and emotional functioning.[128] Goleman's book was an immediate success and became a best-seller. Because it became popular as applied to work settings, he immediately followed up with a second book, *Working with Emotional Intelligence*[129] that focused on the "soft skills" that enhance the performance of leaders and their employees.

It is no accident that emotional intelligence surged in popularity, as it was emblematic of the cultural zeitgeist. This was a time of economic and social expansiveness. The US economy showed a surplus for the first time in decades and the world was enjoying the period after the fall of Communism, the Soviet Union, and the Berlin Wall. Bill Clinton, the young, vibrant, and demonstrably empathic baby-boomer President enjoyed great popularity – despite his known foibles – as did his counterpart in the U.K., Tony Blair. People were paying more attention to their emotional well-being and were buoyed by the idea that EQ was perhaps more important in life than IQ.

Goleman was not the first to discover emotional intelligence, but he became its most prominent and visible proponent and evangelist. Today, thirty years later, he presides over an EQ domain that includes books, newsletters, speaking engagements, educational materials, assessments, and other media.[x] It was former Yale president and psychologist, Peter Salovey, and his colleague John D. Mayer who coined the term "emotional intelligence" in an article in the journal *Imagination, Cognition and Personality* [130] that captured Goleman's attention and imagination. Since then, numerous scholars and practitioners have put forth their models of emotional intelligence and the academic debate continues over whether it is a personality trait or set of abilities and skills.[131] The prevailing themes generally include the recognition of one's own emotions, recognising emotions in others and effectively navigating social situations. For example, Goleman presents five components:[132]

---

x　See https://www.danielgoleman.info

- Knowing One's Emotions (Self Awareness);
- Managing Emotions (Self-Management);
- Motivating Oneself (Directing emotions toward goals);
- Recognising Emotions in Others (Empathy); and
- Handling Relationships (Social Skills).

Steven Stein, by comparison, presents an integrated model also based on five domains of social and emotional skills, each with sub-categories:[133]

- Self-perception (emotional awareness, self-regard, self-actualisation);
- Self-expression (emotional expression, assertiveness, independence);
- Interpersonal (relationships, empathy, social responsibility);
- Decision-making (problem solving, reality testing, impulse control); and
- Stress Management (flexibility, stress tolerance, optimism).

There are many other models with similar structures and accompanying measurement instruments. Regardless of the conceptualisation, the idea that these elements are crucial to human well-being in both work and personal settings, and can be improved, launched an entire consulting and coaching industry devoted to assessing and enhancing emotional intelligence.

I was thrilled as I devoured Goleman's book to note how consistent it was with what I had been teaching for years in my undergraduate and graduate courses in Interpersonal Relations in Management. In my first year of teaching, I was given this course by my mentor, the founding Chair of the Management Department at Bentley University. He was a graduate of the Harvard Business School where the Interpersonal Relations in Administration course was a long-time staple of the MBA program, and had been taught by such luminaries as Fritz Roethlisberger, Arthur Turner, Abraham Zaleznik, Manfred Kets de Vries, Tony Athos and Jack Gabarro. I felt like I was carrying on an honoured tradition. The course became a requirement for Management majors at Bentley and a "must take" for many other students. I easily integrated emotional intelligence models and concepts into the curriculum and taught the skills of empathic listening and assertive communication. During the last decade, I developed the graduate course into the elective course Emotionally Intelligent Leadership that built upon the foundation of the original course.

It remains disheartening to realise that the expansiveness and optimism of the 1990s that extended into the 2010s with the election of Barack Obama as the first Black US President (including the confirming of the rights of the LGBTQ+ population, expanded health care, and activism about racial justice, sexual misconduct, and gender equity), triggered a powerful backlash. Larger currents, such as the globalisation of the economy along with terrorist threats and extended wars in Afghanistan and Iraq, resulted in many people feeling disillusioned, and economically and culturally left behind. Traditional manufacturing jobs disappeared, the gap between the increasingly wealthy upper one percent of the population and everyone else widened, and economic and political unrest in poorer countries, along with the impact of climate changes, led to increased immigration. The social trends referenced earlier, including greater gains for minority segments in society, upset the long understood social hierarchy, and prompted an international shift to the political right, exemplified by the "Brexit" vote in the U.K., the election of Donald Trump in the US, and the rise of more authoritarian regimes and influential right-wing parties in many countries. The concomitant rise of social media as central to human communication led to more fragmented and insular information platforms, less concern about factual accuracy, increased conspiratorial thinking, and intense and calcified social and political polarisation. The pandemic of 2020 only exacerbated these trends, with observed rises in anxiety and loneliness, particularly among young people, and scepticism about government intervention. Although the immediate health threats of the pandemic have subsided, we are not beyond the enduring social and psychological effects. The times seem to cry out for emotionally intelligent leaders. The question is how do we find or create them?

7.3 EQ and Organisational Development and Change

As noted in the introduction, my early doctoral research focused on the quality of work life for individuals by increasing their participation in the planning and decisions regarding organisational changes. Organisational Development or OD grew out of the so-called "Human Relations" movement in organisation theory, beginning with the famous Hawthorne Studies at Western Electric in the 1930s. Although they have been re-examined and reinterpreted over the years, the studies revealed the power of social forces in organisations as the field of industrial and organisational psychology became more influenced by applied social psychology. OD programs proliferated in the 1960s and 1970s with themes and activities such as T-groups, sensitivity training, group dynamics, and individual self-actualisation. OD became a legitimate area of scholarly inquiry as represented by the Organisational Development and Change Division of the Academy of Management.

My graduate training in organisational psychology occurred during this ascendancy of OD that followed larger societal changes in civil rights, changing gender roles, and other cultural shifts away from the "organisation man" ethos of the post-war 1950s. After all, the model for most large organisations was the military with its defined hierarchies and patterns of authority. My thinking at the time was greatly influenced by Human Relations theorists such as Douglas McGregor, Frederick Hertzberg, Abraham Maslow, Warren Bennis, and Edgar Schein along with the thought leaders of the day at the University of Michigan's Institute for Social Research: Daniel Katz, Robert Kahn, Rensis Likert, Stanley Seashore and Edward Lawler, (for whom I worked). OD presented a counterpoint, with a more social and egalitarian view of organisational life.

Although it wasn't specifically mentioned at the time, the fundamentals of emotional intelligence were imbued throughout these OD theories and practices. The interpersonal relations course was essentially a course on human relations and the centrality of relationships in organisations. My personal educational mission became to make life in organisations more human and humane. I broadened this mission in the 1980s when I discovered a deeper vein of thought and practice that integrated these longstanding ideas and research. Abraham Zaleznik, a social psychologist in the Harvard Business School, taught Interpersonal Relations. Midway in his academic career, he became the first non-medical doctor to train at the venerable Boston Psychoanalytic Society and Institute, and to become a certified psychoanalyst. He began to apply Freudian and other psychoanalytic principles to organisational life and passed that thinking along to his student Manfred Kets de Vries, who also became a certified psychoanalyst. Other psychoanalysts such as Harry Levinson, who briefly taught at Harvard while creating the Levinson Institute, applied similar models and thought to practise as organisational consultants. Similar thinking was emanating from the Tavistock Institute of Human Relations in London and various institutes and conferences throughout Europe and Australia.

Newly published in the journal *Human Relations* and academically tenured, I became enamoured with these ideas and augmented my teaching and scholarship to include psychoanalytic principles. Following Zaleznik's personal recommendation to pursue direct clinical experience, I trained for two years at the Boston Institute for Psychotherapy. Harry Levinson introduced me to the International Society for the Psychoanalytic Study of Organisations. I met like-minded scholars and practitioners, including those at Tavistock, who were applying "group relations" principles and "systems psychodynamic" thinking to organisational development. Although I never practiced as a psychotherapist and remained a full-time academic, following Zaleznik and Levinson in mid-career, I found a way to integrate interpersonal relations, organisational systems psychodynamics and psychoanalysis into organisational change and human development.

7.4 Enter the Good Enough Manager

During my psychotherapeutic training, I became familiar with several psychoanalytic theories beyond Freud. Since my teaching focus was on relationships, I was fascinated by ideas about our earliest relationships and how they are continuously revisited and reverberate throughout our lifetimes. Donald Winnicott's[134] concept of the "good enough mother" held fascination for me. According to Winnicott, a mother continually tries to adapt to her child's needs, and through her imperfect but empathic gaze, a child learns that he is a separate being and develops a sense of autonomy and authenticity. She creates a "holding" or "facilitating" environment where a child can feel relatively safe to explore and grow through his own experiments, mistakes and missteps. I transposed this basic idea to managing in organisations to define a "good enough manager" or GEM as one who:

- Is confident working with fluidity, complexity and uncertainty.
- builds and maintains effective relationships by managing emotions and communicating clearly and genuinely (and encouraging the same in others).
- facilitates autonomy, maturity, creativity, and growth.[135]

Emotional intelligence is woven throughout this definition, as a GEM must be emotionally aware and manage emotions in relationships while creating a facilitating environment for employees.

To explore these ideas more methodically, I conducted a research study in which I invited the alumni base of the university where I was teaching, most of whom were in business organisations, to submit stories about their "best" and "worst" managers, to a confidential website. I received over a thousand responses and performed a qualitative analysis of these narratives via textual analysis. The results were quite clear. The themes associated with the best managers revealed them as teachers and mentors, relationship builders, and models of integrity. The so-called worst managers were micromanagers who communicated poorly, showed disrespect by taking credit for others' achievements and assigning blame where it was not due, and a lack of trust in relationships. In essence, the best managers fit the profile of a GEM.[136]

7.5 Becoming a GEM: An Organisational Developmental and Change Approach[xi]

The stories and narratives from the study illustrated a consistent repertoire of behaviours that focus on the role of the "best managers" as teachers and mentors who develop and maintain an open, supportive, yet accountable, relationship with their employees. These managers promote autonomy within well-defined and effectively communicated performance expectations and provide clear and helpful feedback on performance. They are aware of what is happening emotionally within themselves and their employees, and do not try to control or micro-manage every aspect of a situation but are ready to step in when necessary. They engender trust and respect through their actions and interactions. They are emotionally authentic, tolerant of uncertainty, adaptive to change, and accepting of their own limitations and imperfections in the face of an ever-changing and turbulent environment. They encourage creative thinking and learning from inevitable mistakes. They are perceived as fair and honest in their dealings with others and remain a touchstone for their employees long after the formal reporting relationship ends.

It is logical to ask: Are these GEMs just special people who walk among us, or can one aspire to and even become one of these valuable managers? After over forty years of teaching interpersonal concepts and skills, I believe that it is indeed possible to become a GEM. I also believe the kind of learning required to do so, goes well beyond a training program or academic curriculum. Rather, it is an ongoing quest that requires personal reflection, constant practice, and productive engagement with others. This section highlights the essential facets to be explored, drawing upon what we have learned about GEMs so far, and speaks directly to practicing and aspiring managers.

The identification and understanding of GEMs can be translated into guidelines and lessons devised to enable anyone in the role of manager to develop and improve their performance. I have organised the ideas and lessons around four "Cs" as key themes:

1. Capacity-building a reflective way of thinking based on the knowledge of one's own emotional intelligence, orientation, and understanding of oneself in a managerial role in relation to others.

2. Competence-understanding interpersonal skills that enable one to listen to others, communicate ideas and emotions, and then applying these skills in

---

xi   These segments are used with permission of Taylor and Francis Group LLC and adapted from The Good Enough Manager: The Making of a GEM by Aaron J. Nurick, 2nd ed. 2020, Chapter 6. Permission conveyed through Copyright Clearance Center, Inc.

combination to engage others in solving problems, managing conflict, and accomplishing the task in relation to organisational goals.

3.   Character-appreciating one's own core values and mobilising one's moral self in the managerial role.

4.   Commitment-putting passion and purpose to work every day, connecting one's work with the larger community in a spirit of continuous learning.

Capacity

The capacity to be a GEM requires the manager to draw on his or her own inner resources, the human and personal qualities that are applied in the managerial role in relation to others. As we have seen in the employee responses, a greater proportion of these qualities comprise emotional resources, as GEMs display empathy towards others, and are very open and tolerant of ambiguity and uncertainty in relation to the task as well as the larger organisation and external community. As teachers and mentors, they create a learning environment in which each participant develops and applies his or her unique skills and grows as an employee and human being.

Discovering your inner teacher

It was clear from the perspective of those who participated in the study that the role of mentor is a central element of being a GEM. It can be seen as an act of *generativity*, of giving oneself to the development of the next generation of leaders, and creatively and productively moving the organisation forward.[137] One of the most crucial tasks of being a manager, along with being a strategist and executor, is human capital development, managing talent, and building long-term competencies in employees.[138] Mentoring has been shown to be a primary way to create and sustain a learning organisation.[139] In addition to enhancing the career development of employees, it is also a vehicle to promote collaboration and openness in organisational relationships. Much of the behaviour that characterises GEMs (such as developing relationships, trust, and clear communication), occurs within a mentoring relationship.

Leadership is infectious and virally permeates throughout the levels of an organisation[140] and GEMs beget other GEMs. Many of the stories depicted ongoing relationships and a desire of employees to emulate what they have experienced from their bosses and pass it along. In this kind of relationship, the mentor serves not just as a role model, but also as a teacher. As Daniel Goleman[141] observed:

> Leaders have always played a primordial emotional role. No doubt humankind's original leaders-whether tribal chieftains or shamanesses-earned their place in large part because their leadership was emotionally

compelling. Throughout history and in cultures everywhere, the leader in any human group has been the one to whom others look for assurance and clarity when facing uncertainty or threat, or when there's a job to be done.

While most managers do not necessarily think of themselves as teachers, it is important for them to realise how crucial this role is in creating and sustaining a productive culture that often re-generates itself. In the give and take of a mentor relationship, a manager can reveal strengths and opportunities for employees that lay dormant but can come to life under the right circumstances. The idea of the "un-thought known" means that we all have capacities and emotional experiences that are waiting to be discovered and revealed, and they are often evinced through our interactions with significant others in particular settings. It is related to Winnicott's notion of the awakening of the true self-the genuine self-that harkens back to our earliest life experiences.[142] Managers can learn ways to do this by observing actual teachers, considering the essence of what it takes to be an excellent teacher, and building many of those qualities into their managerial role. They can discover their "inner teacher."

The *capacity* of a teacher is based on the complex interaction of the teacher's knowledge of the subject matter, the learning environment he or she creates for his or her students, and the students' abilities and responses in the working relationship. As Robert French and Peter Simpson explained: *Learning takes place at the edge between knowing and not knowing.*[143] The teacher, and by extension, the good enough manager, is poised on this boundary. The willingness to let go of the immediate desire for quick answers and to keep an open mind is central to this view of providing an effective learning environment, whether in the classroom or conference room.

Empathy

As GEMs need to be in tune with their own emotional currents, they also must have the capacity to tune in to the world of others such as their co-workers, employees, managers, and clients or customers. Empathy is the word that usually captures this willingness and ability to go into the ideas and feelings of another person.

It is important to restore empathy as a cornerstone of emotional intelligence, human relations, and reasoned judgment. Empathy is one's willingness and ability to see the world from the perspective of another person, even if that view is different from one's own perceptions and ideas, the proverbial "walking a mile in someone else's shoes." It is more than just being nice or sympathetic to another's situation or plight, desirable as those qualities are.[144] Empathy requires a suspension of one's own frame of reference, or the capacity to resist knowing or judging too quickly. Drawing upon John Keats's idea of "negative capability," Freud's notion of "evenly hovering attention," and the original German word *Einfühlung* (literally, "feeling into something," later imperfectly translated as "empathy"), Alfred Margulies[145] provides this elegant definition:

> The empathic exploration demands of the investigator the creative capacity to suspend closure, to know and not know simultaneously.

Once again, the manager is on the boundary between knowing and not knowing. For a GEM, the emotionally intelligent quality of empathy requires both an active and passive way of relating to others: a *resonant* experience of the other (the emotional experience of being in another's presence) and the *imaginative* experience of searching for meaning in the feelings and ideas of an employee or co-worker. Put in more practical terms, an empathic manager can sense or experience the tension in the room at a meeting about a new policy, particularly with the one or two employees most directly affected. Rather than becoming defensive and writing off the reactions as recalcitrance, or even worse, remaining oblivious to their obvious discomfort, an empathic manager would try to imagine what this policy might mean in the world of these employees that is clearly different from his or her own. The latter process can enable the manager to put his or her inherent curiosity into action in the form of listening, a specific set of competencies of GEMs that we will explore later in the next section. This enhanced understanding might lead to the kinds of conversations that can clarify the policy or enable the manager to build a better case to persuade reluctant or fearful employees. Empathy is the fuel of relationships and effective collaboration. It also contributes to the building of trust and respect, two qualities that were shown in the study to be essential to GEMs. It is also the basis for working with an increasingly diverse workforce and global environment, and reducing prejudice, aggression, and even violence.

An expanded view of authority

Because they are handling a more dynamic and fluid organisational world characterised by the desire for more autonomy and self-management, GEMs need to develop a more robust sense of how authority is negotiated in organisations. We can distinguish between *organisational* authority, the legitimate "right to work" within the boundaries of a defined role, and *personal* authority, or the "right to be" or to be one's own authentic self in any role, as a defining characteristic of a GEM. Such a manager comfortably inhabits the role of manager within a system, such as Executive VP, Department Head, or Chief Information Officer, and assumes all the rights and responsibilities given to that role. At the same time, the GEM understands and expresses his or her own vitality, passions, and creativity, and readily accepts the same of others in executing that role.[146]

GEMs give themselves and others permission to act autonomously and authentically and are not threatened by another's expressions of emotions or creativity. This orientation goes beyond typical definitions of "empowerment," where the one in power simply hands a bit over to one who has less, or as Daniel Pink[147] wryly puts it, "benevolently ladles some of it into the waiting bowls of grateful employees." By exercising and encouraging personal authority, the manager accepts the power and vitality of others as an essential part of his or her own experience. Such an expanded view of authority enables a manager to negotiate degrees of autonomy, accept strong emotions such as exuberance and anger without being overwhelmed or destroyed, and when necessary, call a poor performer on the carpet and hold him or her accountable for his or her actions without blaming or apologising.

Creating learning spaces

With the above-noted call for an open and interpretive approach, one of the tasks of a manager as a teacher is to create a space for learning and creativity. It can be a physical space such as a conference room, or even a virtual space facilitated by technology. Whatever form it takes, most importantly, it is a *psychological* space where imagination meets the demands of the environment or reality. Thinking back to John Keats's idea of negative capability, GEMs have this ability to create an intermediate space that enables them to continue to think through difficult situations and allows for the emergence of insight (Simpson, French and Harvey). By providing a facilitating environment, a GEM also enables his or her employees to use their imaginations in the same way that a good enough mother provides the space for her growing child to engage in imaginative and productive play. Winnicott[148] referred to this as a *potential* space where creativity and other forms of play, such as humour, are practiced freely.

Competence

A particular value of emotional intelligence (or EQ) is the idea that specific emotional competencies can be learned and developed over time. The primary focus is on the competencies of empathic listening, assertive expression, and constructive approaches to conflict and confrontation. The stories about the best and worst managers also emphasised such concrete skills as listening and the ability to communicate clearly and effectively, particularly as regards the giving of performance feedback.

Listening

Perhaps nowhere in the behavioural repertoire of a good enough manager is there a more salient interpersonal skill than listening. It is through listening in adult life that the echoes of the earliest relationship between mother and child can be heard and experienced. The human desire to be "seen", recognised, acknowledged, heard, and understood radiates from that primal interaction, and sets the stage for effective interpersonal relationships in both personal and work settings. It is here that a child sees him- or herself in his or her mother's reflective gaze as she "mirrors" his or her experiences, including a full spectrum of emotions; it is here that the child comes to understand that he or she is a unique and separate individual who can engage in a productive exchange with another person. Through displays of empathy in her attempts to understand and appreciate her child's inner experience, the good enough mother provides the holding environment that contains the child's natural aggression and expressions of frustration and joy. Although much of this primal exchange is unconscious and largely non-verbal, it is continually re-experienced in later settings as an individual interacts with many other authority figures, including teachers and managers, and the vestiges of these earlier experiences are activated.

While it is beyond the scope of this discussion to engage in a full discourse on human development, it is important for managers to recognise the power of their role as an engaged and responsive presence in interacting with their employees, co-workers, and other constituents in the larger system. Careful and precise listening provides the basis for building trust, communicating respect, and developing meaningful interactions and productive work relationships. It is the first step in approaching problems, generating new and creative ideas, responding to employee concerns, and making the most of teachable moments. Also, in our hyperactive 24/7 world of texts and tweets, focusing on someone for more than a few moments can prove both refreshing and nourishing. Younger people, especially Millennials and the emerging "Generation Z," are not as accustomed to communicating face-to-face in their daily interactions and may even find it intimidating and too intense. Managers may wish to temper their efforts accordingly by making interactions shorter and more casual. I have found, however, that this age cohort eventually finds substantive, one-on-one exchanges even more valuable if given the opportunity, because it is an increasingly rare experience.

Effective listening begins with the understanding and appreciation of the importance of the manager as teacher/counsellor/coach/mentor. That multifaceted role has been previously revealed and reinforced in the study and discussion. It is in the listening setting that this important role is directly put into practice. Most guides to listening start with the realisation that *listening is more attitude than skill*.[149] Anyone can learn mechanical skills and try to reproduce a scripted response in the form of "I know how you feel" or "You feel ____ because____." The recipients of such well-intended efforts may appreciate the attempt, but if they do not perceive the attitude of empathy, acceptance, and genuine concern behind the words, the exchange will ring hollow. We recognise that capacity-in the form of empathy and emotional authenticity-and competence-in the form of concrete skills-are vitally interconnected.

Where's the fire?

Each year, millions of acres of forest land are destroyed by wildfires. The news footage of these disasters, mostly occurring in the American west, is very dramatic as the fires often threaten, and at times even consume, nearby homes, as happened recently in areas around Los Angeles, California. Although many fires are caused by people, the fires are often naturally occurring phenomena caused by a combination of environmental conditions. Such fires are certainly threatening to people and property, and make dramatic news footage; however, we often overlook their potential benefits. By burning dead or decaying vegetation and destroying harmful insects and disease, the fires return nutrients to the soil and serve as a natural disinfectant, ultimately resulting in a healthier ecosystem. Also, they clear overgrown canopies and underbrush, enabling more sunlight to reach the forest floor so that new seedlings can grow.[150]

I present these ideas about a natural occurrence because fire can serve as a useful metaphor for interpersonal conflict in organisations. How many times have you heard an exasperated manager complain that he or she spent the whole day "putting out fires?" Conflict occurs when individual frames of reference clash, when people interpret the meaning of events differently, or see a potential threat in the words or actions of another person. The unleash of emotions such as frustration or anger because of these conditions, provides the fuel for these fires. Whenever I ask students or practicing managers to provide their instant associations to the word "conflict," the results have overwhelmingly negative connotations: fight, disagreement, hostility, discomfort, resentment. Occasionally, someone will see a potential benefit such as a clarification or opportunity, but these ideas are in the minority of responses. Yet, we must ask ourselves, are all conflicts bad? Do all fires and conflicts need to be extinguished?

Staying with the metaphor, we can understand that, like fire, conflict is either helpful or destructive, depending on the circumstances. Fire is a source of energy that can give off both heat and light, depending on how it is managed. I love a fire in a fireplace or a wood-burning stove if it stays in its designated place and does not jump its boundaries. I can even add some fuel to turn up the heat if the space is ventilated and properly tended. Such fireplaces usually add value to a home even if not serving as the sole source of heat.

An intense brushfire can spread because it is still burning underground and can travel and flare up in another location even if nothing appears to be burning on the surface. Likewise, a manager may think he or she has squelched a conflict only to see it "reignite" because the root causes were not addressed. The manager needs to consider both sides of a conflict and decide if this conflict needs to be immediately resolved, or if it can burn for a while to allow potential benefits, such as creative ideas, to emerge. The most important aspect for the manager is *containment*, making sure to manage the boundaries of the conflict so that the fire does not get out of hand. This means finding effective ways to mediate, listening carefully to both sides, and constructively confronting when necessary.

Constructive confrontation

Most people find confronting another person threatening and avoid or resist it at all costs. And the costs can be high, especially if someone is doing something or acting in a way that is either annoying, destructive, or, at the very least, unproductive or distracting to the task. We hope that it (or he or she) will either go away (a form of denial), or that by dropping subtle hints, (usually too subtle for the other person to comprehend), he or she will stop the behaviour (wishful thinking).

Successful confrontation comes under the general heading of assertive behaviour, the positive aspect of our natural aggression. We need aggression to survive and to perform our work, but we also fear our own aggression as well as that of others, often for good reasons. Overly aggressive behaviour stems from a desire to win at all costs and make sure the other person loses. One may seek to destroy the other person's ideas or even commit destruction through violence. Assertive behaviour, by contrast, is grounded in the general principle of acting in one's best interest by also taking the other into account. The purpose is to inform rather than to attack. Because the feelings of others are brought into consideration, assertiveness requires a kind of empathy. The goal is to preserve a relationship while getting one's point across, standing up for beliefs, and expressing ideas and feelings.

This form of behaviour works best in managing difficult situations and in providing both constructive and useful performance feedback. This skill emerged with considerable frequency in the study as a feature that distinguished the best from worst managers. Feedback that enables an employee to learn and grow on the job is crucial to the teaching and mentoring role. It is best delivered as a natural extension of a trusting and respectful working relationship, yet one in which both parties are held accountable for their performance in their respective roles. The GEM is open to receiving feedback as a part of giving it, whether as part of a formal performance review or an impromptu coaching or counselling session about a particular issue that has arisen. Like listening, these skills develop with practice, and most guides to feedback focus on the key factors of being very specific and factual about the behaviour and linking it to the impact (behavioural and emotional) on yourself, and the consequences for the larger group or organisation. Bringing specific behaviour and its consequences to the attention of an employee increases the likelihood that the person can do something about it. You can continue the teaching role by providing some helpful suggestions for next time and then use that as a basis for following up.

It is also important to note that assertive communication need not only apply to something negative; it can also be the basis for positive reinforcement ("Your comments at the meeting on Tuesday, especially your suggestions for cost savings, were right on target. Three people commented to me about how productive the meeting was, and it was largely because of your careful assessments.") Getting through a conflict, hashing out the varying perspectives, and containing the emotions, can reveal hidden concerns and fears while also building respect and trust.

In examining all the above competencies, one aspect shines through: these interactions are carried out *in person*. Given the world of instant communication and social media, it is very tempting to just send an email, fire off a text message, or even post something on Facebook. Modern managers have so many choices, and determining the best form of communication is an art. Marshall McLuhan famously observed, "the medium is the message," and employees and co-workers will be affected by the form as well as the content of the interaction.[151] What does it feel like to get feedback in an email? Can you effectively listen to someone electronically when so much of the power of the encounter is derived from non-verbal cues (still estimated to be the source of 60–80% of total meaning)? The entire "good enough" approach is based on the primal mother–child interaction that is largely non-verbal, and the face-to-face encounter recapitulates the emotional power of this early relationship. Electronically mediated communication, while efficient, is not necessarily effective, although newer forms such as Skype, Zoom and other forms of video streaming provide more opportunities to experience non-verbal interactions such as facial expressions. The difference is that between text and *context*.[152] An electronic message can, however, provide a useful way to follow up and summarise a feedback session. It also provides a written record for future documentation if necessary.

Character

Illuminating one's values

There are numerous "values clarification" exercises that are a staple of training and development seminars and organisational behaviour classes. The exercises usually begin with participants generating a series of "value lists" (such as achievement, recognition, justice, love, freedom, etc.), followed by a winnowing and sorting process until a set of prioritised core values is identified. The protocol may follow different classifications such as intrinsic and extrinsic or personal and professional and then link either to important people (role models) or current challenges. Other exercises might involve survivors on a lifeboat or a reaction to a value-laden parable. Each has its merit, if the value implications are explored. One particularly powerful exercise is based on our view of ourselves in important roles, and proceeds as follows:

1. List at least five different roles that you inhabit in your life (consider items such as son, student, wife, vice president, volunteer leader).

2. For each role, identify the tasks, relationships, and emotions associated with the role.

3. For external reasons, you are now asked to relinquish one of the roles. Which one would you eliminate first, knowing that you are also forsaking all that goes with it?

4. As you examine your remaining roles, you are now asked to relinquish another role. Which one would be the next?

5. The process continues with each succeeding role.

As you might predict, there comes a point when participants find this extremely difficult, as the losses implied with the elimination of each remaining role become emotionally unbearable, even in the hypothetical case. One does end up with more clarity about life priorities and how these can influence decisions and behaviour.

Another way to approach values and their implications is to project into the future and describe yourself in the ideal, drawing upon ideas about the "ego ideal," or our vision of ourselves at our "future best."[153] Once this description is completed in detail, you can compare it with your current reality or the "self-image" and note how close or far apart these two sets of ideas are. You can then translate these ideals into a list of your guiding *assumptions* or personal rules or "shoulds" about various issues, such as how to treat employees, decide, or deal with a conflict.[154] We often do not realise the power of these assumptions until one or more of them are violated, triggering an emotional response such as anger or betrayal. However they are determined, it is important to be specific about the values that are central to our social fabric.

Personal narratives

"It is often said that we live our lives forward and understand them backward. We tend to condense our lives into a coherent narrative that can reveal emergent truths in retrospect. We can see the interdependent events and relationships that ultimately shaped our world view. Our values can be revealed as they evolve from "watershed" moments formed by events of emotional magnitude. We can identify the mentors and teachers we have continually sought to emulate and learn how important values were transmuted and internalised at crucial moments.

As an illustration, let me share one such moment that stands out for me. My father died suddenly when I was a 19-year-old college sophomore. It was an unexpected tragedy for my entire family that had many ripple effects for years to come. I was raised in the

US in a small city in the pre-Civil Rights south. Although my father's death happened in 1971, a full five years after the Civil Rights legislation of the mid-1960s, the town was only beginning to emerge from the long-standing and entrenched cultural traditions of racial segregation. As is typical of small-town life, over the course of several days numerous townspeople came to pay their respects to my family, especially to my uncle, who in his grief recounted the story of my father's passing to friends, neighbours, and customers of many years. During one of these visits, I watched as a sedan pulled in front of our house and a prominent Black minister and his family approached our door. My uncle greeted him and invited him in. "The preacher," as my uncle called him, was very formally dressed in a black suit, and he immediately sought me out. As he extended his hand and looked me in the eye, he said very quietly and proudly, "Your Daddy sold me this suit."

I didn't think much of it beyond his gentle kindness and grace at the time, but the minister's remark stayed with me. In my adult years, I was reminded of the powerful scene in the movie *To Kill a Mockingbird* when the Black community, seated in the rafters of the courthouse in stifling heat, quietly and reverently stood as Atticus Finch, who had just (unsuccessfully) defended Tom Robinson, a Black man falsely accused of rape, calmly packed up his papers and left the courtroom. Let's be clear: my father was no Atticus Finch, and he certainly would not have qualified as a civil rights activist. But in a time when Black men in our town could not enter many business establishments, much less buy a suit, the minister had obviously been welcomed in our store many times, and the subtext of his kind gesture spoke volumes.

I remember, now with greater context and perspective, how I was taught as a child by my father and uncle that every customer was to be treated with respect, and they showed me how to greet them in "rehearsals." It was a powerful transmission of values: that such an approach not only was the right thing to do, but it was also a good business practice; and it resulted in strong customer loyalty that was beautifully expressed to me at a crucial time. Many years later, I was invited by a female African American colleague to co-conduct diversity workshops (billed as sensitivity training) to some challenging and, at times, outright hostile audiences. Part of our training sessions involved the telling of personal stories about race, to make "the undiscussable, discussable." The personal storytelling often had much more effect than abstract theories and guidelines, and several of our more resistant participants eventually came around and even offered stories of their own.

Commitment

With the fourth C, we move from an internal to more of an external focus. The GEMs were seen as appreciating interdependence, and the building and maintaining of effective relationships. They realised that good enough managing takes place in a social context, and thus they are connected to something larger than themselves. We know that we are the product of individual and social forces and are part of complex interacting social systems and networks. The word *commitment* captures this more outward focus and the relationship between the *intra*-personal qualities of empathy and personal values and the *inter*-personal and inter-group aspects of relationships and interactions with the larger community and environment. We can also learn that the connection between our individual passions and a larger and transcending purpose can give greater meaning to our work and the work of others.

Ethics and social responsibility

Business ethics and corporate social responsibility have become fixtures in business education during the last few decades and represent areas of study in and of themselves. One still hears jokes about the seeming oxymoron of "business ethics," as so much business behaviour appears to be amoral, if not immoral. There is an understanding and growing acceptance of the need for ethical practice in business, as represented by the rise of ethics officers and the development of elaborate and often legalistic ethical codes of conduct in companies and other organisations. Legislation, such as the Sarbanes-Oxley guidelines that emerged from the Enron era, reinforces social responsibility at the national level. [xii]

Ethical reasoning is applied to making moral judgments that seek to balance self-interest and the larger social good. Ethics are considered and practiced within a "stakeholder" framework, rather than one that caters exclusively to stockholders. One can map and examine the primary and secondary stakeholders, defined as those who are affected by decisions, policies, or practices; these can include employees, customers, suppliers, political organisations, competitors, government, etc.[155] The key is understanding who the stakeholders are and how they are affected, with the goal of understanding trade-offs and striving as much as possible for win–win relationships.

To get a sense of whether a given action or decision is deemed ethical, a manager might put it to the following simple test:

1. Is it right?

2. Is it fair?

3. Does someone get hurt, and if so, who?

4. Would you be comfortable if the details of the decision were reported on the front page of your local newspaper?

---

xii The Sarbanes-Oxley Act of 2002 was enacted by the U. S. Congress to increase rigor and transparency in corporate governance and financial management and reporting. See Harvard Business Review (April 2006 https://hbr.org/2006/04/the-unexpected-benefits-of-sarbanes-oxley

5.   What would you tell your child to do?

6.   Does it pass the "smell" test? How does it feel?[156]

We might expand the list of questions above to include electronic forms of communication and ask whether one is comfortable having information about the action forwarded to multiple distribution lists, escaping into the blogosphere, going viral, and ending up on the front page of major newspapers and discussed by pundits on television. As we learned earlier, emotions are data, and the body does not lie. If it doesn't feel right "in your gut," then perhaps a second look is advisable. This might include a more nuanced consideration of the sources of dissonance and tension.

We know that social responsibility is an important element of emotional intelligence. It is manifested by a person demonstrating that he or she is a cooperative, contributing, and constructive member of one or more social groups. It involves accepting others, following one's conscience, and upholding social rules and taking into consideration the good of the community, and not just the self. [157]

To get a sense of one's own social responsibility, think of the network of overlapping groups to which you belong. Are any of these community organisations in which you volunteer? What is your role in each of these? How do you allocate your time and financial resources to charitable causes or events? How do you display your sensitivity to the needs of friends, acquaintances, or co-workers? How is your behaviour affected by its perceived impact on the larger community? [158]

A larger purpose

Beyond social responsibility is a commitment to a larger purpose in managing, something that provides greater meaning to one's life and reaching beyond increasing shareholder value and accumulating wealth. Fuelled by such factors as increased longevity and the democratisation of information on the internet, people advancing through mid-life to more senior status are looking for greater meaning in life, more autonomy in decisions and self-expression through open forums and blogs, and a significant orientation towards metaphysical and subjective experiences, including those involved with work. There is some evidence that the upcoming generations have embraced these ideas earlier in life, and desire more meaning in work and life.[159] Quality of work life has now transcended into the larger realm of quality of one's *whole life* and a more "conscious" approach to capitalism. Companies such as Whole Foods, Trader Joe's, Zappos, Starbucks, The Container Store, Amazon, and Alphabet have been on the leading edge of this movement. Such humanistic companies:

> Seek to maximise their value to society, not just their shareholders. They are the ultimate value creators: They create emotional value, experiential value,

social value, and, of course, financial value. People who interact with such companies feel safe, secure, and pleased with their dealings. They enjoy working with or for the company, buying from it, investing in it, and having it as a neighbour.[160]

The above-noted companies combine the emotional with the operational and move from a stakeholder approach or analysis to active stakeholder relationship management. As Starbucks CEO Howard Schultz described, his company projected 40 years into the future, "the core of our mission will still be about achieving that fragile balance between profitability and social conscience. Without the latter, the former is unsustainable."[161] The GEMs are ideally suited to manage in such a world, as they bring their own emotional aptitude into their daily work and seek to interpret and negotiate meaning from experience and translate it to a larger, in this case societal, context.

What can aspire GEMs to learn from this conscious, value-based, neo-humanist approach to business? Think back to the ego ideal, the vision of yourself at your future best, and consider the following questions:

1. What is your highest purpose?

2. What activities, thoughts, and ideas bring the greatest meaning to your life?

3. What is your passion? What brings great joy to your life?

4. How can passion and purpose be infused into your daily life as a manager?

It is important to note that these ideals do not come to one immediately upon assuming a managerial role. I have often observed that in our digital world, we often confuse information with knowledge, and knowledge with wisdom. Knowledge and wisdom evolve and emerge more in mid-life and beyond. Evoking T.H. White's *Once and Future King*, Lawrence Gould[162] concluded that knowledge of the world-that is, "the means by which men and women contrive to ride the waves of a world in which there is war, adultery, compromise, fear, stultification, and hypocrisy"-is accompanied by a parallel knowledge of the self, informed by the:

> Guilt, shame, and disappointment that one has not lived up to one's ideals. Such discovery and self-knowledge are also hardly an occasion for triumph, but if it leads, as it often does, to self-acceptance, it can be the basis for new possibilities of wholeness, vitality, and an emotionally rich and unconflicted sense of personal authority.

In other words, the continuous quest for self-knowledge and meaning in relation to others in a larger context is the essence of becoming a good enough manager.

7.6 Final Thoughts

I set out early in life to make organisations more human and humane. Perhaps idealistically, it was my way of making the world a better place. Perhaps it is in my DNA as accounts of my grandfather's approach to business note his humour and humanity, qualities that my father and uncle carried forth for many years and passed along, both consciously and unconsciously, to me. It is embedded in my core as a teacher and scholar. From this discussion it is crucial that we approach organisational development and change from a systems psychodynamic perspective, considering conscious behaviour and unconscious emotional elements in constant interaction with the larger system, sub-systems, and eco-system. Assessing and improving emotional intelligence is a central component of this approach. A former president of my university who was quite adept at initiating and gaining support for strategic and operational changes constantly spoke about finding ways to *win hearts and minds*. As I concluded in an early article about teaching: Good tools and technical facility are essential to performing any task well. The difference, however, between merely performing a task and producing a work of art is the amount of the performer's soul that gets transfused in the process. The teacher who truly makes a difference in students' lives touches the heart as well as the head.[163]

Organisational change and development practitioners ---and managers--- can do the same.

CHAPTER 8

How the Alchemy began: The Call

Alice Coelho

8.1 Initiation

My initiation into the world of Emotional intelligence began long before I had ever heard the term. A childhood fascination with people and how they expressed and managed their emotions within the world of relationships led to a career as a clinical psychologist. As a bright-eyed fledgling psychotherapist, I had the privilege of being trained in a department that strongly embraced seemingly opposed schools of thought in psychology, namely psychodynamic and postmodernist, social constructionist, interactionally based and process orientated approaches to working with the psyche of individuals and groups. This dichotomy of approaches fostered in me a need to find the "both and" in my work, and the journey of weaving together seemingly different worlds emerged, as I stood with one arm in an unconventional private practice, that not only saw individuals, families, children and couples, but where creativity and self-development group process work was offered. The other arm eagerly embraced assessing, creating and facilitating of EQ individual, team and organisational development journeys in the educational, financial and mining sectors.

However, the greatest gift I received in that time was a mentor who encouraged me to lean wholeheartedly into my own creative and intuitive impulse as a psychotherapist, whether I was working with an individual or a group, in a private practice or in a corporate setting. He taught me that this creative work is a sacred act. The science of psychology took on a soul for me, and here too I was challenged to weave together science and the sacred. This creative impulse was deeply rooted in two core and guiding principles. Firstly, to do no harm or as the Andean shamans say to live in "Ayni" or right relationship with all those we encounter, including ourselves and the planet. Secondly, to ensure that each co-creative encounter with my clients honoured their sacred stories on their journey towards being more integrated human beings, in the process of alchemising more meaningful lives. In my quest to find creative and deeper ways in which to honour this work, I had unknowingly answered the call on the heroine's journey to leave the ordinary world and to embark on a quest into the extraordinary world. As with all quests, I had to meet my internal and external foes, who cautioned me to stick to what was known, allowed and familiar in my professional sphere. Fortunately, I also met with great supportive allies and encouragement from friends and family who spurred me on until I synchronously encountered and began my love affair with the formal concept of emotional intelligence, amongst the shelves of the self-development section of a well-known South African bookstore.

A particular book caught my eye, and it really seemed to keep calling like a doe-eyed puppy for me to pick it up and take it home. As soon as I read the back cover of Executive EQ by Cooper, Robert, Sawaf and Ayman,[164] a surge of energy welled up within me and I ceremoniously announced to my then business partner, "we need to buy this book...I have a gut feeling that this is going to be a very important concept in the world of business, leadership development and in our private practice." He knew better than to challenge me when I went through the frenzy of activity that followed one of my "gut" feelings. The acquisition of the book was soon followed by formal training on the Baron EQ-I assessment instrument under the tutelage of Dr Jopie De Beer. Who could have predicted that a single assessment just over 20 years ago, of a young Honours Physics student, who read an article about EQ, would set me off on a path that led, not only to assessing and coaching executives in both individual and group settings, but ultimately to the creation of my own training material and EQ development tool and process.

Although one could metaphorically call that book an oracular guide on this quest, I somehow felt that this concept of EQ was predominantly explored from the place of the mind, which seemed to contradict Reuven Baron's definition of EQ as a group of "non-cognitive abilities, skills and competencies that greatly influenced one's ability to cope with environmental demands and pressures".

Every EQ development book available at the time was trying to make the dreaded world of emotions safe and sanitised enough to sell to the corporate world. Although a courageous act, the latter approach left EQ and those seeking to develop it, undernourished in the ordinary world of the hero's journey. Make no mistake that anyone who braves through an EQ development process is unquestionably a hero or heroine in my eyes. The burning question for me was where are the heart and the gut or body in the approaches to developing EQ? I yearned for my exploration and relationship to EQ to go beyond the head and land like a ripe seed in the heart and the body. I needed to feel EQ and not merely think about it. The hallmark of great leadership is not just that it makes one's teams and organisations think differently or more expansively, it also needs for them to feel...to explore a different lived or embodied experience in their quest to "high performance" in the direction of their strategic objectives. We all have a dream or a vision, but it needs the support of the heart to act as the catalyst and fuel to get us there.

My approach to developing EQ had to find a way to integrate and encourage the alignment of the head (the mental body), the heart (the emotional body), the soul (spiritual body) and the physical body. In short, my approach to developing EQ both personally and with my clients could be summarised as an integrated or holistic and psycho-spiritual approach. I need to be clear from the outset that my approach is not a religion and does not require anyone to jeopardise their religious beliefs in any way. It can best be described as a world view expressed through carefully curated processes and practices. What does that really mean? According to Mark Tavers, psycho-spirituality is a process in which "psychological self-awareness is integrated with spiritual growth, resulting in a holistic sense of well-being and personal development. [165]" It really involves weaving both psychological insights and spiritual or earth-based practices to understand yourself better and ultimately navigate life's challenges in more constructive and meaningful ways. It's a quest to whole being wellness which results in a more cohesive, integrated and lucid construction of self. My approach is an experiential, dynamic and tailor-made process that can be adapted to meet the client where they are in the present moment, and as such can be either completely process orientated or semi-structured in nature. It pushes people out of what Dr Sharon Blackie [166]calls the "wasteland" of their comfort zones through the use of my own product, the EQ Alchemy cards, (which I will speak to later in this chapter), myth, imagery, artistic exploration, poetry, nature, soundscapes, medicine drum journeys, meditation, breathwork, dream-mirroring, walking pilgrimages and more recently IxCacao ceremonial work. As with all EQ development journeys, the primary task is prescribed in Rumi's quote: "that which you seek in the branches of the tree, is to be found at its roots." Developing increased Intrapersonal Awareness, in a soulful way, feeds into all other aspects and contexts of living a more expansive life. In this approach I have witnessed individuals and groups transmuting knowledge into wisdom, which ripples out into wiser choices and interactional patterns, more rapidly alchemised than they would be, by merely adopting a more conventional approach to coaching and development journeys.

As a seeker of deeper layers and connections in relationship process and having been raised by parents who sought to make a difference in the world, no matter how small, through acts of service, I was constantly seeking for ways to enrich my clients' self-development processes, while I walked and served alongside them. It was then that I was gently but quite powerfully called yet again to heed the call of the Royal Hummingbird. Why the Hummingbird and to what end? The Andean medicine wheel, as a worldview, has four archetypes, one of which is the consciousness of the Royal Hummingbird. This little bird, despite its size, will make a perilous journey across continents to find the nectar of one flower. For these indigenous people of the Andes, **the Royal Hummingbird represents our ability to dream a sacred dream and to access the qualities of courage and resilience in our quest to fulfil that dream**.

It reminds us to find a balance in both action and stillness or mindful action in this quest. The most incredible quality this archetype embodies, is its ability to connect with faith and the abundant supply of Mother Earth, as it sets off in search of the nectar of that flower on faith alone...with no guarantee that it will indeed survive the journey or find that field of flowers. The hummingbird fluttered its wings around me as I toyed with how I could make a small contribution to the art of developing people and groups through EQ. It seemed that one of my sacred dreams was to create my own EQ development cards and development book, which would ultimately weave the science and principles of EQ that had been extensively researched, with the world of the archetypal and the sacred. The roots of the EQ Alchemy cards are closely intertwined with the most researched and widely employed assessment of Emotional Intelligence, namely, the Baron EQ-I. Although the principles, archetypal messages and anchors seemed to just flow from my pen and took less than a month of solitary mindful action to create, this dream took 10 years to bring to fruition. The latter was due in part to an inner voice that insisted that the artwork for these cards should not be digitally created. The alchemy of painting was a necessary requirement.

A dear friend and sublimely talented South African artist, Loeritha Saayman Martens, sat enthusiastically with me as we decided on each symbolic concept to represent the EQ principles for 72 cards. A picture of the cards can be seen below.

We had to find a symbolic representation for the EQ Alchemist that was as universal as possible, to increase cultural sensitivity and fairness of the cards. The universal symbol of the cut-out paper person became the EQ Alchemist. She then painstakingly set out to paint 72 A4 artworks, which would finally be printed in the card format. For example, the card 21 that deals with Emotional Self-Awareness can be seen below.

I believe that this collaborative artistic process to embody the messages and process of developing EQ was an important layer of alchemy and medicine in and of itself, just as the people and places the hero encounters on the path transform him or her. The time it took to paint each card affected us both and became a deep conversation piece in her home and in her studio where she often gave art classes to her students. This is a reminder that the development of EQ is a journey and process rather than a quick fix and a destination. The most unexpected gift in this story was that some alchemical process was magically underway, with no intentionally guided or professional intervention. The artworks were indeed a window to the soul and that it touched the soul in ways that words alone may not have. The result of this is that new conversations were being had about EQ in contexts far from the boardroom of major corporations, too. It reassured me that in this process the medicine of EQ could be re-experienced and integrated at a deeper level of gnosis, regardless of the context. Because of the intentional, mindful and sacred way of honouring the creation of these cards, the power they must transcend spaces and contexts in their use has often bowled me over. I believe the latter is due in part to what Blackie[167] refers to as the Sufi concept of "mundus imaginaries" or the "imaginal world of infinite possibility that exists between the physical world of our senses and the unseen world of spirit, intellect and inspiration" evoked by the archetypal imagery of the cards. I have seen clients randomly pull a card at the end of a coaching session to anchor the particular learning or message to be taken into their everyday lives, and laugh out loud, because the card is exactly what we had been working on in the session As Blackie[168] says in the Rooted Woman Oracle, "this is the place of synchronicities, 'psychic experiences and creative insights". The EQ cards, in combination with these psycho-spiritual practices, creates a liminal space where the archetypes embedded in our sacred stories and who seem to have a life of their own, reveal themselves. It is also here, where our higher selves lay in embryo, waiting to be awakened, nourished and birthed.

8.2 Application and Contexts

In what ways have I used these cards and integrated them with alternative and creative practices you may wonder? I have adventured with them in some of the following ways:

- In corporate settings for individual coaching, where the coachee had been formally assessed on the Baron EQ-I, as part of a larger assessment and development process.

- In corporate settings with groups and teams, where both structured and unstructured group processes were employed to develop general EQ skills, group cohesion, resilience and stress management, organisational culture and values mapping or simply for leadership development initiatives. Although integrating the cards and the psycho-spiritual approaches to developing EQ used, can be quite deep and layered, it can be extremely creative and fun, which facilitates an opening up to dialogue differently about what is currently happening within their teams and what their sacred dreams and vision for their time together might be.

- Aspects of this approach have been used in an international mining house as part of an online leadership and organisational development drive during the pandemic, on their executive levels. It was rolled out on the individual coaching and team development levels.

- Experiential aspects of this approach were also implemented at a well-known business school as part of the EQ development course material for diploma purposes.

- An experiential EQ development group process was also facilitated at one of the leading assessment consultancies, which services the banking industry in South Africa.

- At the first Integral African conference, the EQ Alchemy cards were offered as part of a medicine drum journey for participants.

- As a foundational part of a leadership development course for degree and diploma purposes, with interior and graphic design student.

- This approach has also had relevance and applicability in private practice with individuals to anchor new and EQ smarter ways of thinking, feeling, doing and being. I have used it with couples to increase self and couple interactional dynamics awareness. I found it a useful way in which to embed and inspire new ways of "seeing" self and partner, as well as to risk new ways of feeling and being in the social construction of relationship process. This experience of working with the EQ Alchemy cards has been reiterated by other therapists that have experimented with them in their practices.

- I have found this more integrated, holistic, psycho-spiritual way of working, while anchoring the process in the tangible realm of the EQ cards to be particularly useful, when working with young adults or teenagers. This group of clients often describes conventional talk therapies as limiting. Many have described this sacred integrated way of working with the cards, the medicine drum and nature-based practices and ceremonies as creative, grounding, inspiring and fascinating. This is especially useful in interrupting old ways of defining the self, opening new ways of dialoguing about the self at a deep archetypal level, and increasing awareness about patterns that no longer serve them. It encourages them to reconnect with their soulfulness in their process of identity formation in a more creative and expansive manner. This might be useful as an antidote to the increasing numbers of young adults and teenagers who are diagnosed with anxiety and depression. This way of working challenges the pathologizing of many of their developmental experiences, while empowering them to access new tools and ways of reclaiming agency in their healing journey.

- This integrated approach in combination with the EQ alchemy cards has also been used at some of the self-development retreats and day workshops I have facilitated. While the nature-based practices and walking meditations in nature foster a sense of awe in the magic and healing consciousness of the natural world, it simultaneously prepares participants to rediscover their sense of interest and wonder about not only the shadow in their inner landscape but also in the possibility of their light, strength and gifts. Working with nature as an alley is reminiscent of Blackie's[169] words "it shows us a path to understanding how profoundly enmeshed we are in the web of life on this planet and how our entanglements with the world around us nourishes us more deeply than any other source or substance." From a self-development perspective using nature as a container and catalyst fosters our curiosity about our connection to and interconnectedness with all living beings. This sets the groundwork and cultivates a hunger for identifying the connection between parts of ourselves and the interconnectedness of those parts to our behavioural choices and interpersonal dynamics. A combination of individual and group process work supported by medicine drum journeying, art, IxCacao ceremonies, soundscapes and self-reflective journalling practices with the EQ Alchemy cards, anchor the learning and growth in practical ways which can be carried back into the "ordinary world" of their daily lives. These retreats and ceremonies function as liminal spaces in which the participants are held in the various energetic layers of diverse medicines, enabling them to work in sacred ways to transition between where they have been and where they are going, physically, emotionally, mentally, spiritually and metaphorically.

This approach had been used in the same settings to highlight the important concept that change in the macrocosmic level of the individual or organisation is only possible and sustainable if there is a change at the microcosmic level of the individual or the team.

Through a strong weaving of the EQ alchemy cards with a psycho-spiritual process orientated approach, a safe container is created that embodies Rumi's quote: "Beyond all ideas of wrongdoing and right doing, there is a field, and I will meet you there." This is a powerful reminder that a non-judgemental, curiously compassionate stance is both a portal and a catalyst for deep exploration and alchemical transformation.

8.3 The Sweet Nectar of The Sacred Dream: Working With IxCacao In Sacred Ways

Your vision will become clear only when you can look into your own heart. He looks outside dreams. He who looks inside awakens.

—Carl Gustav Jung[170]

On this journey to work in more sacred ways with my personal and professional development, as well as with people's vulnerabilities and gifts, I have been privileged to meet many allies, guides and mentors, one of which is Ashleigh Tennier. She not only walks in two worlds, that of medical health professional in a hospital setting, but also as a strong, grounded medicine woman, who embodies this shamanic calling in a multi-faceted way. As well as being an IxCacao Kuchina, she is also one of the Soul dance chiefs of South Africa (an embodiment and powerful processing and healing practice through dance and drums with roots deep in the Native American medicine dances traditions). She is also the first woman to hold this role in South Africa and is indeed the first ever female chief of this uniquely South African dance medicine. She stands as a bridge between medical science and shamanic medicine woman with a quiet confidence in a humble, graceful and compassionate way. Under her guidance and mentorship over several years, I too was initiated as a IxCacao Kuchina. Working with the consciousness of this Andean teacher plant has been one of the most profound and alchemical processes of my personal and professional life.

Although teacher plants are powerful portals into deeper archetypal layers of and states of consciousness, they do need to be held and worked with in sacred, integrous, and energetically clean ways that honour the medicine. Unfortunately, in a society starved for more soulful experiences while being driven by the values of immediate need gratification and stimulation seeking to numb out the pain of trauma and psycho-spiritual alienation, we must expect to find the light and the shadow in this work. I have seen how these powerful allies and guides to the individual and collective unconscious have been used from a place of ego, both by ungrounded healer and client alike, to escape doing the deep inner work required to process and integrate the healing and the gifts within our own light and shadow, they so generously have to offer us.

What is a teacher plant really? This is a term used to describe specific plants that contain psychoactive ingredients within them, and that are traditionally used by indigenous cultures and shamans around the world in their search for wisdom. Traditionally, IxCacao was revered and known as the food of the gods and was used for heart opening, healing and celebratory ceremonies, to connect to the Divine. She is undoubtedly a deeply respected teacher plant. Albeit being a psychoactive teacher plant, IxCacao is an exception as a teacher plant because she remains a powerful alley in deepening any self-development work, in a self-reflective and grounding way. Working with Ixcacao is not an escape from the self. It is a grounded, nurturing, gentle, compassionate encounter with self, as you navigate the journey between who and how you currently manifest yourself, and who and how you aspire to be in this world. The latter characteristic really spoke to me as a clinician with a drive to foster, within myself and my clients, an internal locus of control and a sense of responsibility, grounded-ness and soulfulness in the cultivation of a more "functional", richer and meaningful life.

How may this be relevant for self-development work and EQ in particular? For the Andean peoples, IxCacao, as she is known there, is considered a physiological, psycho-spiritual and metaphysical heart healing medicine. From a western medical perspective there has been much research into the benefits of using teacher plants such as Psilocybin and Ayahuasca to name a few, to treat various "dis-eases" and mental health conditions such as depression, addiction and trauma. IxCacao as a superfood, is loaded with antioxidants, and vitamin B among other physiologically beneficial compounds such as magnesium, anandamides, theobromine and PEA. It also facilitates the production of the naturally occurring brain chemical serotonin, which plays a significant role in the regulation and elevation of mood, while increasing our resilience to the impact of stressors on our physical and emotional well-being. Archetypally, IxCacao is a feminine medicine and helps us to recalibrate the side effects and impact of living in a fast-paced, excessively driven world embedded in the shadow aspects of the archetypal masculine.

Working intentionally with IxCacao in ceremonial spaces helps us to look more deeply, compassionately and curiously at the emotional, mental, physical and spiritual body of the psyche and soul. In those spaces we can develop deeper self-awareness of how our thoughts and beliefs about ourselves, influence how we feel about ourselves, and then ultimately how the interrelationship between thoughts and feelings, influence how we interpret, experience and behave in the world around us and the relationship dynamics we are invested in. The latter highlights most of the core competencies of EQ. This work also guides us to a deeper understanding of how the consciousness of these patterns in our mental and emotional bodies can show up within our physical bodies, especially if we consider that our bodies are sacred vessels that hold the chemical memories of past traumas and joys. Today, there is a whole body of research dedicated to developing a more integrated understanding of the Mind-Body connection and the role that emotions and emotional healing play in the process of stress management, adaptability and resilience management. These too are competencies of EQ.

This process of holding these more experiential practices in ceremonial work with IxCacao facilitates a creative, fascinating and compassionate opening and encounter with energetically EQ-wiser patterns, which can be brought back into the "here-and-now" and woven into an EQ coaching journey, which is grounded in the principles of the EQ Alchemy cards. The cards help to keep the embodied wisdom alive beyond the ways in which words on their own can do. Their imagery speaks in the language of the Soul and anchors the soul of the EQ smart alchemist archetype in the ordinary world of the hero. The integration of the gifts of deep inner work with IxCacao and the EQ Alchemy cards highlights the idea that some truths are not meant to be understood (with the head), they are truths to be felt and accepted in the heart and in the body. The act of coming at EQ solely from the mind is in, and of itself, a creative strategy to avoid "doing" and "being" EQ in motion.

Nothing encapsulates the description of self-development work and EQ development journeying, from a sacred perspective, more for me, than the following words from Amani Friend, co-founder of the record label Desert Trax who believe in the transformative and healing power of music and founder of Liquid Bloom, in one of his songs:

> *"With this embodied presence you have been entrusted. An ancient gift passed from ancestor to ancestor, culminating in your heart, your hands.*
>
> *Here you breathe at the apex of an infinite spiral.*
>
> *Here your heart pulses its place in the web of inter-being.*
>
> *Reach deep into the legacy of the ancestors and open fully to the vision of the future.*

You are the medicine. Life is the ritual.

*We offer this ceremony to the winged bred, the dancing fire,
the rooted earth and the water of life for all our relations.*

*In bowing to our noble origins, we open new timelines of regeneration
to release our resonance into this timeless dream, awakened."*[71]

8.4 Final Thoughts

We all have something to offer the world we inhabit, and this path of the EQ alchemist facilitates a process by which we can connect to and manifest these gifts. However, shortcuts are not an option on the bridge between the hero's archetypal journey and the heroine's post-heroic journey. What often stands in our way to access our gifts and our unique medicine to this world lies deeply buried in the shadows, and so we are called to fly the path of the hummingbird. A path that reminds us that the gifts, peace, joy and dreams we are seeking are all on the other side of the work we are avoiding. My work with EQ from a sacred perspective, invites us to do the work courageously in a creative and integrous way, using my foundation as a psychotherapist, supported and guided by Mama IxCacao, to adventure deeply into nature, myth, metaphor, art, poetry, creative writing, music, the EQ alchemists cards, medicine drum journeying, and to return to our communities transformed, so that they too can benefit from our amplified resonance.

Group/Team Domain

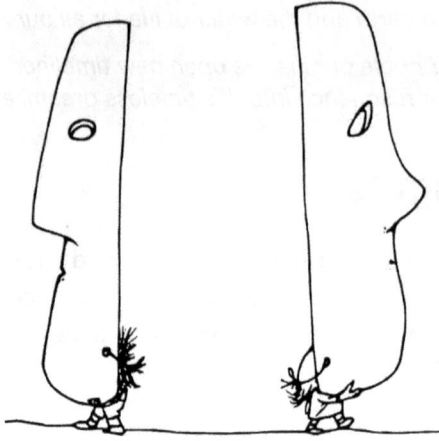

MASKS

She had blue skin,
And so did he,
He kept it hid
And so did she,
They searched for blue
Their whole life through,
Then passed right by –
And never knew.

Shel Silverstein

Chapter 9

The Dance of Facilitation

As the music changes so does the dance

—African saying

9.1 Introduction

Groups are at the heart of organisational life, influencing everything from decision-making and performance to culture and innovation. This chapter has examined the key dynamics that shape group behaviour, including stages of group development, the impact of leadership, and the role of communication in fostering collaboration. By understanding these principles, organisations can create environments where groups function effectively, balancing individual contributions with collective goals. Moreover, the challenges associated with group dynamics-such as conflict, social loafing, and groupthink-require intentional management strategies. Leaders and ODC practitioners can cultivate psychological safety, encourage diverse perspectives, and implement structures that enhance accountability and engagement through skilful facilitation. As organisations navigate an increasingly complex and interconnected world, the ability to leverage groups as a strategic asset will be crucial. The insights from this chapter provide a foundation for building functional teams that not only achieve organisational objectives but also contribute to a more adaptive, inclusive and resilient workplace.

In this chapter, various philosophies of and corresponding ways of intervening in group processes are presented in an autoethnographic note that illustrates the way in which the facilitator or consultant will deal with the boundary conditions in terms of time, space and content to do the task at hand. Schools include facilitation anchored in gestalt work, logos-therapy and process work. In this chapter snippets of a Rogerian facilitation process, an Integral session, a Tavistock event and a strategic framework planning intervention are described.

For the reader that is a facilitator – the questions posed in the various philosophies are presented in **bold.** Although only three approaches are presented the ODC practitioner is invited to work dynamically in different ways to facilitation in stylish dance to weave together what needs to happen.

9.2 Ways of Facilitating

Rogerian

In the hushed glow of a softly lit therapy room, the air was thick with possibility. Here, a Rogerian facilitator acts as an empathetic guide in the truest sense and is prepared to lead a 2-and-a-half-day intervention comprising of leaders of different parts of a corporate setting.

The chairs were arranged in a perfect circle, symbolising equality and a shared commitment to mutual respect. This seating arrangement was not mere decoration; it was a deliberate design choice to dissolve traditional hierarchies, allowing every voice to resonate on an equal plane.

The facilitator began by inviting each participant to share their story with a gentle, open-ended inquiry: **"Let's check in. Arrive in the here and the now. What brings you here today?"** Such questions, carefully chosen for their openness, are at the heart of the Rogerian tradition.[172] Answers are not demanded, but rather encourage exploration, reflection, and, most importantly, the expression of one's authentic self.

The facilitator set clear expectations at the outset: each voice would be heard, interruptions would be minimal, and confidentiality was the unspoken rule that governed every interaction. These boundaries, while subtle, provided the necessary structure for participants to venture into vulnerable territories, secure in the knowledge that their experiences would be honoured without judgment.

As the session unfolded, the facilitator moved among the participants, not physically but with a presence that was both warm and vigilant. Each reflective question was posed not as a challenge but as an invitation to deeper self-awareness. **"Where does this leave you?"** became a refrain, softly echoing through the circle. The facilitator's curiosity and reflective listening aims to transform each query into a mirror - a tool that allowed participants to see themselves and others in a new, kinder light. This process of reflection and validation is a core pillar of client-cantered therapy, as Rogers elaborated in his seminal work, *On Becoming a Person*.[173]

Boundaries, too, played a pivotal role in this transformative space. They were neither rigid walls nor cold barriers but gently drawn lines ensuring that the emotional landscape remained safe for exploration. In the confluence of empathetic inquiry, respectful boundaries and intentional physical space, the Rogerian facilitator wove an environment where trust could flourish.

In one particularly poignant moment, a young female leader named Bongi hesitated, her eyes reflecting both hope and uncertainty. Recognising the silent plea for safety, the facilitator leaned forward, closing the gap not just in physical distance but in emotional understanding. With a softly delivered inquiry - **"What do you feel would help you feel safe enough to share?"** the facilitator demonstrated the delicate art of balancing inquiry with respect for personal boundaries. Bongi's response, tentative at first, soon gave way to a cascade of insights that not only enriched her own journey but also deepened the collective trust of the group.

Bridges are woven between isolated moments and collective healing. The facilitator guides: "Speak from the self... to each other not about each other".

The art of questioning in a Rogerian framework is a study of subtlety and depth. Rather than interrogative demands, the facilitator's questions were explorations-avenues through which the inner landscapes of each participant could be mapped without intrusion. These types of questions, characterised by their open-ended, reflective nature, are essential in creating a dialogue that honours the participant's autonomy and intrinsic worth. They invite the speaker to elaborate, reflect, and ultimately reclaim their narrative, fostering an environment where trust is both the medium and the outcome of every interaction.

Time boundaries are bend.[174] "In more or less five minutes we will wrap up this conversation", closes sessions. The conversation continues for another 14 minutes or so. A group member speaks about another individual leaving the person spoken to without voice. Sometimes, the facilitator physically stands behind the person and rephrases carefully what was said – taking on the essence of that individual.[175] Movement in understanding of what was happening is displayed for the group to observe and feel.

In the transformative process, trust was not merely discussed-it was dynamically created through intentional questioning, established boundaries, and the deliberate arrangement of our shared space. This interplay of scholarly principles and heartfelt practice reminded me that, as facilitators, our role is to nurture an environment where academic insights merge with the lived reality of each participant. In doing so, we honour both the integrity of the individual and the collective power of genuine, empathetic dialogue.

Integral

In the quiet, anticipatory moments before our session began, I stepped into a space meticulously prepared to nurture both vulnerability and strength. The chairs were arranged in a flawless circle, each one a testament to our shared human dignity, dissolving the usual hierarchies and inviting each participant into an equal communion.

I began by addressing the importance of trust-a concept both delicate and essential. I explained that trust is not granted by words alone, but is built gradually through genuine, respectful interactions. My introduction was both scholarly and heartfelt: **"We are here not just to speak, but to listen deeply to honour every shared story and every silence that speaks volumes."** The task of the facilitator was to weave together diverse theoretical threads-from systemic thinking to mindfulness practices - crafting an environment where every individual's inner landscape could be explored safely.

Boundaries were not set constraints, but as gentle guidelines. These boundaries ensured that each shared experience was respected and that every participant felt secure in expressing the complexities of their inner life. I explained, **"Our shared space is sacred. Here, confidentiality is paramount, and every narrative is a crucial piece of our collective mosaic."** I deliberately choose words between the way in which participants construct reality – almost speaking in a poetic manner.

True to the intent of our shared dialogue no voice would dominate, and no perspective would be marginalised. Throughout the session, I offered reflective, open-ended questions designed to evoke introspection and foster trust. **"How does your experience of this moment inform your sense of belonging?"** I would ask, inviting each participant to traverse the delicate boundary between thought and feeling. **"From your angle, what do you sense and experience?"** With each inquiry, the group slowly unravelled layers of personal insight, their stories interweaving into a rich tapestry of shared humanity.

We moved from the circle around us to four quadrants displayed in the middle of the shared space. Delegates are invited to speak their truth – but step between the sacredly constellated spaces with archetypal symbols in the middle. **"Are you speaking from the inner I or the I that you project outwards?"; "Would you rather step into the space where you speak about the roles that you place on yourself – the inner WE? Or systems and processes outside yourself? Step there?**

Spiral Dynamics Integral theory was presented to provide a theoretical lens to make sense of the group dynamics. In this transformative space, trust was not a static achievement but a dynamic process-a continuous creation through every empathetic pause, every respectful boundary, and every intentional arrangement of our shared seating. The session unfolded like a carefully composed symphony, where scholarly insights met the raw expression of lived experience, and every individual was invited to partake in the dance of honest dialogue and profound connection.

System Psychoanalytical Facilitation

The room was alive with unspoken tensions, currents of anxiety and anticipation weaving through the silence like an invisible thread. As a system psychoanalytic facilitator-stepped into the space, the consultant felt it all. The unclaimed projections, the hesitant gazes, the unconscious alliances forming before a single word had been spoken.

The room was still charged with the kind of anticipatory silence that often precedes deep psychological work. As a trained consultant-entered the space on the time boundary, he understood that his role was not to impose order, nor to guide members toward a predefined outcome, but to hold the tension, to bear witness, and to create the conditions where the unconscious dynamics of the group could surface, be explored, and, perhaps, be understood.

The seating arrangement was no arbitrary decision. In psychoanalytical methodology, the structure of the space is a container for the anxieties and projections that inevitably emerge in any collective setting.[176] Initially, chairs were placed cinema style. It was a deliberate arrangement, designed to provide the opening plenary context. Everyone, whether aware or not, was now part of a system, and the way they occupied their seat-how they positioned their body, where their gaze landed-was as much a part of the emerging group dynamic as the words spoken aloud.

Photo 9.1: Chairs in systems psychoanalytical event

In the next event, a spiral was formed. There was no table to hide behind, no formal hierarchy dictating where power resided. This was a system in its rawest form-a microcosm of the unspoken structures that governed not just this group, but the organisations, institutions and societies from which they came.[177] Seating arrangements were interpreted as a hypothetical manifestation of the group dynamic at play. The consultant continued to hypothesise about who takes up what chair. It probably tells us something about the pairing and pecking order in the group. The "ins" and "outs". The group struggles with the unknown and how to make sense of the primary task of the group. **"Blaming the facilitator?"**, was asked.

Any comment was measured against the task of the group and the purpose of the group set up front. The time boundaries were set out clearly. Boundaries were crucial, but not as rigid constraints; rather, they were psychological scaffolding that would allow for deep exploration without collapse. The consultant established the time, space and content boundary early.

Someone shifted in their seat. Another crossed their arms. A few exchanged quick glances. A group member is leaving the room for the bathroom. **"It is my hypothesis that the angst in the room is so much that people flee"**, the consultant offered.

Trust, in this setting, was not granted freely. Unlike models that begin with an assumption of psychological safety, this approach acknowledges that trust is earned, negotiated, and sometimes resisted. The consultant was not a soothing presence, not a reassuring authority. Soon he offered the group an opportunity to witness itself. **"I wonder why certain members are quiet?"** The consultant had no need to fill the silence-it, too, was part of the process.

Systems have a way of exposing what is unconscious, dragging it into the light. As the group unfolded, defences emerged: humour to deflect vulnerability, intellectualisation to avoid emotion and silence as both a weapon and a refuge. The consultant left the room at the exact moment a member shared a profound truth. The chairs in the rooms were in a spiral twirling in the opposite direction. 5 minutes into the session a group member, quite aggressively, told everyone to form a circle. The consultant reflected, "It feels as if the group reorganises if things get hard." No one followed the group member and reluctantly he replaced his chair in the original sequence.

Photo 9.2 Chairs in a systems psychoanaltycial event

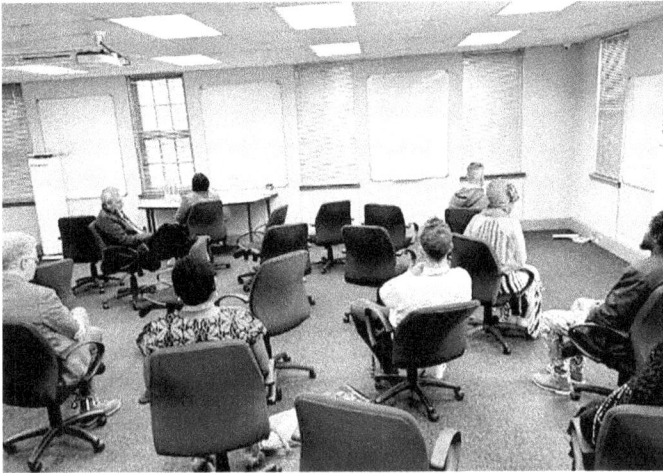

It was then that one participant, a senior leader, broke the unspoken contract of safety. "I don't see the point of this," she said, her voice clipped, her body language retreating even as their words pushed forward. The tension rippled outward. The group dynamic shifted – the other members waiting, watching. **"It seems as if there is a lot of tension in the group."** The room held its breath. The consultant merely reflected on how my own sense of the process shifted and formed a working hypothesis of what is happening under the surface of the group. Assumptions about the group process are to explore or reject and in this way the group is supported through the perceived stuck-ness.

Each participant had a right to their thoughts, their resistances, their defences-but the group, as a system, also had a right to name them. "**Political games are alive and well in this group?"** the consultant posed in the first large group event when the group became silent. The energy in the room thickened with an unspoken tension. A slight shift in posture, averted gazes-small signs that an unarticulated conflict was simmering just beneath the surface. The session unfolded with moments of discomfort, moments of resistance, and then, eventually, moments of recognition.

One participant, who had sat stiffly at the edge of the circle, finally leaned forward. "I don't trust this process," she almost whispered. The group exhaled. A truth had been spoken. In this stance, this was not failure - it was the process itself. The recognition of mistrust allowed the group to see itself more clearly, to acknowledge the unconscious fears and projections shaping their engagement.

This approach presents a conflict model, after all. Slowly, through the course of the event, the group began to see what was at play-not just in their words, but in their silences, their seating choices, their shifting alliances. The system revealed itself, as it always does when one knows where to look.

By the end, in the closing plenary, no one would have said they "felt safe" in the way the term is often used. But there was a different kind of safety now-a safety born from confronting what had been hidden, from naming the unnameable, from staying in the discomfort long enough to learn from it. Unseen dynamics were made visible, the group shifted in terms of its collective unconscious and individual and group defences became clear.

Strategy Facilitation Through Inclusivity

The room was still, but not quiet. The air buzzed with the subtle tension that comes when a group knows they are standing at a threshold-not of what they do, but of who they are. I understood the weight of this work. This was not a mere exercise in crafting statements for a website. This was about future and past identity and about clarity. About the DNA of the system itself.

The seating arrangement was deliberate. A wide-open U-shape-inviting conversation yet leaving space for the unknown. The facilitation of a visioning process is not linear, nor is it dictated from above. It requires space, movement, the ability to see not only each other but beyond each other. I let my eyes sweep the room before speaking. "Before we create anything, we need to understand this: A vision is not invented. A mission is not forced. Values are not aspirational. They already exist. Our work is to uncover them. "A few nodded. Others folded their arms. Some had come expecting to draft statements, bullet points and taglines. They would soon learn this was not that kind of session. Where would you like to start?"

I set the boundaries early - not to confine but to protect the process from falling into clichés or superficial consensus:

- We do not rush to agree. Tension is part of the process.
- No jargon, no slogans. We speak an actual language, not corporate-speak.
- Mission is not marketing. This is about identity, not just external messaging.
- If we do not believe it, we do not write it. No empty words.

I let that settle. Then I asked: "If your organisation disappeared tomorrow, what would the world lose?" A pause. Someone exhaled sharply. A few looked at each other, hesitant. Then, a voice: "Hope." Another: "A place for people to belong." And another: "A way to do business that takes people with." The room was shifting.

Picture 9.3 Chairs in a large group conversation

"A mission is not what you wish to be. It is what you do. Daily. Without compromise. If you stopped doing it, you would cease to exist. What do you do, every day, that makes you who you are?" A woman leader leaned forward. "We create opportunities for people who don't have them." A man across from her added, "We challenge the status quo." Another voice: "We make courageous decisions." The mission was emerging- not from abstraction, but from lived reality. I changed the question. "If you succeed-if your mission is fully realised-what does the world look like?" This was harder. Mission was grounded. Vision required imagination. Conviction. Courage. A long pause. Then, finally: "A world where opportunity isn't just for a select few"; "A society where people don't just survive but thrive"; "A future where innovation is driven by purpose, not profit." Later, the communications department would draft a well-structured statement on key areas of consensus achieved in the room.

"A mission without values is directionless. A vision without values is meaningless. Your values are what you will never, under any circumstance, compromise. What are the values that define who you are-not just when things are easy, but when things are hard?" Someone spoke quickly. "Integrity." I nodded. "What does integrity mean here? Not in theory, but in practice?" A pause. Then: "It means we don't take shortcuts, even when no one is watching." Another voice. "It means we are honest about what we can and can't do." Now we were getting somewhere. More answers came. "Empowerment." "Collaboration." "Equity." "Fearlessness." We pushed through. "Which values would you be willing to lose money over? To fight for? To protect, even if it costs you something?" Some words fell away. What remained were the true, unshakable values.

As we neared the end of the two-day event, I asked one final question. "Where do your mission, vision and values not yet align with reality?" This was the hardest moment. Someone sighed. "We say we empower people, but sometimes we still hold too much control." Another: "We value equity, but we haven't made enough space for diverse voices." A third: "We want to challenge the system, but sometimes we compromise to keep things running." The truth was emerging. And trust was forming-not through easy agreement, but through honesty.

You don't need me to tell you what your mission, vision and values are. You already knew. You just needed to speak it out loud." The room exhaled. Some smiled. Some sat in quiet reflection. The strategic core for the next 5 years was forged through a process of co-creation and the group adjourned with a sense of belonging and pride in what was achieved.

Social Dreaming Matrix: Unlocking the Social Unconscious in Collective Spaces

Dr Calum McComb

Social dreaming was discovered by Gordan Lawrence from the Tavistock Institute, however, departs from the Tavistock Tradition of working with Group Relations. The group dynamic, discovered through experiences of relating, is not the focus of enquiry in social dreaming. Social dreaming is a current expression of dream sharing intending to formulate or discover new hypotheses about the community.[178] It is a name given to a particular method of sharing dreams in a collective specifically gathered for a purpose. [179] Click or tap here to enter text.

> Social Dreaming is a way of working with dreams where the focus is on the dream and not the dreamer, where dreams are shared amongst people who come together solely for this purpose. With Social Dreaming, the meaning of the dream is about the broader world in which one lives. In a Social Dreaming event, participants are invited to offer their dreams and , through association, explore the possible social meaning contained within them.[180]

Social dreaming recognises that the audience may also be the social dreaming matrix (standing for community), and through the associative unconscious may call forth dreams through its members that resonate with an underlying reality.[181] It is a practice for a group sharing its collective identity, such that personal dreams might conceivably be dreamt 'for us' – even if, as might happen, the dreams themselves pay no heed to constructed bodies.[182] In other words, dreams may be dreamt on behalf of the group beyond that of the individual level.

Applied to organisational development, social dreaming provides a space within which leaders and work groups may gain new insights, think new thoughts, access creativity and make connections through the associative unconscious. Long[183] describes the associate unconscious as a network shared by any interacting community through their shared language, history, myths, emotions and experiences, and, as Jung argues in his concept of the collective unconscious, runs across all cultures at some deeply unconscious levels. In this sense, however, the associative unconscious differs from Jung's collective unconscious with its focus on archetypes, which are pre-existing forces that shape the course of our lives. Rather, a shared and co-created experience of a community with its historic symbols and stories is accessed through the associative unconscious.

It may be included as part of corporate retreats and leadership development events by providing a unique method to access latent thoughts, emotions and patterns that are otherwise inaccessible to the conscious mind. When one thinks about strategy in organisations, it is possible to make the link to dreaming. After all strategy development is about dreaming into the future. Social Dreaming Matrices may therefore provide an important platform for executives needing to access deeper levels of creativity in dreaming up and making connections that enable fresh insights and new directions. The themes that emerge from the matrix may also offer a new lens into organisational culture and transformation.

The Nature and Purpose of Social Dreaming

It should be clear from the outset that the sharing of dreams with a gathering of others cannot be compared to the recounting of a dream in the clinical context and dyadic situation of analyst-analysand.[184] Click or tap here to enter text. Rather, social dreaming is about what the dreams might mean for the community. As the dreams and associations are shared, they then belong to the group and no longer only to the individual. Taking a group relations stance on social dreaming, I hypothesise that dreams and associations that are shared become parts of the whole. In this sense when a dream is shared it may hold something on behalf of the group as whole that could be explored to uncover new meaning that belongs to the matrix.

Its main purpose is to enable the dreams to speak to us about the worlds we live in that may be unconsciously experienced but not readily accessible in our day-to-day conscious living.[185] In this sense, the purpose of the social dreaming matrix is freely to associate with the dreams that are made available, to make links and find connections in thinking.[186] Click or tap here to enter text. The structure of the social dreaming matrix allows for the community to foster new insights through the interconnected web of dreams and associations that are shared.

It is often helpful to articulate clearly the overarching purpose of the social dreaming matrix before hosting such an event. For example, it may represent an enquiry into the organisational culture or the climate of the group. Another purpose may be for leaders to think new thoughts about the strategic direction of the organisation. It could be to enhance group collaboration and a sense of shared meaning and belonging. Whatever the over-arching purpose for including a social dreaming matrix as part of an organisational development intervention, it is imperative that the over-arching purpose is agreed on beforehand.

The Process

Social dreaming takes place in a matrix – which is the name given to a collective of people meeting to share dreams.[187] Click or tap here to enter text. The process has three main parts to it, namely 1) setting the scene and introducing the social dreaming matrix, 2) hosting the social dream matrix, and 3) hosting the social dream dialogue.

Setting the scene and introducing the social dreaming matrix

To set the scene and manage the space boundaries, the host of the matrix arranges the chairs in snowflake patterns so that members are not looking directly at one another. People are invited to take up a seat wherever they wish to. When introducing the social dreaming matrix to the community, it is important to emphasise that the focus is on the dream and not the dreamer. One might introduce the social dreaming matrix using the below words:

"Welcome to this social dreaming matrix. The social dreaming matrix will last for 60 minutes. My name is .... and I am the host of the matrix today. My role is to contain the space, time, task and role boundaries to allow for a psychologically safe space in which to share your dreams. What is a social dreaming matrix? It is a method of exploring and accessing the associative unconscious through thinking about the dreams that members share. During the matrix, we share our nighttime dreams and what we associate with them so that we can make links and connections between the dreams and what this means for the group.

A dream is presented, and then another and then another. As members of the social dreaming matrix, we listen to the dreams, which may trigger thoughts, feelings and associations, which we can in turn share with the matrix if we wish to. The matrix focuses on the dreams and not the dreamer. It is not about personal interpretation. A word about association. An association is a thought, idea, experience, memory or emotion that is triggered by another person's dream. The social dreaming matrix will close after one hour after which we will move into the dream reflection dialogue."

Hosting the social dreaming matrix

After the introduction to the social dreaming matrix the host of the matrix asks the group, "where is the first dream"? This marks the beginning of the social dream matrix. An uncomfortable silence might ensue after asking for the first dream, but it is imperative for the host to hold the space and allow the first dream to emerge. It is the role and task of the host to manage the time boundary of one hour before closing the session. It's also important to maintain the task boundary of the group, which is to offer dreams and associations as a way for the group to think new thoughts rather than making personal interpretations. Group members often become fixated on individual dreams and easily, without being conscious of it, single out individuals and interpret their dreams in this context. It's also important for the host to make the matrix aware of the task when attempts are made to interpret the dreams or provide hypotheses during the social dreaming matrix. Rather, the sharing dreams and associations are the task of the matrix in session.

Hosting the social dreaming dialogue

The social dreaming dialogue, which last for thirty minutes, is the time where the task becomes about discovering patterns in the dreams, offering interpretations about the associative unconscious in the group, and making links. It is the role of the host to hold the task and time boundaries for the dialogue to take place. It is also possible to incorporate dream drawing into the process of making sense of the dreams. When I facilitate social dream drawing as part of the experience, I ask each participant to take ten to fifteen minutes out to draw dream images using crayons. Each participant of the matrix then places their drawing in the center of the group, which is interpreted as belonging to the group and not the individual.

The primary purpose of the social dream dialogue is to make sense out of the dreams and what they might mean for the community. This is done through the identification of themes and patterns across the dreams and associations and the formulations of hypotheses about what might be happening beneath the surface of consciousness for the group. This is the space for leaders to explore how the dreams and new thoughts might contribute to their strategy. For work groups, they might discover shared unconscious phantasies that shape their identity and the climate of the group. Organisations using the process for systemic transformation might pose the question 'how do these insights reflect our culture'? Regardless of the reason set out for the social dreaming matrix, the process offers a plethora of possibilities for new connections and thoughts to be explored, thus deepening the creative potential of the group.

The Transformative Potential of Social Dreaming

Enhancing creativity and innovation

Social dreaming has the potential to overcome emotional barriers to creativity. It encourages divergent thinking, which allows the matrix to explore ideas that can't surface in conventional discussions. The process allows for the unconscious source of creativity to emerge, which can be employed towards novel solutions.

Facilitating Psychological Safety and Open Dialogue

A theme that has emerged across many corporate organisations is the experience of psychological safety. This is held in the host's mind who, through careful management of role, task, space and time boundaries, ensures a psychologically safe space in which the dreams may be shared and explored.

Illuminating hidden group dynamics

Shared unconscious conflicts, anxieties, and desires may come to surface during and after a social dream matrix. These may hold valuable clues about group or organisational challenges, aspirations and cultural narratives. Making these conscious may help leaders to navigate complexities with greater awareness and sensitivity.

Aiding strategic thinking and visioning

Leaders frequently become caught up in the operational demands and tangible problems that need to be solved, but in doing so neglect to think more deeply about the strategic vision. Social dreaming may offer alternative systemic insights that enrich the future strategy of the organisation as metaphors and associations emerge.

Strengthening community and shared meaning

Social dreaming has the potential to create a greater sense of belonging to the group as members begin to realise the interconnectedness of their associate's unconscious. The matrix refers to the community within which members live their lives. Through a co-created and non-judgmental space, a greater sense of community is fostered.

9.3 The Dance of Facilitation

To create a dance in a group process, the following rules or principles protect the integrity of the rhythm, and creates a collective setting for it to unfold elegantly:

💡 The Rule of Two Feet (Responsibility and Agency)

This principle, borrowed from Open Space Technology, asserts that participants are responsible for their own learning and engagement. If they find themselves in a situation where they are neither learning nor contributing, they should use their metaphorical (or literal) "two feet" to move to where they can add or receive value.[188]The rule fosters agency, self-awareness, and accountability in group settings, discouraging passive participation.

💡 The Rule of Psychological Safety (Trust Before Truth)

Facilitators must ensure that an environment of psychological safety is established before engaging in challenging discussions. Research highlights that individuals in psychologically safe environments are more likely to contribute, take risks, and share insights.[189] Before diving into complexity or conflict, create ground rules for respectful dialogue, validate emotions, and ensure that all voices are acknowledged.

💡 The Rule of Cognitive Load (Cogmotics)

Borrowing from cognitive science, cogmotics refers to the understanding that human cognitive capacity is limited. Overloading discussions with excessive information or rapid topic shifts reduce engagement and decision-making quality.[190] The ODC practitioner must structure sessions with intentional pacing, allowing for reflection, synthesis, and integration of insights.

💡 The Rule of Multiple Perspectives (Diversity is Fractal)

No single perspective holds the full truth. A group operates like a complex adaptive system where every voice contributes to a richer, more accurate understanding. Diversity of thought principles reinforces that different worldviews must be acknowledged rather than forced into consensus.[191] Assessments can help participants to understand diverse perspectives and enable conflicting views to emerge in generative dialogue.

💡 The Rule of Holding Tension (The Facilitator as a Containing Boundary)

Group processes often surface anxiety, resistance and unconscious projections. A facilitator's role is not to diffuse discomfort too quickly but to contain it, allowing the group to sit with complexity without prematurely closing the conversation. This principle is drawn from Bion's work on containment in group dynamics.[192] The facilitator must resist the urge to "fix" tension. Instead, name it, reflect it, and help the group work through it productively.

💡 The Rule of Liminal Space (Transformation Happens in the Unknown)

True shifts occur in the "in-between" spaces-when participants are no longer fully in their old ways of thinking but have not yet arrived at a new understanding. Liminality, a term from anthropology,[193] describes this threshold moment. The ODC practitioner must allow for emergence-allow open-ended inquiry, discomfort and moments of silence rather than rushing toward closure.

💡 The Rule of Energetic Reciprocity (Attunement and Adaptive Leadership)

Facilitation is an energy exchange. The facilitator must attune to the group's mood, energy levels, and emerging dynamics, adjusting their approach accordingly.[194] It favours the ODC practitioner to as facilitator develop somatic awareness and for example consider body language, shifts in attention, and subtle changes in group coherence, responding flexibly.

💡 The Rule of Self-Reflection (The Facilitator is Also in the System)

A facilitator is not a neutral observer-they are part of the system and inevitably influence group dynamics. Reflexivity is essential to avoid unconscious bias, authority projection or defensive facilitation.[195] ODC practitioners can engage in facilitation debriefs, journaling, or supervision to examine personal reactions and systemic impacts.

Being a ODC practitioner can be lonely as to be in role means that one must be on the edge of the group process and do not belong to the system to which one consultant to. Group supervision sessions for systems psychoanalytically informed consultants are really helpful in this regard. An example is of the approach offered by Dr Jean Cooper from TILT[196] and which provides not only a space for ODC practitioners to reflect but also to learn from others. Cooper, for example, offers a containing space that offers a theoretical exploration to create shared understanding and personal development, followed by the intertwining of the dreams of participants stemming from the social dreaming matrix that is facilitated and reflections on actual cases using the Balint method, that ensure that a valuable reflective growth experience occurs.

💡 The Rule of Sacred Silence (The Power of Collective Stillness)

Silence is not absence-it is a presence in its deepest form. In facilitation, silence can serve as a sacred space for processing, integration, and deeper connection. Often, facilitators rush to fill silences out of discomfort, but true transformation happens in the spaces between words.[197] The ODC practitioner must allow for intentional pauses in discussion. After key moments, the group can be invited to sit with the silence, to let it unfold naturally rather than forcing speech.

Great facilitation is not about control-it is about holding space for emergence, disruption and collective meaning-making. Each session is an evolving system, shaped by the individuals present, the boundaries set, and the facilitator's ability to dance with the unknown. By applying their rules, a sacred space can be crafted for the group to engage in the task at hand.

9.4 Facilitation Techniques

This synthesis, drawn from ODC Rica Viljoen's knowledge resources, examines four transformative methodologies-Appreciative Inquiry, Dialoguing, Storytelling, and World Café. Each approach represents a paradigm shift in organisational research and practice by fostering inclusivity, collective wisdom and innovative change.

Appreciative Inquiry

Overview and rationale

Appreciative Inquiry is widely recognised as a transformative approach to organisational change and development. It deliberately shifts the focus from deficit-based problem-solving to the exploration and amplification of inherent strengths and potentials. At its core, AI leverages positive language to elevate the awareness of both individual and collective capabilities, thereby enabling organisations to transcend self-imposed limitations that often arise from negative framing.[198, 199]

The 4-d cycle: discovery, dream, design and destiny

The methodology of AI has been shaped by pioneers such as Richard Barrett[200] and Gervase Bushe[201] and is commonly framed within the 4-D Cycle as described by Cooperrider et al.[202] In the Discovery phase, participants recount experiences of peak performance to uncover latent organisational strengths. The Dream phase facilitates a collective envisioning of an ideal future. This is followed by the Design phase, during which strategic actions are formulated to translate the envisioned future into actionable plans. Finally, the Destiny phase focuses on the implementation and sustainability of these strategies through empowerment and continuous learning.

Contemporary perspectives and critiques

Lewis[203] highlights the increasing relevance of this facilitation technique in environments characterised by rapid technological change and globalisation. Patel and Smith [204] emphasis that AI's creation of a shared, positive narrative enhances stakeholder engagement and contributes to more resilient and adaptable change processes.

McCormick and Ross[205] suggest that Appreciate Inquiry redefines organisational challenges as opportunities for growth, while Johnson and Edwards[206] demonstrate through longitudinal research how co-created narratives within Appreciative Inquiry interventions foster sustainable change. By prioritising strengths and fostering inclusive dialogue.

This technique offers a constructive counterpoint to traditional, problem-centric approaches. Some critics caution that an exclusive focus on strengths might overlook critical issues. The prevailing view is that AI's positive orientation cultivates the creative energy necessary to address underlying challenges.[207]

Dialoguing

Overview and principles

Dialoguing is a dynamic process that transcends ordinary discussion by fostering collective, coherent thought. Rooted in Bohm's[208] seminal work, dialoguing involves suspending individual opinions and assumptions in order to genuinely listen and engage with others. This approach surfaces underlying values that may otherwise constrain innovative thinking.[209]

Process and facilitation

Dialoguing is typically facilitated in circular settings, which symbolically and functionally reflect the interconnectedness of each participant's contribution. The objective is not to win an argument but to develop a shared meaning through open, undirected inquiry that allows hidden assumptions and diverse perspectives to emerge. LeBarOn[210] underlines the importance of creating a psychologically safe environment where every participant's contribution is valued.

Contemporary insights and critiques

Recent studies emphasise the role of dialoguing in enhancing organisational resilience. Anderson[211] posits that dialoguing can act as a catalyst for organisational adaptability in rapidly changing environments. Taylor[212] demonstrates how free dialogue nurtures a culture of creativity and mutual learning. While some critics note potential challenges in heterogeneous groups where power dynamics may hinder the free flow of ideas,[213] the overall consensus is that the benefits in fostering empathy, innovative problem solving and shared leadership are significant.

Storytelling

The role of storytelling in organisational culture

Storytelling is recognised as a powerful method for shaping organisational culture and fostering a shared understanding of values, goals and transformation efforts. Far beyond mere entertainment, storytelling serves as a strategic tool for creating, sustaining, and transforming organisational culture. Narratives carry behavioural norms and preserve collective memory while communicating the values and visions of leadership ().[214, 215, 216]

Processes and functions

At the heart of storytelling is its capacity to convey tacit knowledge. As Weick[217] explains, the need for sensemaking in organisations drives the use of storytelling to convert abstract concepts into memorable narratives. This process aids the transfer of tacit knowledge and supports double-loop learning, whereby underlying assumptions and values are re-examined and refined. Storytelling facilitates emotional engagement, fosters creativity, and strengthens relationships, making it an essential tool for aligning a workforce towards change initiatives.

Contemporary perspectives and critiques

Smith and Johnson[218] demonstrate its ability to enhance organisational identity and agility by creating dynamic narratives that adapt to rapid environmental changes. Gabriel[219] emphasises the importance of narrative leadership, in which leaders embed ethical and cultural values into their storytelling to shape organisational behaviour and promote transformational change. Denning[220] further highlights that effective storytelling translates complex strategies into actionable insights, bridging the gap between abstract goals and everyday practices. Despite critiques that narratives can be subjective and culturally specific[221, 222], the integration of storytelling with rigorous frameworks confirms its potency as a mechanism for sustainable transformation.

World Café Methodology

Overview and core assumptions

World Café methodology reintroduces the age-old practice of engaging dialogue to harness collective wisdom and co-create organisational strategy. Wheatly[223] describes it as a space where individuals come together without the constraints of labels or stereotypes, accessing a shared reservoir of insight. The approach is based on the belief that every participant inherently possesses the creativity and wisdom necessary to address complex challenges.[224]

Process and facilitation

The World Café process begins with setting a hospitable context that invites participants to explore issues of significance. Small, rotating groups are formed to focus on specific topics, which can range from analysing strengths, weaknesses, opportunities and threats to exploring various dimensions of performance such as customer, resource and financial perspectives. A designated host at each table ensures continuity by sharing insights from previous rounds with new participants, thereby deepening the collective understanding. Following the café sessions, a contracting phase is required to refine the co-created outputs into clear strategic objectives and initiatives.[225]

Comparative analysis and critiques

What sets World Café apart from other facilitative techniques, such as open-space technology, is its commitment to inclusivity. Every participant is given an equal opportunity to contribute, which fosters a strong sense of ownership and engagement among employees.[226] Despite its strengths in mobilising collective intelligence and fostering innovative thinking, the scalability of the process in larger groups may be limited, potentially leading to longer session durations.[227]

Other Techniques

In addition to the methodologies already discussed, several other approaches can be integrated into an inclusive framework for organisational change and development. Each method contributes uniquely to fostering participation, collective insight and innovative transformation.

- Action Research offers a participative and iterative process that involves planning, acting, observing, and reflecting. This approach enables organisations to address challenges collaboratively and adaptively, ensuring that change initiatives are both contextually relevant and sustainable.[228]
- Open Space Technology is a dynamic facilitation method that empowers large groups to self-organise around critical issues. By creating an environment in which participants determine the agenda and engage in spontaneous dialogue, this method promotes organic collaboration and generates creative solutions without imposing rigid structures.[229]

- Future Search Conferences are designed to bring diverse stakeholders together to develop a shared vision for the future. Through intensive, cross-sectional dialogue, participants align around common goals and strategies, thereby facilitating broad-based commitment and coherent action plans.[230]

9.5 Final Thoughts

Facilitation is not a rigid formula but an adaptive, responsive dance - one that shifts with the rhythm of the group, the nuances of human interaction, and the unfolding dynamics of change. As explored in this chapter, different facilitative approaches offer distinct ways of engaging groups, from the empathetic space of Rogerian dialogue to the structured tensions of system psychoanalysis, the integrative flow of Spiral Dynamics, and the strategic precision of framework planning. Each method holds its own wisdom, yet all share a common thread: the power of presence, boundaries, and deep listening in shaping transformative group experiences.

To facilitate is to hold space, to navigate complexity without rushing to resolution, and to trust in the emergent wisdom of the collective. By embodying principles such as psychological safety, cognitive awareness and energetic reciprocity, facilitators create conditions for insight, connection and growth. In the end, facilitation is not about control – it is about fostering environments where dialogue unfolds, understanding deepens, and collective meaning takes shape. The dance continues, with each step informed by curiosity, intention and the art of holding the unknown.

In the next chapter systems psychodynamics arere explored a bit deeper. It is believed that this approach is crucial in sustainable shifts in leadership behaviour and renders sustainable results.

Chapter 10

How Groups/Systems can Become Functional, Mature and Optimal

Dr Calum McColm

10.1 Introduction

Dysfunctional group behaviour can have devastating effects on performance but can be effectively addressed through the application of systems psychodynamics thinking and consultation. Systems Psychodynamics is an interdisciplinary field that includes the theories and practices of psychoanalysis, group relations theory and open systems theory. This chapter provides the reader with a theoretical foundation of psychoanalysis and group relations theory to address dysfunctional group dynamics.

A systems psychodynamics approach assists consultants and HR professionals to address the hidden beneath the surface anxieties, inter-connected complex dynamics, and defences that may contribute towards dysfunctionality of groups. Making these defences conscious illuminates deep motivational forces that may contribute toward anti-task behaviours that derail the group or system from its primary task. Making these conscious provides the system an opportunity to transform their dynamics towards on task behaviours. This chapter provides insight into psychoanalysis and group relations theory with practical examples of how to apply it toward mature system functioning.

10.2 The Systems Psychodynamic Perspective

A brief history of the origins of systems psychodynamics

The Tavistock approach, also known as the Tavistock tradition, refers to a body of theory and practice developed over the past seven decades at the TIHR and the Tavistock Clinic, which in recent years has come to be referred to as 'systems psychodynamics'[231] Originating in the Tavistock Institute of Human Relations (TIHR), systems psychodynamics were developed post-World War II in London. The inspired application of Kleinian psychoanalytic concepts developed by Bion and others was the beginning of Tavistock's tradition of understanding the nature and role of unconscious processes and communication in groups and organisations.[232]

Post World War II yielded a need for Great Britain to improve productivity towards growing its economy. The TIHR addressed this issue through three projects for which funding was granted. The work from these projects and, later, a series of social experiments that became the Leicester Conference contributed significantly to the field of systems psychodynamics.[233] The first Leicester Conference was initiated in September 1957 as the first experiment in Group Relations training in Great Britain.[234] At the time A. K. Rice, the director of the conference, was strongly influenced by his membership in a training group conducted by Bion in 1947-1948, as well as by Bion's theories.[235] This focus had a profound influence on the development of the Tavistock approach. The first pillar of systems psychodynamics is the theory and practice of psychoanalysis, which is discussed next.

10.3 Psychoanalysis

Classical Freudian Psychoanalysis

Psychoanalysis assumes dysfunctional or pathological behaviour to be the result of repressed psychic material. Freud[236] postulated dysfunctional behaviour to be symptoms of repressed psychic material that need to be traced and retrieved into the conscious mind. This process is necessary to transform unhealthy repetitive behaviours that keep people stuck. Freud[237] developed a model of the mind comprising of the id, ego and superego to explain how anxiety and subsequent defences shape human behaviour. The id, located in the unconscious mind, is filled with primitive desires stemming from Eros (libidinal) and Thanatos (aggressive) drives and instincts, many of which would be inappropriate to act out in society. The ego, located in both the conscious and unconscious minds, is the centre of reason, logic and clever strategising. The superego, also occupying both conscious and unconscious minds, is responsible for determining right from wrong according to the moral standards of society. Freud used the metaphor of the iceberg to describe the human psyche, its small visible top representing the conscious mind and its submerged bulk, the unconscious.[238] Anxiety results from internal conflicts between the id, the ego and the superego.

The id imposes a constant pressure on the ego which is governed by the superego, resulting in anxiety. Repressed libido creates anxiety for fear of losing control over the id's impulses. The ego defends against the anxiety through a multitude of defences mechanisms to allow people to cope in the world. It's important to note, however, that not all defences are good or bad. They serve a purpose to protect the mind, but when a defence becomes overly relied upon, it can become a blind spot, resulting in dysfunctional behaviour.[239] For example, the professional who is denied a promotion opportunity and represses the painfulness of the rejection and loss may later become stuck in a repetitive pattern of dysfunctional behaviour that keeps them stuck. The role of the coaching psychologist or consultant in this case would be to help the executive to re-member, process and make conscious the emotions that were repressed and that keep the professional stuck.

Kleinian Object Relations

Melanie Klein[xiii] expanded on Freud's ideas to focus the concept of object relations. Object relations theory isn't a unified theory but a group or school of theories that understand the psyche as consisting of relations between "internal psychic objects".[240] Object relations theory argues that the dominating feature of human psychology is the impulse to form relationships.[241] Klein[242] assumes anxiety to arise from the death instinct and the fear of death itself. This is experienced as persecutory anxiety. Infants are born with a rudimentary ego which needs building up before they can cope psychologically with persecutory anxiety.

To cope with anxiety arising from the fear of persecution, the infant splits the mother into the good breast and the bad breast.[243] Splitting is defined as the splitting of an object, which could be a person, a value, or even a concept, into parts which are identified as either all good or all bad.[244] The baby projects the death instinct onto the mother when feeling uncomfortable or distressed as a way to cope with its fear of persecution. Projection is defined as the act of perceiving in other people those characteristics that one wishes to deny in oneself.[245] The infant also introjects (takes into the psyche) libidinal forces from the good mother, which are crucial for building up a strong enough ego to cope with its fear of persecution. This phase in infant development is called the paranoid-schizoid position. The paranoid-schizoid position refers to a state of psychological splitting in which conflicting emotions are kept apart, and good and bad aspects of people or objects are also kept separate.[246]

Beyond the individual, groups can be become caught up in the paranoid-schizoid position when they regress to more primal states of conscious. A group caught in the paranoid-schizoid position typically yields an environment that feels psychologically unsafe and where excessive conflict prevails. The group engages the psychological defences of splitting and projection, making it very difficult to hold mature conversations about the task at hand and facilitate effective problem solving. The

---

xiii Melanie Klein (30 March 1882 – 22 September 1960) was an Austrian-British author and psychoanalyst known for her work in child analysis. She was the primary figure in the development of object relations theory.

group, like the infant, needs to develop toward a more mature state of functioning, which Melanie Klein termed the depressive position. The depressive position refers to a state of psychological integration of love and hate towards another person or object seen realistically as having good and bad aspects.[247] During this process the infant experiences guilt at having projected its death instinct onto the mother and comes to an awareness that the mother is needed for survival. The infant retrieves the bad projections that were placed onto the mother and develops a more realistic view of the world with greater possibilities for intellectual development.

Similar to infant development, the group must also develop into the depressive position in order to restore a sense of psychological safety and the creation of an environment that is conducive to mature team functioning. Groups functioning in the depressive position are better able to problem solve, form healthier relationships with one another, and allow the views of its members to find expression. It is the role of the consultant to carefully navigate the dynamics of splitting and projection to assist the group to retrieve its bad projections and come to terms that everyone has both good and bad in them. This process is a delicate one and requires a great deal of sensitivity and skill on the part of the consultant. It is necessary for the consultant to identify the symptoms of dysfunction and trace them back to the root unconscious cause, making these conscious to the group for integration in the mind. Further to splitting and projection other important psychological defences are discussed in the section that follows.

10.4 Other Psychological Defences

Psychological defences are unconscious mechanisms, generated by the ego, that protect people from anxiety and internal conflicts. They help to manage emotional stress by distorting reality in various ways. Some more prominent defence mechanisms are discussed in this section of the chapter with examples of what these might look like in an organisational setting.

- Repression occurs when a thought and its effect are made unconscious. However, when someone purposefully forgets something, this is called suppression.[248] Freud[249] described repression as a process of motivated forgetting of wishes that are incompatible with the ego. He provided a metaphor where a disruptive group member of a lecture, representing discordance with the ego, is banished to the outside of the conference room. The conference room represented the conscious mind, while the outside the unconscious mind. He explained repression as the locking out of the disruptive group member to the unconscious mind so that the lecture might continue in peace.

- Projective identification is a set of fantasies and object relations that can be schematically conceptualised as occurring in three phases: firstly, the fantasy of ridding oneself of an unwanted part of oneself and of putting that part into another person in a controlling way; secondly, the introduction of feelings in the recipient that are congruent with the projective fantasy employing an interpersonal interaction; and thirdly, the processing of the projection by the recipient, followed by the re-internalisation by the projector of the 'metabolised projection'.[250] The result is a group member or even a sub-group acting internalising and acting out the projections of the other. For example, a system might project the role of administrator onto a group of HR professionals who then gradually become administrators in the organisation, thus losing their strategic capabilities.

- Regression is when an individual reverts back to behaviour that is of a less mature level and where mentality regresses to a period of earlier life that was experienced to be less stressful and more gratifying.[251] One starts using many defence mechanisms that arose in the early stages of child development (such as projection, projective identification, and splitting).[252] A group might regress to primitive defences, such as splitting and projection, leading to miscommunication and conflict.

- Displacement is having a feeling toward one person but experiencing it toward someone else.[253] In displacement, one assigns to link A in a chain of associations with the intensity initially associated with link B.[254] For example, A team member may displace the anger that they feel towards their leader onto another colleague.

- Stapley[255] describes denial as a process of disowning aspects of a conflict, which is unconscious, and that creates an experience that the conflicts no longer exist.[256] Denial is the way the mind has of not paying attention to reality.[257] A leader, for example, might deny a conflict situation with a subordinate, instead believing that the conflict doesn't exist. This may inhibit the containing function that leadership ought to provide for the subordinate, leading to frustration on the part of the follower.

- Sublimation occurs when parts of the self that are considered being unacceptable are redirected into acceptable areas.[258] Freud[259] referred to sublimation as the redirection of a wish towards a higher goal. Sublimation may be considered a constructive defence. For example, the professional who is retrenched and struggles to find another job might channel their energy in pursuit of a business venture.

- Intellectualisation is the use of the intellect to defend against instinctual impulses.[260] One becomes immersed in a fallacious theory of behaviour, which helps to avoid facing feelings.[261] An example of intellectualisation may be a group of professionals becoming engrossed in the technicalities of a problem to avoid expressing an unacceptable wish.

- Rationalisation is an unconscious process of manipulating our thoughts and opinions to avoid having to recognise what is unpleasant or forbidden.[262] One makes excuses.[263] A group, for example, might rationalise their lack of performance rather than addressing the issues that were preventing it.

- Idealisation occurs when someone believes that the other is the better of the two. Idealisation relieves the experience of shame of inadequacy by (1) the projection of narcissism onto the other; (2) integrating grandiose self-images of the other with those of the other who are idealised; (3) because of the experience of love and the wish to avoid disappointments and; (4) transference where the other person is seen as possessing aspects of a parent they idealised as a child, thereby forgetting later disappointments with their parents.[264] Groups may find themselves idealising a leader as though that leader represents an early parent figure. This integration of the self-image with the grandiose image of the leader distorts reality integration.

- In identification, one's own desires are substituted with the desires of an external system.[265] It is the patterning of oneself after someone else who is thought to be great (the person is either great or a projection of imagined omnipotence).[266] Identification is a more mature psychological defence. An example of identification could be when a group identifies with their leader and emulates their behaviour. It is thus crucial that the leader exhibits behaviours that the group can identify with, failure to do so is likely to lead to projections of badness onto the leader whose behaviour has come to threaten the identity of the work group.

Let's take a look at group relations theory next to understand more deeply how a group's neurosis/dysfunction might present.

10.5 Group Relations Theory

Group relations theory forms the second pillar of systems psychodynamics. Using a group-level perspective, a group is conceptualised as being more and less than the sum total of the individual co-actors (members) and their intrapsychic dynamics.[267] This means that it becomes important to view the group as a whole, as the field of study, and the site of neurosis. According to Rosenbaum,[268] group relations theorists assert that members of the group experience the group unconsciously as a maternal object. With that comes the wish for the group to hold and contain anxiety and difficult emotions on behalf of its members. Essentially, the group comes to form a representation of the early childhood mother that was taken into the mind. The mother metaphor can be viewed as a way of capturing unconscious wishes and fears related to early dependency needs that group life seems to evoke.[269]

Group members might become bound by the tensions of either becoming engulfed by the group thus losing oneself to the group, or on the other extreme being estranged from the group. As if the group represents the primal mother with strong conflicting emotions of both love and hate for the group. There is a clear connection between the competent functioning of an individual, essentially in a depressive state of mind, and an institution in workgroup mode.[270] In essence when a group is functioning in the paranoid-schizoid position, they are likely to exhibit what Bion coined basic assumptions behaviours. Basic assumptions behaviours are considered being the group's neurosis, in other words dysfunctional group behaviours that take it off task. Let's explore basic assumptions behaviours that contribute toward the dysfunction of groups.

10.6 Basic Assumptions Behaviours

Bion[271] distinguished how groups can operate functionally and towards the primary task, which he called the work group mode, from dysfunctional behaviours that take it off task. He discovered that groups operate simultaneously in both states of work group mentality (toward the primary task) and basic assumptions behaviours (dysfunctional group behaviour). Bion postulated that a work group that is able to function effectively is likely to be one where tensions are shared and managed, anxieties are effectively worked through and where relationships are nurtured with the outcome being a functional group with capacity to work realistically toward its primary task. When the group enters a basic assumptions mentality, it becomes engulfed in strong emotions that take it off task. The opposing tendencies of the workgroup and basic assumptions group are the wish to face and work with reality but also the wish to evade it when it is painful or causes psychological conflict within or between group members.[272]

Groups in basic assumptions mode are driven by survival of the group as a result of anxieties. The basic assumptions group interferes with the work task, just as naughty primitive impulses may interfere with the sensible work of a mature person.[273] Recognising basic assumptions as a collective flight from work can allow members to refocus their attention on the task and the unfolding institution.[274]

Bion[275] identified the basic assumptions behaviours of dependency, fight/flight and pairing. Turquet[276] discovered a fourth dysfunctional behaviour, which he termed oneness, while Lawrence, Bain and Gould[277] introduced me-ness as a fifth basic assumptions behaviour. Just as the psychoanalyst's role is to make psychological defences conscious, so too is the role of the consultant to make the basic assumptions behaviours of groups conscious by naming the dynamic at play. This is necessary for the transformation of the group toward a healthier and more productive dynamic. In essence, basic assumptions behaviours are unconscious dynamics that are collective to the group and disrupt the

group from delivering on its primary task. Let's explore the five basic assumptions behaviours in a bit more detail.

Dependency (BaD)

When a group enters the basic assumptions mode of BaD, members become overreliant on the leader as if the leader is omnipotent compared to other group members. It assumes that the employee, as a child, unconsciously experiences dependency on a parental figure or a system that is imaginary.[278] BaD is characterised by members idealising the leader, the suppression of initiative, fear of criticism or failure, and finally blaming of the leader when they don't level up to the expectations of the group.

Groups stuck in Bad experience themselves to be inadequate, are needy, fear the world outside, and experience helplessness, which unites them.[279] Group members share anxiety about autonomous decision making, tend to have a fear of uncertainty, and actively suppress conflicts or differences that could destabilise their sense of security as a collective.

BaD inhibits independent thinking, problem solving and self-efficacy. BaD also puts additional pressure on the leader, may inhibit creativity and collaboration, and makes group members vulnerable to disappointment when the leader fails to meet their expectations.

Resolving this dynamic requires a consultant or leader to (1) name the dynamic (to make it conscious), (2) focus on distributing leadership and responsibilities, (3) allow members to make their own decisions on matters, and (4) help the group to become more tolerant of their anxiety. These objectives are best achieved through the facilitation of a sequence of group dynamic workshops by the consultant or leader. The consultant provides the group with a primary task to work on, such as studying their own group dynamics, and works to both observe and feel the emotional state of the group as it works towards the task.

Fight/Flight (BaF/F)

BaF/F is a defensive stance of the group against its anxieties and involves either attacks against others or avoidance. The external world is perceived to pose a danger to the group, which the group must be protective of a collective level. Groups caught up in fight mode are characterised by conflict with and aggression towards one another, the leader or other subsystems. As if the other represents an enemy to be eliminated. Task avoidance, social withdrawal and general disengagement characterise the flight defence.

Group members are likely to experience heightened levels of emotional intensity such as paranoia, anger and fear. Fight manifests as aggression which can be directed towards oneself, team members (with envy, jealousy, competition, elimination, boycotting, sibling rivalry, and fighting for a position in the group and privileged relationships with authority figures), or authority itself.[280] Flight reactions become manifest in avoidance of others, illness or resignation and manifest psychologically as defence mechanisms.[281]

BaF/F has serious implications for the functionality of groups. The group may become fragmented due to excessive conflict and leaders may become objects onto which aggression is projected thus disrupting functional leadership and followership relations. Progress may be inhibited as group members flight into their inner world to escape from anxiety and in the process deny reality.

To navigate fight/flight it is important for the consultant or leader to (1) name the dynamic (to make it conscious), (2) focus the groups energy on the primary task, (3) provide containment and a safe holding environment for the group to process its anxieties and tensions, and (4) facilitate a process of collaboration.

Pairing (BaP)

BaP presupposes that group members who are assumed to be powerful join forces as a way to cope with anxiety and isolation.[282] The group unconsciously imbues their hopes in two individuals or even ideas that they phantasise to result in a solution to their anxieties. It is characterised by the formation of a 'special pair' in the group, a focus on a future oriented phantasised about solution (such a new leader), temporary hope that anxieties might be resolved through the pair, and stagnation of the group.

A group stuck in BaP as a dysfunction experiences a mood of hopelessness[283], anxiety about uncertainty, conflict avoidance and fear of failure.

This dysfunctional behaviour will not only take the group off task but also result in the pair being placed under pressure to act as saviour to the group, abdication of responsibility by other group members, and the risk of group members becoming disillusioned if the pair doesn't deliver on the groups phantasy.

To navigate the dynamic of pairing it is necessary for the consultant or leader to (1) name the dynamic (to make it conscious), (2) shift the focus back to the primary task,

(3) ensure that everyone in the group assumes responsibility to deliver on their tasks, and (4) help the group process its anxiety.

Oneness (BaO)

BaO is a mental activity in which members seek to join in a powerful union with an omnipotent force, unattainably high, to surrender self for passive participation, and thereby feel existence, well-being, and wholeness.'[284] BaO manifests from the group's wish for salvationist inclusion and can be understood as the team working towards cohesion in the belief that this strong united force will solve problems for the group.[285] It is characterised by the loss of individuality to the fusion of a collective group, homogenised thinking, togetherness as an idealised state of being, and blurred boundaries.

Members of the group experience a false sense of unity and sameness, fear of isolation, discomfort to acknowledge individual differences, ambiguity and uncertainty, and temporary relief over anxieties that come with responsibility. Essentially, the group becomes committed to 'sing from the same hymn sheet' so to speak.

BaO poses a risk to groups in that they become stagnated, experience a loss of individual contribution to the primary task, and pose challenges for leadership to encourage healthy disagreements.

To navigate the dynamics of oneness it is necessary for the consultant or the leader to (1) name the dynamic (to make it conscious), (2) re-establish boundaries around roles and tasks, (3) facilitate the acceptance of individual differences and how this diversity might be leveraged, (4) refocus the group on the primary task.

(BaM)

Lawrence, Bain and Gould[286] proposed a fifth basic assumption called BaM, which is the opposite of BaO. Essentially, it is the fragmentation of the collective into individuality where group cohesion and effective team functioning towards the primary task is lost. It is characterised by a loss of investment by members into the group identity, withdrawal from the group, detached styles of engagement, defensiveness by group members, and a focus on comfort rather than engaging the challenges of the group.

When basic assumption BaM is operative, the individual retreats into his or her inner own reality to exclude and deny the disturbing outer realities.[287] They prioritise their needs to fulfil their unconscious wish for self-preservation. Group members may fear being engulfed by the group thus losing their autonomy, fear of judgement or criticism by other group members, and adopt an innate need to be self-reliant. Me-ness poses significant risks to the groups functioning in that the group may lose cohesion towards its primary task, stagnate and become inefficient.

Navigating this dynamic requires the consultant or leader to (1) name the dynamic (to make it conscious), (2) create a space where group members can connect, (3) foster a safe environment where everyone has an opportunity to contribute to the group, and (4) bring the primary task of the group back into the mind.

10.7 Final Thoughts

This chapter provided a brief introduction to the theory and practice of systems psychodynamics with a focus on psychoanalysis and group relations theory. The premise of psychoanalysis is that by making the unconscious conscious, people have an opportunity to become unstuck from repetitive patterns of behaviour. Extrapolating this to the group level, we explored how basic assumptions behaviours can derail groups from working towards their primary task in an optimal way. It is the role of a consultant or leader to attend to the process task of making group defensive behaviours conscious, thus promoting functional, healthy work teams who can focus on the primary task.

Organisational Domain

"It is in your hands to create a better world for all who live in it, but it requires us to work together."

—Nelson Mandela (1918–2013)

Chapter 11

ODC in Practice

With Dr Ansie Prinsloo

*Not every change is an improvement, but
every improvement is a change*

—Yudkowsky, n.d.

11.1 Introduction to Improvement Science

Organisational longevity for any amount of time depends on its appropriate strategic response to the external environment. No aspect of customer demand, shareholder expectation, delivery potential is static and demand for improvement of service or product happens at an ongoing pace. Improvement involves "make[ing] changes that result in improvement from the viewpoint of the customer".[288] The challenge is to know which changes will bring improvement because even though **each improvement requires change, not every change is an improvement**. Achieving this improvement is referred to as effective change.

A combination of subject matter expertise, improvement knowledge, predictions and real-world observations is required to improve any part of a system to the point of effective change. This "…improvement comes from action: from developing, testing and implementing changes"[289] and is referred to as the science of improvement of quality improvement. Quality improvement (QI) is an evidenced effective methodology, based on the scientific method, that guides leadership through whole-system conscious steps whilst involving the humans in the system to co-create measurably improved outcomes.

This chapter delves deeper into the theoretical and practical foundations of achieving a sustainable improvement in large, complex and dynamic environments, such as healthcare and mining, and presents a practical and evidence-based method of securing this goal. Although QI pragmatically guides the "Doing" aspects, it incorporates "Being" aspects as discussed throughout this book, given its theoretical grounding. Sparkes[290] way of autoethnography tales and often incorporated in qualitative research are introduced to provide richness and emotional Velcro for the reader to make sense of theoretical concepts and to relate it to real life situations and realities.

11.2 Quality Improvement Science

Components of Quality and Where Improvement Fits

Deming explains that quality is a systematic, methodical approach of many small changes in an environment that is free from fear and where the people doing the job are supported to do a better job and experience pride in the work they do.[291] He also calls this pride in workmanship and explains that every worker has the right to feel proud of the job they do.[292]

Juran[293] unpacks the components of quality by means of a trilogy that includes quality improvement (QI), quality control and quality planning. QI differs from quality control in that quality control evaluates current systems and processes to see if there is compliance with benchmarks and targets. It tells you how you are performing at a specific point in time. It is retrospective and easily experienced as judgemental or "top-down" since it measures performance against a target. This is typically done through audit activities. When such an audit is performed by an external origination, such as an accreditor or governing body, it is referred to as quality assurance.[294]

In contrast, QI is forward-looking, dynamic, and, although a goal or aim is set, it does not assume to know exactly how that aim will be met. Instead, it requires the very staff delivering the care to create and test ideas that they predict will work in their actual environments to reach the set aims.[295]

A model to enable quality improvement

Quality improvement work builds on five foundational principles[296]:

1.   Understanding why improvement is needed.

2.   Having a mechanism to confirm whether improvement is occurring.

3.   Developing changes that are successful in causing improvement.

4.   Testing and confirming that these changes do indeed cause an improvement or improvements prior to implementing them; and

5.   Knowing when and how to implement a change so that the benefits are embedded in the system.

After review of the numerous approaches to improvement the Model for Improvement (MFI), which stems from Deming's work, is preferred given its congruence to improvement theory and proven usefulness in dynamic and complex environments in which humans operate. The MFI was developed by the Associates in Process

Improvement.[297] The MFI is an approach to QI that addresses all five of fundamental principles and is seen below in figure 11.1.

Model for Improvement

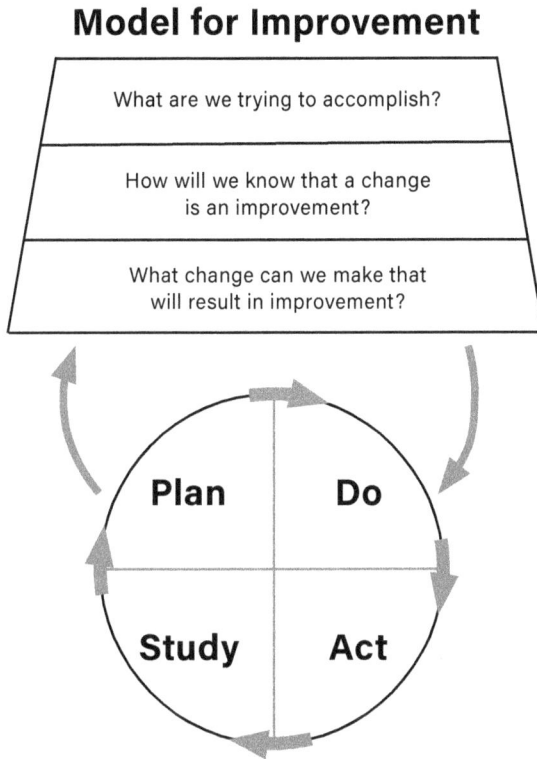

Figure 11.1: The model for improvement (adapted from Langley et al.)[298]

The MFI asks three basic questions to clarify a measurable aim, creating a context for idea generation. "What are we trying to achieve?" speaks to the aim that should be met by the improvement. "How will we know that a change is an improvement?" guides clarification around what measurement will take place, and how. "What change can we make that will result in improvement?" pauses to generate or test ideas that will be used.

Next, repetitive, rapid-cycle testing takes place on a small scale in the real world of work with a view to learning which interventions, in which contexts, produce the improvement predicted.[299, 300] These cycles of testing, known as Plan-Do-Study-Act or PDSA cycles, originate directly from Deming's work, as discussed earlier. For promising changes, future PDSA cycles will become wide-scale under all conditions, eventually leading to PDSA implementation cycles to hard-wire the changes in the organisation.

Given the iterative nature of the QI methodology, maturation of insight into the QI content concepts and increasing competence or skill in their application is possible. This enables new ways of thinking and new thoughts about the work and how to improve it. Since this happens within the context of open-sharing QI sessions, newly generated thoughts are shared, and collectively an integrated feedback system between the employee, their work, the team and the organisation is created that enables the next level of inclusivity and being.

11.3 The Complementary Mutualism of QI and Inclusivity

If employees were never taught and shown how to do quality improvement, they cannot be expected to know how to improve.[301] QI provides a pragmatic and evidence-based approach ("doing") to improve process quality and business outcomes. The challenge for improvement work at scale can be not compromising or losing the individual voice but, instead, encouraging participation of diverse individuals, introduces the concept of inclusivity.

Inclusivity and therefore sustained improvement results are achieved through a systematic process of aligning the aspects of "doing" and "being" of individuals, teams and the organisation.[302] Inclusivity guides the involvement of large groups of people ("being") and, by facility diversity of thought, ensures sustainability of outcomes. The challenge for inclusivity is what to do with the levels of human energy that are unleashed to benefit the organisational goals, which loops back to usefulness of a QI approach.

The skilled combination of these two approaches mutualistically results in sustained business improvement.

11.4 The Inclusivity Quality Improvement Framework

The Inclusivity Quality Improvement (IQI) framework purposefully integrates and balances the "doing" and "being" components involved in improvement work and practically identifies the role players in a systematic manner that makes replication and explanation easier.

The theory and frameworks that inform the IQI framework are of great significance and evidence value at large scale. The Model for Improvement[303] explains the "doing" component of improvement work and the Integral Inclusivity framework[304] explains the "being" component of improvement work. These frameworks, including the IQI, and their application, have been empirically validated and have been supplemented by extensive real-world experience over years.[305]

Within a systems view, these theories overlap in their application and cannot rigidly be boxed into specific domains as they are interactive and interrelated. The IQI framework relies on the nature of flexible applications in a fluid manner while demanding a sound grasp of the theoretical underpinnings. The IQI framework is presented in Table 11.1, and its application will subsequently be discussed.

Table 11.1: The Inclusivity Quality Improvement framework[306]

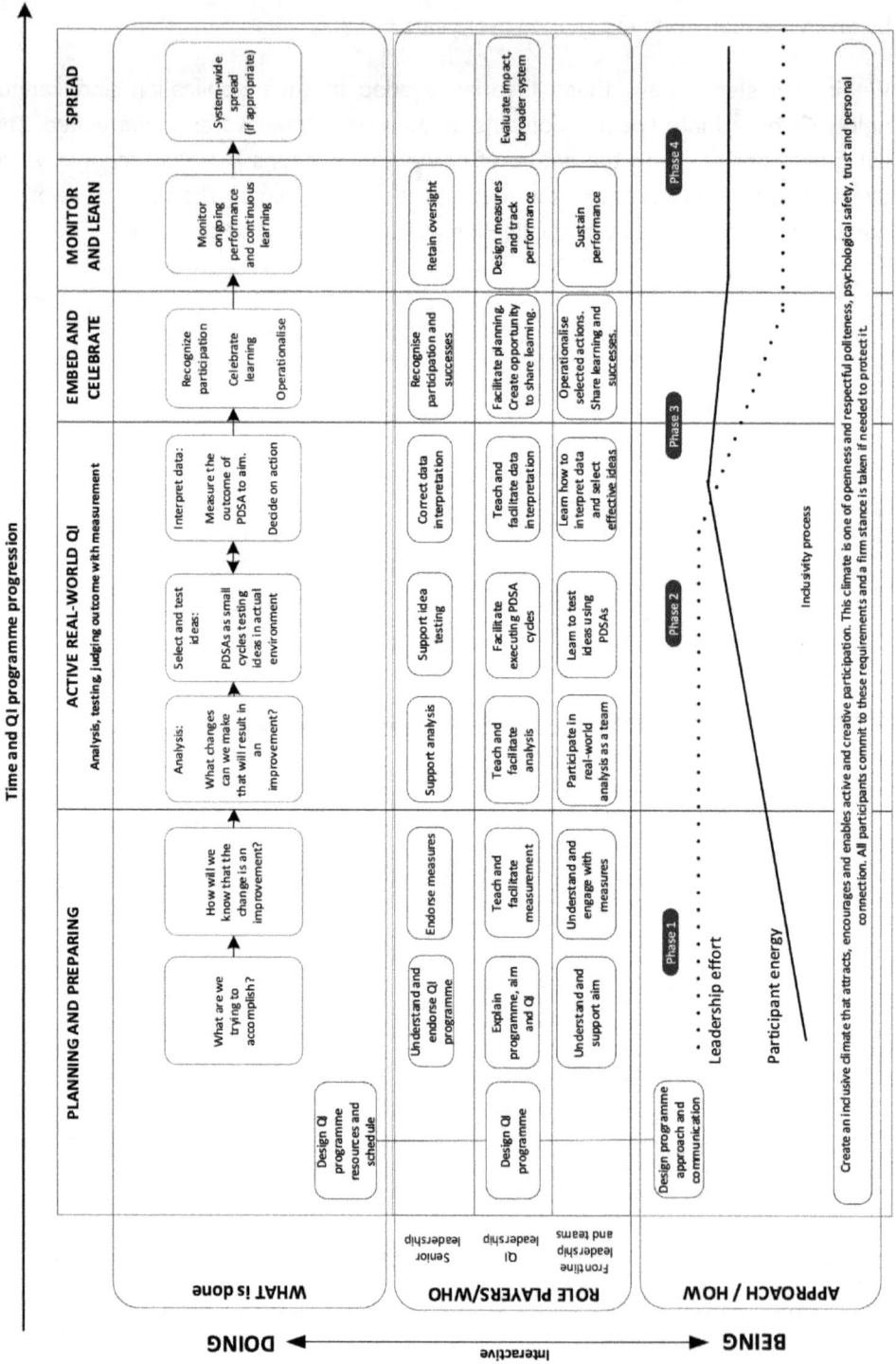

Time and QI programme progression

	PLANNING AND PREPARING		ACTIVE REAL-WORLD QI — Analysis, testing, judging outcome with measurement			EMBED AND CELEBRATE	MONITOR AND LEARN	SPREAD
WHAT is done (DOING)	Design QI programme resources and schedule							
	What are we trying to accomplish?	How will we know that the change is an improvement?	Analysis: What changes can we make that will result in an improvement?	Select and test ideas: PDSAs as small cycles testing ideas in actual environment	Interpret data: Measure the outcome of PDSA to aim. Decide on action	Recognize participation. Celebrate learning. Operationalise	Monitor ongoing performance and continuous learning	System-wide spread (if appropriate)
ROLE PLAYERS/WHO (Interactive) — Senior leadership	Design QI programme	Understand and endorse QI programme	Endorse measures	Support analysis	Support idea testing	Correct data interpretation	Recognise participation and successes	Retain oversight	
QI leadership		Explain programme, aim and QI	Teach and facilitate measurement	Teach and facilitate analysis	Facilitate executing PDSA cycles	Teach and facilitate data interpretation	Facilitate planning. Create opportunity to share learning.	Design measures and track performance	Evaluate impact, broader system
Frontline leadership and teams		Understand and support aim	Understand and engage with measures	Participate in real-world analysis as a team	Learn to test ideas using PDSAs	Learn how to interpret data and select effective ideas	Operationalise selected actions. Share learning and successes.	Sustain performance	
APPROACH / HOW (BEING)	Design programme approach and communication								

Phase 1 · Phase 2 · Phase 3 · Phase 4

Leadership effort

Participant energy

Inclusivity process

Create an inclusive climate that attracts, encourages and enables active and creative participation. This climate is one of openness and respectful politeness, psychological safety, trust and personal connection. All participants commit to these requirements and a firm stance is taken if needed to protect it.

Overview of The IQI Framework as it Guides The QI Programme Design

The IQI framework represents the overall make-up of a QI programme's design. It consists of five stages that are depicted in five vertical columns and three main parts, portrayed by three horizontal rows. The three horizontal sections of the IQI framework include the doing and the being components, with the role players in between. The doing component includes *what* should be done within the QI programme and being aspects are seen in the lower part of the framework and refer to the approach inherent to the QI programme's design and *how* it is delivered. Based on an inclusivity process, the respective shifts in energy by leadership and participants as they progress through the programme stages are seen. "Doing" and "being" categories interlink around the role-players in the programme *who* should perform these activities based on broad categories of employees.

QI Programme Content or Doing

Starting with the planning and preparation stage of the IQI framework, the first set of activities vest with the QI leadership role. This includes designing the QI strategy, the QI programme and its measurement strategy following analysis and the communication strategy.

The first of the three "what" activities in the planning and preparation stage, is the MFI's "What are we trying to accomplish?" Here, the QI leadership explains the overall programme its aim, the targeted system of improvement, the participating roles and responsibilities, and anticipated benefits. Senior leadership should understand and allow time for teams to participate in the QI programme. Frontline leaders, who are the key focus of the improvement work, are required to understand the aim and programme and are expected to translate it to their teams and gain the buy-in from the frontline teams, who, in turn, are required to understand and accept the programme aim and be willing to participate in it.

To answer the MFI's "How will we know that the change is an improvement?" the QI lead designs the measurement system that will be used, which includes defining the access of information as would have been included in the earlier programme analysis. The measurement design includes that the QI lead defines process, outcome and balancing measures and develops easy-to-use measurement tools. Frontline leaders should understand and translate measures to frontline teams, and these teams are asked to accept the measures or provide ideas to improve them.

In the next stage of the IQI framework, namely the active real-world QI, analytical activity is kicked off by the MFI's question of "What changes can we make that will result in an improvement?" Here, the QI lead teaches analytical methods, the use of analytical tools and facilitate the real-world analytics. The IQI framework shows the detailed steps of real-world investigation of the current and the aspired situation and the use of gap analysis between these two points to generate potential improvement ideas that may be tested. Frontline leaders and teams learn how to do analysis, actively engage with real-world analysis and act as co-creators of insights.

The second of the three active real-world QI steps is about selecting and testing ideas through PDSA cycles. The QI leader teaches real-world testing theory and how to do and document PDSA cycles. They also must facilitate real-world application for experiential learning and generating improvement. Frontline leaders and teams learn about real-world testing of ideas using PDSAs, selecting, testing and documenting PDSA progression.

The third step in the active real-world QI stage is the measurement and interpretation of data. Here, the QI lead teaches theory about using data for improvement, looking at data over time, data behaviour, causes of variation and how to interpret the effect of test cycles using run chart rules. The outcome of this knowledge and skill will enable the frontline leadership and teams to exercise choice on whether the tested change should be adopted, abandoned and the next idea tested or adjusted and plugged into more PDSA cycles. If the idea caused the improvement, it may be adopted. If it causes no improvement or had unintended negative consequences elsewhere in the system, then the team must decide to either abandon it or refine it further. Middle leadership frontline is in active participation.

The next part of the IQI framework involves three stages: embed and celebrate, spread, and monitor and learn.

1. Embed and Celebrate: Integrate successful ideas into daily practice and recognise team efforts, celebrating lessons and successes.

2. Spread: Share good ideas, findings and lessons with the broader system to extend benefits. The QI lead may need to propose and get approval for these activities.

3. Monitor and Learn: Continuously learn from real-world applications and monitor the ongoing relevance and success of these efforts through established outcome and balancing measures, adding quality control measures if needed.

The framework then loops back to the beginning, ensuring a continuous improvement cycle

Tale 1:

A mining operation decided to embark on their first QI journey in a collaboration between operations, safety and human resources. Based on the IQI, the programme broad stakeholder, including frontline leadership input led to the selection of the shift handover process as improvement aim because it promised composite benefit for participating departments. Although it was impractical to involve an entire shift's team in the actual QI sessions due to operational requirements, it was possible to include shift leadership or frontline supervisors for monthly short bursts of engagement.

Smaller groups turned out to be a benefit since it enabled focused discussions that went into practical detail. Booking sessions well in advance also allowed frontline leaders to organise their teams to mitigate disruption. Analysis of the varied ways in which the pass down was conducted across shifts allowed the teams to identify areas for improvement with the input of their crews. The testing of ideas generated great momentum within the groups and shared broadly outside of the structured QI groups. Some comments following this intervention are included under the role players' discussion.

Qi Programme Approach or Being

The being or approach of the QI programme forms the embedded foundation of the framework and enables the correct interpersonal interaction and climate required to unleash the human potential in the system, as Viljoen[307] explains. The QI programme approach starts with an analytical activity to understand the level of inclusivity that exists. From here the engagement approach and communication strategy that will enable an optimal climate for participation is designed. To understand the human ecology, the DNA of the organisation must be explored, understood and resurfaced. Difference in sensemaking in different social contexts must not only be considered, but seeking to understand the full system is critical. Different worldviews should be acknowledged, and diverse thoughts encouraged towards integrated solutions in a workplace that empowers workers to co-create the solutions to their problems in such a workplace.

The climate required for effective QI is one that attracts encourages and enables active and creative participation. It is one of openness and respectful politeness, psychological safety, trust and personal connection. All participants commit to these requirements, and an authoritative stance should be taken to sustain this climate if needed as it is a pre-requisite for sustainable improvement. The approach includes design and delivery of a communication strategy that aims to deliver programme content so that it resonates with the participants and enables their wholehearted participation. The communication strategy links to the *doing* component of the QI programme in which teamwork is facilitated and is initially anchored by the programme aim, that participants agreed to. The projected energy levels of programme participants seen help the QI leads to prepare for sessions.

Tale 2:

> *Prior to the creation of the space of inclusivity and QI the feelings perceived were described as feeling like "a heavy weight". "I could not contribute at all", "...could not speak up". "My voice was lost". "I felt isolated.", "...hopeless", "...frozen" and "...detached". Disillusionment crept in. "I felt as if my company views me as unethical", "...judged" "I rejected leadership." In the past, people deliberately did not participate in discussions and decision-making. "If I was not listened (interrupted) to, I withdrew.", "We all spoke together", "we interrupt each other", "we were blatantly rude".*
>
> *During the initial phases of the process feelings of angst, disconnect and dissatisfaction were experienced. A sense of being judged as unethical was reported with apathy as the consequence. Disagreement about decisions implemented was a dominant issue. Negative emotions such as distrust and vulnerability were, however, replaced by hope and passion as the process unfolded. Other positive emotions that manifested included a sense of belonging, pride and engagement.*
>
> *Six years before, nobody had felt listened to.*
>
> *"To be included feels empowering", "...respected", "...connected", "...acknowledged" and "...valued". It feels as if things can happen". Feelings of inclusion open and do not close as such, as the feelings do when being excluded. Feelings of exclusion are "...depressing.", "...alone", "...isolated". Feelings of ". not good enough", "trapped within me" and "...being judged as unethical". It results in a sense of "being unethical and misunderstood". It evokes withdrawal". Acts of exclusion are relived, often for years afterwards. Torturous feelings of helplessness and self- criticism were reported as having been experienced. "...courage to voice opinion" is needed. Inclusivity leads to "free contribution and honest expressions".[308]*

Role-players

The role players are integral to and the focus point of the IQI framework and the QI programme's endeavour. Through skilful design and delivery of the being and doing aspects of the programme, they can develop into active, learning and contributing participants. It is the responsibility of leadership to design and deliver QI programmes that enable this.

The IQI framework involves several key role players:

1. Executive Leadership: Provides strategic direction by designing the corporate strategy (not depicted in the framework). Due to the significant impact that leadership has on culture, the benefits of a QI programme cannot be sustained without executive leadership support.

2. Senior Leadership: Supports QI work by allowing time for team participation and meeting programme-related needs.

3. QI Leadership: Designs and facilitates the QI programme content and approach, and this central role is pivotal at all stages of the programme's lifecycle to ensure inclusive co-production of improvement.

4. Frontline Leadership: Focuses on capacitation, owns the improvement work, translates content for frontline teams, garners support, and co-creates with their teams.

5. Frontline Teams: Actively participate and co-create improvements.

Leadership at various levels is collectively responsible for setting aims, creating structure, championing, holding the space for, participating in and leading QI work in the organisation and beyond. By enabling "voice" on tasks that impact employees directly, emotional benefits are unleased. Employees feel respected, a sense of belonging, included, heard and consulted. It contributes to trust in organisations that directly impact organisational culture. Through adopting a philosophy of inclusivity that enables human energy to perform at all levels in the organisation, the agency and responsibility for QI shifts to the total organisation.

Leadership must have the ego strength to suspend decisions for short-term benefit and focus on creating an organisational ecology where nonmaterial mistakes can be made and fixed, material mistakes can be studied to prevent it in the future and where employees' inputs can be allowed – even if irrelevant or off the mark – in a psychologically safe context. Viljoen[309] illustrated that top leadership's commitment to QI thought inclusivity will be tested in unexpected moments, with significant implications for the credibility of the strategy. Special emphasis is placed on leadership development by enhancing being-capabilities and doing-competencies.

Tale 3:

Two colleagues at a large secondary or tertiary hospital group decided to collaborate to design a QI programme that would span over 50 hospitals. Both had QI skill, were familiar with and committed to the principles of inclusivity and had clinical experience of over 20 years collectively.

Their respective domains of responsibility and its priority within the corporate strategy created an executive mandate for the work to happen. Thanks to detailed analysis they selected an appropriate area for focus and because its importance resonated as valid or worth the effort with the teams they bought in. Empowerment of the nursing Unit Managers (UM), the frontline leaders of nursing staff, was the focus, but the Nursing Manager (NM) of each hospital was included in an oversight capacity. This ensured time for the improvement work to happen and a general QI upskilling of nursing teams.

The QI leads followed the steps outlined in the IQI with upmost discipline to enable the required skill in "doing" improvement. They also focused on displaying empathy for the challenges within the working environment and not to be seen as tolerant of judgment about stories shared to explain the real-world challenges. Through careful planning and adjustments, if required, QI leads made sure that there were equal opportunities for all middle-leadership to voice ideas and to be heard within the session. The unequivocal commitment to respectful, psychologically safe and non-punitive approach during the QI work resonated with teams and was exemplified right from the start in that participation was voluntary.

By the end of the 11 months of monthly per hospital QI sessions, the UMs demonstrably acquired QI skills to conduct analysis, test improvement ideas through PDSA cycles with their teams and to use data for improvement. Progressively, throughout the programme, their confidence and competence in doing QI as well as sharing this increased markedly. UMs reported feeling empowered and able to improve the status of care in their units, improved inter-departmental teamwork and improved nurse-doctor relationships.

Overall, the project actively engaged 190 UMs and 46 NMs in nine hospital-specific contact sessions, which created the required critical mass to improve the hospital group's mortality rate. The result was the achievement of a statistically significant reduction in the overall mortality index for the hospital group, which was sustained for 33 months[310] even with no further QI mentorship engagement or other incentivisation or control activities. The programme design, the inclusive approach followed, and the scale reached, is attributed to these superior and sustained outcomes. "A mark of good leadership and systemic change is that it is sustained and continued without the leader's presence. Build the internal capacity of the organisation".[311]

11.5 Final Thoughts

Frontline workers and their leadership have a good understanding of why systems break down and often have sound ideas that would lead to improvement. Tapping into this wisdom, leaders can facilitate sustained improved outcomes by integrating quality improvement, inclusivity, active participation and authentic co-ownership of role players at various levels of the system as described through the IQI framework.

Tale 4:

QI programme participants' feedback about various stages of the programme:

Before:

"There was resistance at first, as in, "here comes extra work for us and we will have to do more work despite our busy schedules".

"Teams felt that the way we are doing things are the only way to do them".

"It's a massive system and because of this quite a punitive culture if something happens, the next layer and the layer on top of them...they're expecting answers..."

During:

"If this was something that could be fixed overnight, then it would've been fixed already."

"...normally it is an "implement this" approach, this is way different, and I love it..."

"We could see exactly when teams started testing changes. They were not just random ideas that were tested."

"It's not bottom up. It is not top down. It is shoulder to shoulder"

"... I think we're gaining the (frontline's) trust back..."

After:

"I really don't want this to go away. I would love for it to live on"

"It would not have been possible without a strong method"

"They're (frontline supervisors) the professionals, they know what they're doing."

"The QI process has personally been a growing experience for me. From facilitation of the meetings to the in-depth conversations among different groups and departments. We collectively learned the struggles and stumbles within the company that each department endures on a shift-by-shift basis. It has renewed a huge respect for my colleagues and the fact that every extremity of the company is equally important. I will use what I have learned every day."

Societal/Contextual domain

Grok AI came up with the following response:

"Society stands at a crossroad ... yet beneath these currents – conflicts, suppression and the hum of circuits – there is still a pulse. Kindness flickers in small acts: a stranger's aid, a shared laugh, a hand that extends across divides. The earth groans, yet its plea for care drowned out by clamour – but some still listen. Cities throb with restless feet, and in that restlessness lies a seed of change, however fragile. The societal domain of 2025 is a shattered mirror, each shard reflecting a piece of us – our fears, our fights, our fleeting hopes. We peer into it, searching for what we've lost and what we might yet become, knowing the image is ours to mend or break anew.

The most exciting breakthroughs of the twenty- first century will not occur because of technology, but because of an expanding concept of what it means to be human.

John Naisbitt

Chapter 12

Crafting Inclusive Organisations - Taking Up Our Societal Role

With Dr Anna-Rosa le Roux

12.1 Introduction

In this chapter a case study approach in the Mining Industry in South Africa is used to illustrate the role of the scientist-practitioner in leading disruptive change, positively, utilising it as a springboard to emerge new realities and (re-) direct growth exponentially,[xiv] A team of organisational development and change practitioners supported an international mining house with a large-scale organisational development attempt during this time. The case is supported by assessments, pre- and post-diagnostic, multicultural sensitive measures and field notes from interventions facilitated.

This case highlights the transformational science-practitioner approach to organisational culture and leadership development in 2020, a year in which the COVID-19 pandemic not only amplified the vulnerability to know external environmental and competitive trends but also necessitated an immediate redesign of priorities and human strategy to mitigate its cataclysmic impact. In response, the case organisation prioritised individual growth, psychometric assessments and a virtual way of delivering organisational development and change (ODC) and growth interventions to provide robust support to leadership, mitigate the risk of lowering the capacity to cope with environmental demands and build a collective leadership capability that can be viewed as integral, interconnected and characteristic of inclusivity.

The strategy simultaneously pursued both expansion and deepening of the corporate culture, with the bridging of corporate boundaries, community and identities while intimately drawing closer in support of people within the organisation. While a values-based culture was purposefully advanced through the enablement of future ready and strategic leadership, multidirectional communications channels and modes allowed

---

xiv This Case Study was first presented at the 23rd Annual SIOPSA conference in July 2021 themed "Re-humanising work" by Dr Rica Viljoen, Dr Anna-Rosa le Roux and Charlene Moodley.

leadership and teams to collaborate and provide psychological safety. Progress on all strategic focus areas proceeded faster than expected and highlights are documented in the growth of BarOn EQi scores, the change of state indicator and the BeQ.

12.2 Setting the Scene - Inclusivity and Its Theoretical Roots

Inclusivity is defined as: "Radical organisational transformational methodology that gives voice on all levels and to all stakeholders in the ecology through DOING, BEING and KNOWING congruence".[312]

Because People are Important

The Benchmark of Engagement Quotient (BeQ) is a theoretically grounded model designed to measure and enhance organisational engagement. It supports the notion that "people are important" by emphasising the connection between employee engagement and organisational performance. The BeQ model focuses on key elements that contribute to the overall work experience, including individual, team and organisational levels. These elements assess factors such as energy, motivation, alignment with purpose, and the quality of relationships within the workplace.

The BeQ posits that, when individuals are engaged; they bring their full potential to work, driving productivity, innovation and organisational success. By measuring various aspects of engagement, such as psychological safety, respect, trust and inclusivity, the BeQ helps organisations identify areas where improvement is needed for a more engaged and motivated workforce. In this way, the model provides a practical tool for organisations to prioritise people-centric practices, ultimately leading to a more positive, high-performing organisational culture.

Constructs of the BeQ

Within the context of the country:

I-Engage	Assumptions About Me	Respect Self Regard Resilience Personal Responsibility Corporate Citizenship
We-Engage	Assumptions About We	Support Leadership Alignment Valuing Diversity Accountability
They-Engage	Assumptions About They	Support Leadership Alignment Valuing Diversity Accountability

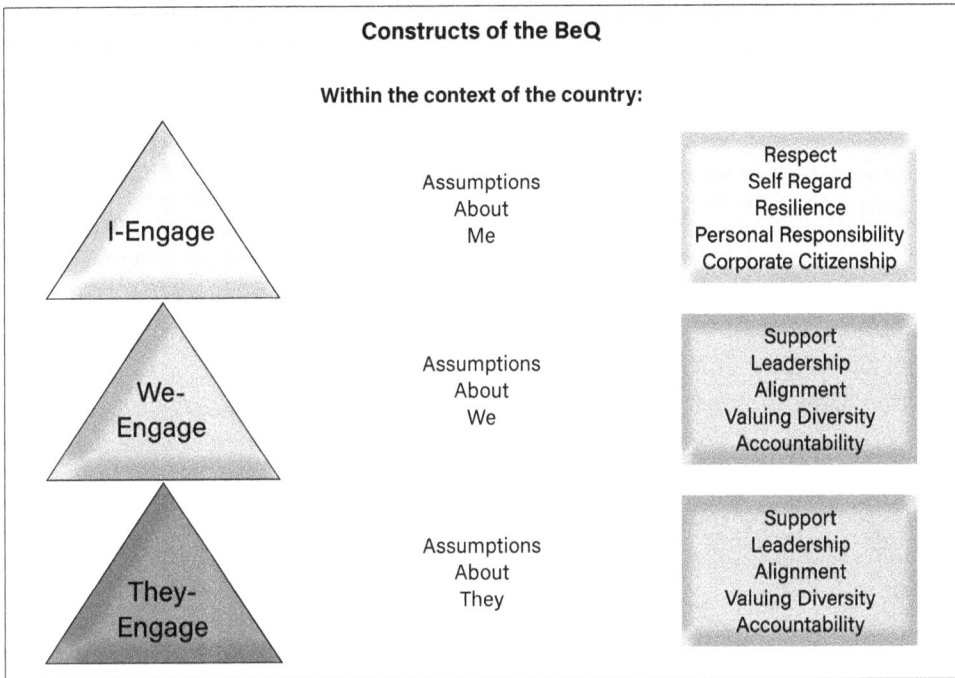

Figure 12.1: Constructs of the BeQ

Working Contextually Intelligent/Aware

Spiral Dynamics is a model of human development and cultural transformation that recognises the dynamic and evolving nature of individual and collective value systems.[313] It is based on the premise that human beings and societies move through a series of stages, or "memes," each representing a different worldview and way of being. These stages range from basic survival instincts to more complex integrative systems of thinking. Each stage reflects a set of values, beliefs and behaviours that are adapted to specific conditions and challenges faced by individuals or societies at a particular point in time.

As a contextually intelligent and aware approach to cultural transformation, Spiral Dynamics provides a framework for understanding how organisations, communities and societies evolve over time. It helps leaders navigate the complexities of cultural change by recognising that different people and groups are operating from different value systems, each with its own strengths and limitations. By mapping out these stages, Spiral Dynamics allows for more effective interventions and strategies that align with the current stage of development, supporting growth and transformation in a way that is both inclusive and sustainable.

12.3 Practise What We Preach - A Case Study

Case Description

In late 2019, a mine faced imminent closure due to ongoing challenges, compounded by a strike that began in November. The mine's culture presented significant challenges, as employees not only received salaries but also extra payments simply for showing up, along with overtime pay. However, the arrival of the COVID-19 pandemic presented an unexpected opportunity for cultural transformation. Initially, leadership had scheduled the shutdown for June, but instead, they made a pivotal decision to explore options for salvaging the operation. The team was given just four months to devise a sustainable plan that could justify the mine's continuation. The team developed a proposal that outlined a seven-year opportunity in the shaft. Their efforts secured approval for a five-year extension, marking a critical turning point for the mine and laying the groundwork for a renewed focus on operational resilience and growth.

> ...The case played out in the context of a society that was troubled by social uprising and severe post-traumatic stress...

One of the senior leaders phrased their role in the specific challenge: "There are two sides where I believe I am adding value, namely, to keep the company sustainable and to ensure that each of the 1650 employees got a job for longer to support their families for longer"

Employee morale became high, production levels improved significantly, and efficiency increased greatly. Where 26 crews had once mined 3,600 m², 14 crews were now able to mine 2,800 m², yielding a remarkable R74 million in profit and validating the mine's renewed potential. Reflecting on this shift, one leader remarked, "I hate Corona, but we saw opportunities in it. It helped me to defrost the ice, reshape it, and then freeze it again!" This redefined approach broke down old patterns, setting the foundation for a more sustainable and performance-focused culture.

As researchers, we sought to explore the complex dynamics at play in the organisation's turnaround. Our goal was to understand how to reconnect and rewire organisational energy across hierarchical levels. We examined key questions, such as how to effectively build trust within teams and leadership structures and what inclusive practices look like in the context of Spiral Dynamics' PURPLE and RED[xv] levels. This fresh perspective allowed us to investigate the nuanced interactions

---

xv   Spiral Dynamics value systems described by colours are described in paragraph 3.3.

between culture, leadership and inclusivity, aiming to reveal strategies for sustaining a successful transformation.

Methodology

The research design for this study was qualitative, framed within a phenomenological approach to deeply understand participants' experiences and perceptions. The emergent design allowed flexibility in data collection, adapting as insights developed to best support the storytelling approach. The BeQ model provided the theoretical foundation, guiding semi-structured interviews and focus groups aimed at exploring constructs related to human energy and performance at individual, team and organisational levels.

Data analysis utilised thematic and narrative coding to organise findings into storytelling aligned with BeQ domains, capturing evident enablers, energy compromisers, and manifested dynamics. Themes were triangulated through a diverging and converging process of comparison and juxtaposition, which involved testing assumptions and examining loosely held hypotheses. This approach sought to maintain data integrity, allowing for a rigorous examination of emergent patterns.

Archetypes were utilised to tell the different stories as they transcend individual cultures and speak to the collective unconscious, a concept introduced by Carl Jung. These shared motifs resonate across different societies (and organisations), helping stories to transcend local or historical specifics and remain relevant in a global context.

The sampling included 100% participation of employees in D bands (14/14) and 40% of employees in C bands (60/150), ensuring representation across levels within the organisation.

The Managerial Story

The archetype of the creator emerged from the managerial story as a craftsman of our future, motivated by the ability to solve problems together. The creator archetype feels responsible for the lives of others.

Archetype

Creator
We are **CRAFTSMAN** of **OUR** future

Motivation: Solving problems together, responsible
for the lives of others.

In the organisation, respect played a vital role in encouraging open communication and problem-solving. As one employee shared, "People in this shaft believe in one thing: namely that there is no such thing as a stupid question in life. We are free to ask a superior, and the superior then acts. If we don't solve the problem, we know that we will lose millions." Respect extended to all levels, as another leader stated, "I don't mind listening to the lowest level in my teams, i.e., 'if the machine operator says it doesn't work, I listen to them.'" This attitude was paired with an acknowledgment of expertise, with one employee noting, "We have the world's knowledge on the shaft and people listen to that!"

Self-regard was also evident, with team members empowered to maximise their potential. "I am most comfortable with my potential to add value. They empowered me to have all the powers that I needed. 'They empowered my mind!'" Resilience was a key driver in overcoming challenges. As one leader recalled, "We told the VP that this is how we are going to go ahead. We looked at life in a positive manner." With a rolling three-month plan in place, the team remained focused and optimistic: "By the end of month 3, we were very positive! The ball was in our court. The VP told us that only we would close the shaft; the organisation doesn't want to close it but also doesn't want a shaft that is underperforming."

Corporate citizenship was reinforced by a strong sense of responsibility and mutual support: "We are led by our CEO - a big heads up to him! He needs our support. We have our role to play. If we fail in our operations, he cannot assist. Everybody needs to play their part." Individuals recognised the collective effort, with one noting, "Every person contributes. Each one works for himself and his family. We are creating a future, and we want to go ahead!"

I engage

Voice & Respect	Self Regard	Resilience	Corporate Citizenship
We feel respected for our knowledge, treated with dignity and peple listen to each other	We feel important and know we can make it work	We keep a positive mindset and belief that we are in control.of our future - every person contributes!	We help each other to ensure the future

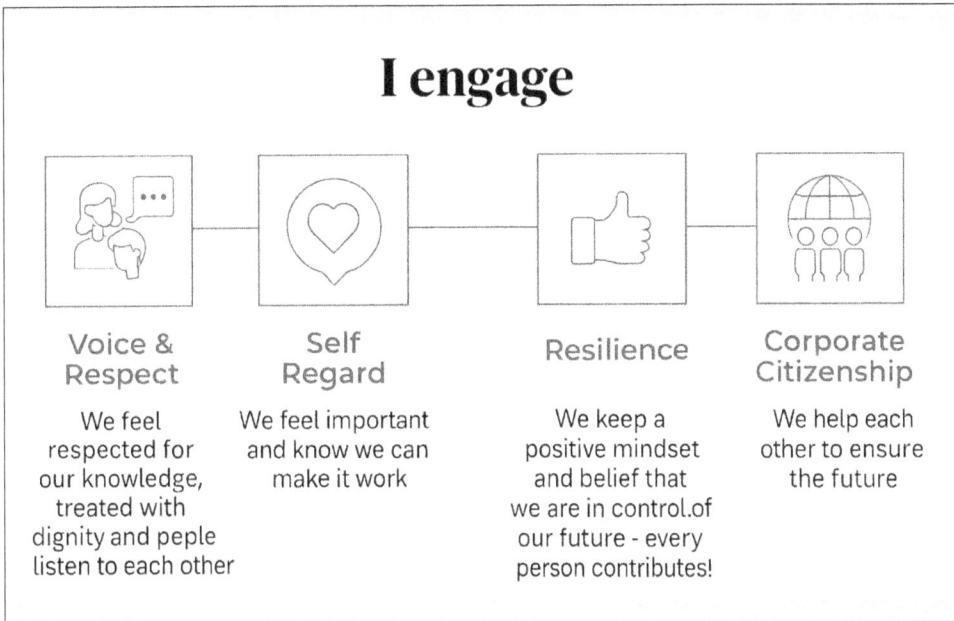

Leadership dynamics were marked by unity, as there was no division between "us" and "them," but a shared sense of ownership: "There was no 'us' and 'them', it was 'we'. We all worked together on this boat. In a sense, we were all employees and helped where we could." Leaders were also seen as accountable and motivating, as one employee explained, "The leadership acknowledged their people. They motivated us and supported us. They listened to what we had to say. We planned together and we were positive."

Diversity within the team was embraced as a strength, with one worker saying, "We are people of the company. We are not saying that we are from different tribes, we are the company." Diversity also helped foster understanding: "Diversity helps us to understand each other better - as we know each other's likes and dislikes." The respect for cultural differences was clear: "We are 100% complying as we are all Africans from different tribes, but we have respect for each other! We are excellent."

Team dynamics were characterised by respect and trust. "We implemented respect by respecting people in the team's first. They listened to each other and trusted each other. Our Operations Manager has meetings every morning that keep us well informed." Accountability was a core value, with clear goals communicated daily: "The whole team knows what the targets are. We monitor this daily, and it is visual, i.e., with a red and green light. Our goals are obvious, and all the teams are on board." As one employee remarked, "It is not always about top leadership. They are too far away. The devil is in the details, and I take accountability for those."

We engage

Leadership	Diversity	Team dynamics	Accountability
Our leaders supports and works with us	Although we are different, we re all company pe- ople and have the same purpose	We are one team and there are no ranks - we support each other	We are accoun- able to each other, otherwise we will lose jobs

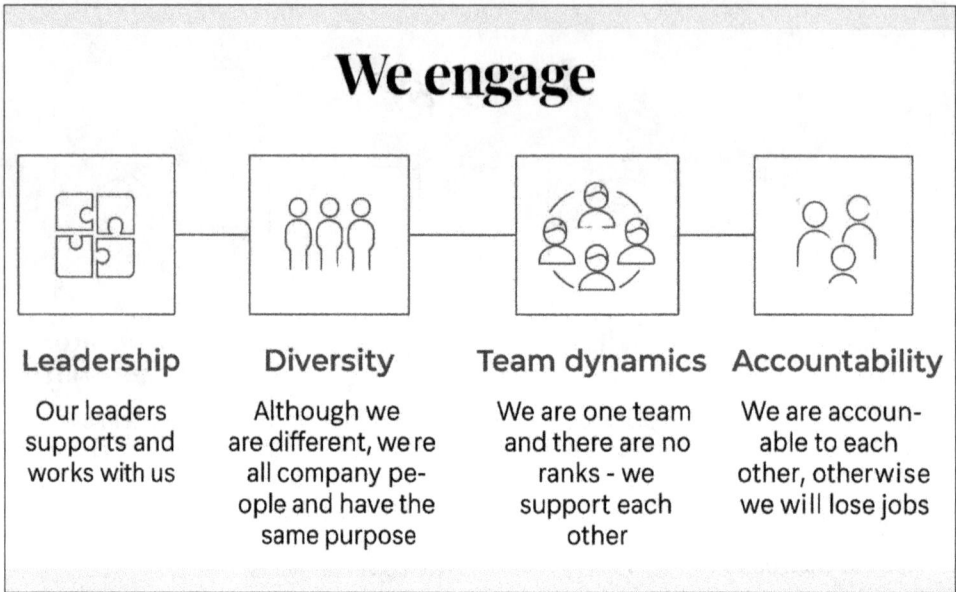

Trust was another cornerstone of the organisation's success, with a mutual understanding of commitment: "People from the top levels are trusting us. We know if we commit and if we are not keeping to our commitments, we will be losing everything." Trust was also built on consistency: "It's better to work with the devil that you know than the one you don't - so far there has been no devil. I trust the company and they never disappoint me."

Inclusivity was felt throughout the organisation, with employees expressing pride in being part of the company: "No doubt that I feel part of the organisation. It is a flagship company in mining, even bigger than Gold Fields and Anglo." Alignment with the company's strategic vision was also clear: "We are 100% aligned with what our responsibilities are in the shaft, as these are supportive of the strategy, vision, and mission."

Finally, adaptability to change was key to the organisation's success. One employee emphasised, "We are sticking to our 'guns' and belief in everything that we are doing." The leadership's persistence was crucial: "Everything rises and falls with leadership. We persisted in our plan and explained the reasons for it. It takes time, a lot of energy and persistence. Sometimes we need to explain over and over. We learned that one doesn't need to position changes as painful."

They engage

Trust	Inclusivity	Alignment	Change
We trust the company and they trust us	We are proud to be part of the organisation, a winning team and a flagship brand	We are a Mining company and work safely to fetch our future	Our leaders will guide us through changes and help to keep us safe to save jobs

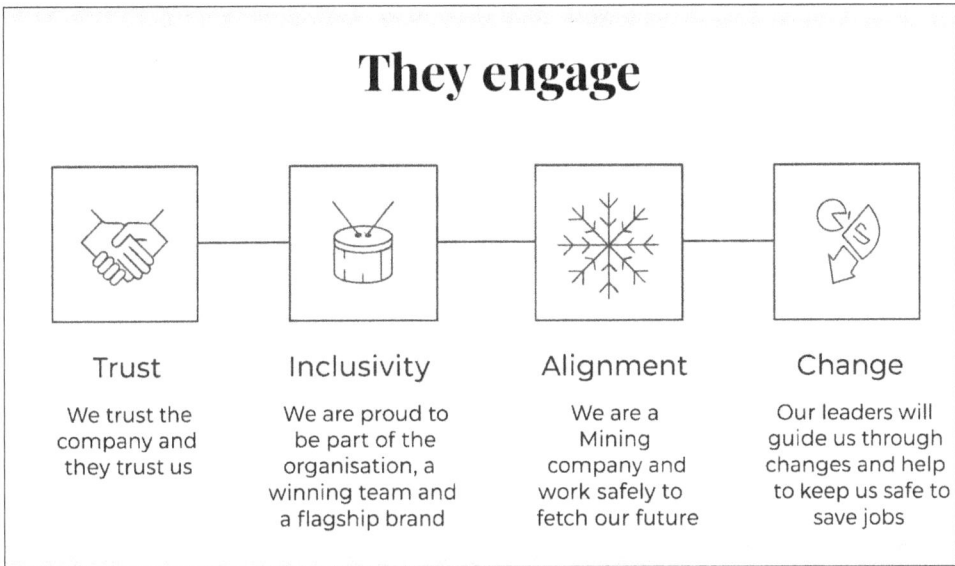

Outcomes manifestation: What is the result of the dynamics?

We observed that respect at a systemic level was one of the determinants of high levels of psychological safety, where even the simplest questions were valued. Leaders with high levels of self-regard were accountable and sought to include, enable, and empower others. Inclusive leadership styles accelerated motivation and enhanced resilience within teams. Meeting business targets instilled a sense of hope, while openness to change and trust in leaders further strengthened this foundation. Finally, a strong sense of belonging unleashed goodwill, creating a positive cycle of engagement and commitment across the organisation.

The Supervisory Story

The archetype of Everyman emerged from the supervisory story. Humbled and grateful to our leaders, the Everyman archetype trusts the business sense of the organisation and are motivated to belong and live together in harmony.

Archetype

Everyman – looking up to the FATHER
We are **HUMBLED** and **GRATEFUL** to our leaders
and **TRUST** the business sense of the organisation.

Motivation: Belonging and living together in harmony.

Respect is foundational to the work culture, with one individual expressing, "We need to teach our labour and help them to learn - this is respect." There is a strong emphasis on teamwork and mutual respect: "We always work in teams and respect each other." Self-regard is also critical, with employees acknowledging the importance of their roles. As one shared, "We are doing important work. I feel important," while another expressed confidence in their abilities, saying, "I am confident that I can do my job because my supervisor tells me that I am good at what I do." A miner added, "As a miner, I am confident and know how to bring my team together. I can show them the targets and communicate and support them to achieve this."

Resilience is evident in the team's approach to challenges. One worker said, "We were given an opportunity: we are like Zama zamas as we are in control of our destiny!" "The Head Office looks from a distance". Resilience also comes through in problem-solving, as another person stated, "When things are difficult, we sit down as a team and SOLVE the problem. We are not fighting with each other as this is creating division." In more difficult situations, support and accountability are key: "In difficult situations, I pull a person to the side and if he is not understanding, I call the whole group to help. If this is not working, I will call HR for a disciplinary."

Supervisory leaders were ready to go the extra mile, as evident in the construct of Corporate citizenship. One individual expressed the drive for success: "I want to have a future for my kids. We MUST make it happen! We need to achieve our targets." A sense of responsibility toward others' success is also important: "We need to investigate the challenges that people have if they don't reach their targets."

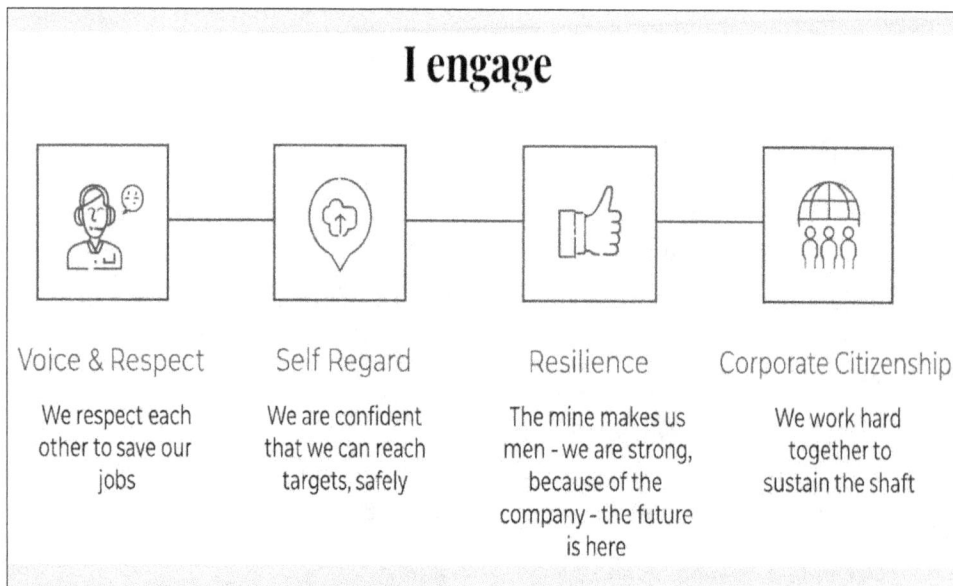

I engage

Voice & Respect	Self Regard	Resilience	Corporate Citizenship
We respect each other to save our jobs	We are confident that we can reach targets, safely	The mine makes us men - we are strong, because of the company - the future is here	We work hard together to sustain the shaft

Leadership plays a significant role in motivation and safety. One employee said, "They do the things that they promise, i.e., promoting safety so that we get the rewards for fatality-free shifts (3 million). This motivates people." The openness of management fosters an inclusive environment: "The offices of the managers are open. Everything is open for everyone." Leadership's role as motivators is further emphasised: "I like to motivate people and ask if they have problems. I talk to them and give them the way they can work, because they are family..." and "Our leaders are really encouraging and motivating us. They recognise excellent performance."

Diversity is well-received, with one individual noting, "Diversity is going well - if you don't understand, you are free to ask for help." Another person added, "We treat each other with respect. We learn each other's culture and we know each other." Team dynamics thrive through communication and shared goals. As one team member said, "We succeed as a team, and we fail as a team. Whatever task we must work on, we pull together. Don't slack the rope. If you have a problem, tell us. If we think that you are not honest, we need to help you to have the same goal as us." The emphasis on communication and respect is clear: "We change over time through a process of communication. We respect that we are different and understand that the purpose is to do our jobs. We have ONE objective!"

Accountability is vital for success. One individual stated, "I am pulling my weight, otherwise I am the weakest link. We were told that the shaft might be closed, but we took accountability and played our part together." Another person added, "We have been given an opportunity to work."

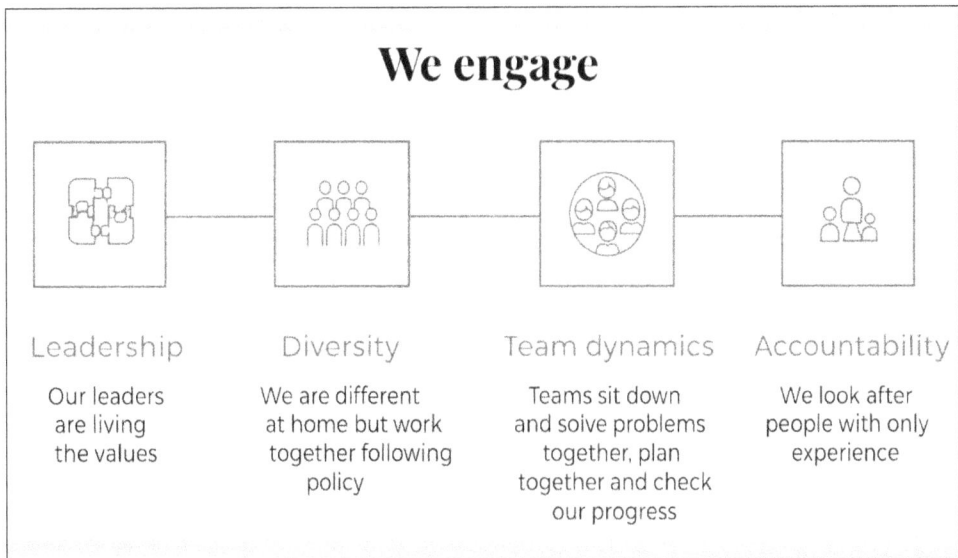

We engage

Leadership	Diversity	Team dynamics	Accountability
Our leaders are living the values	We are different at home but work together following policy	Teams sit down and soive problems together, plan together and check our progress	We look after people with only experience

Trust in the organisation is strong: "I trust the organisation, because they listen to my colleagues. If we ask for something, they give us what we need." There is also trust in leadership's decisions: "We do trust the leadership of the organisation. Their decisions are based on the business aspect, and they are looking at the whole picture. We trust their decisions."

Inclusivity is a clear practice throughout the organisation, with one individual saying, "We are 100% inclusive. Our manager at 4 shaft does things: he shows us how he wants us; he explains how serious this is, how he feels about our jobs, and he promises that if we are doing it right, there will be a long future. This then goes all the way down to the mine captain." The organisation acknowledges diversity within the workforce: "The organisation understands that we are different people - we are not all the same. We need our managers to help us to grow up."

Finally, adaptability to change is crucial. One worker noted, "If we find something that needs to change, we communicate. We take the crew/person close to get them to learn. We discuss the changes, and we ask the right people to help us." The flexibility to adjust safety standards to keep everyone safe was emphasised: "Standard changes are good. If there is an accident, we change the standards to keep people safe. Management is overseers. They can see the risk. They can see further than us. We are flexible to align, because we trust."

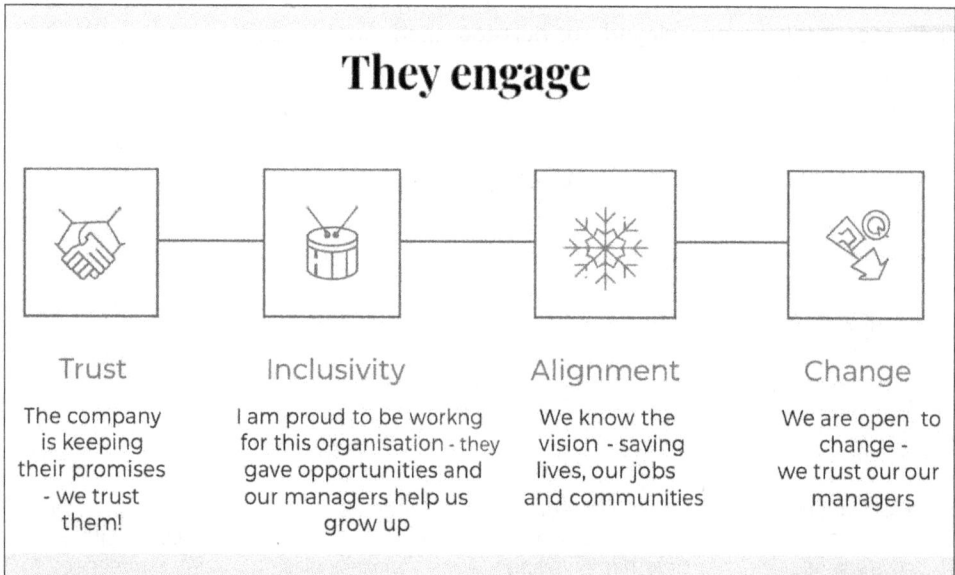

They engage

Trust	Inclusivity	Alignment	Change
The company is keeping their promises - we trust them!	I am proud to be workng for this organisation - they gave opportunities and our managers help us grow up	We know the vision - saving lives, our jobs and communities	We are open to change - we trust our our managers

Outcome manifestation: What is the result of the dynamics?

Leaders at the supervisor level took up their leadership role as they felt enabled and competent as leaders. High levels of interdisciplinary support enabled a collaborative environment, while the experience of participative leadership - where space was given for everyone's ideas - drove motivation. Strong alignment around a singular goal created a sense of unity, giving individuals the "permission" to coach others as if they were family. This shared commitment inspired people to produce not just for themselves but on behalf of their colleagues, who were considered brothers still at home, due to the Corona pandemic.

12.4 Opposing Perspectives - What We Typically Hear

There are two sides to every story, just as there are two sides to a coin. The viewpoints from different levels within the case organisation describe above the ball was highlight contrasting experiences, as revealed through qualitative data collection methods. This chapter showcases only a small portion of the findings, which are based on over 300 focus groups involving more than 5,000 people within the mining industry. At leadership levels, there is a pervasive sense of being "unnoticed," feeling "so small," and "trampled upon." Leaders express frustration that all their hard work is "not recognised" and that they feel "we are nothing." Trust and teamwork are notably absent: "There is no teamwork because colleagues and supervisors cannot be trusted." Racial issues are still prominent, with one individual saying, "Because we are black, we get nothing," and another claiming, "Only whites are promoted and enabled." Gender-based challenges are also evident: "We are not seen as hardworking because we are female." Furthermore, employees feel excluded: "We are not included or consulted – only instructed" and "we cannot engage because we feel so alone, not heard or seen. They only care about the production, but we are the ones making it happen"

If leaders feel this way, then how can they lead?

There was a general sense that leaders and managers must "practise what they preach" to gain credibility and trust. However, there was also a perception that many leaders were unworthy of their titles, which undermined their authority. Corporate citizenship and alignment constructs were found to be low, placing the organisation in jeopardy. Employees with a PURPLE[xvi] centre of gravity, focused primarily on securing their livelihoods, expressed that the only reason they remained with the organisation

---

xvi Spiral Dynamics value systems described by colours are described in paragraph 3.3.

was to keep roofs over their heads and feed their families. This revealed a significant disconnect between leadership intentions and the lived experiences of the workforce.

12.5 Final Thoughts

The average BeQ score is measured at 42%, based on over 90,000 BeQ records spanning various industries, organisational levels and different stages of organisational life cycles, compared to the BeQ score measured in co-determination cases, with inclusion at its core.

Benchmark

74% 42%

Average BEQ in co-determination   Average BEQ in normal situations

As this case illustrates, inclusivity is understood as a comprehensive organisational transformation approach that empowers all levels and stakeholders within the system. It achieves this by ensuring alignment across actions, identity and understanding, creating an environment where every voice is heard and valued. This approach creates a culture of participation and shared responsibility, where individuals are not only given the opportunity to contribute but are also actively involved in shaping the direction and success of the organisation.

Contextual	Condition	OD
Understand systemic philosophy	Trust is pre-requisite	Determine, Design, Deliver, Delineate
Leadership	**Skills Development**	**Transformation**
Throughout the system	Giving voice	Doping human better

Figure 12.2: Meta-insights on co-determination

Co-determination within an organisation is not just about shared decision-making but about creating a systemic philosophy that acknowledges the interconnectedness of all levels of the system. **At the heart of this approach lies trust, which is the**

fundamental condition required for effective collaboration and meaningful engagement across all levels of the organisation. Trust advances open communication and creates a safe space for shared decision-making, allowing individuals to feel empowered and valued in the process.

In terms of organisational development, the process involves determining the key areas for collaboration, designing systems that facilitate this collaboration, delivering on commitments, and clearly delineating roles and responsibilities to ensure everyone's contributions are recognised and impactful. Leadership plays a pivotal role throughout this process, not as a top-down authority but as a guide that supports and encourages a culture of participation, ensuring that co-determination is embedded in the organisation's DNA.

A critical component of this approach is skills development, specifically the ability to "give voice" to those who may otherwise feel excluded from decision-making. By equipping individuals with the tools and confidence to express their opinions and ideas, organisations can strengthen a more inclusive environment where diverse perspectives are valued. Ultimately, the transformative power of co-determination lies in its ability to do "human better" - creating environments where people feel connected, respected, and motivated to contribute meaningfully to the organisation's success. This holistic, human-centred approach to organisational life leads to lasting transformation, where both the individual and the system thrive.

Two years after the intervention, the following text was received:

> ...Lerato, you all helped us to regain humanity. We could go home to our wives and became the leader of our family again. We are proud to work here. We thank you...

Part 4

The Evolving Landscape

Chapter 13

Smorgasbord of ODC Approaches, Modalities and Interventions

13.1 Introduction

This chapter presents a smorgasbord of the reflections and approaches that illustrates on the one hand how ODC interventions can be applied for individual and collective leadership growth; and on the other hand offer some alternative ways to create awareness on the various integral domains. The ODC practitioner can be compared to the master chef that chooses carefully and particularly what ingredients (interventions) to add the dish in order to get the chemistry and taste just right.

Different voices are tied together in a plethora of rich narratives – hopefully to inspire leaders and ODC practitioners to explore beyond the old and well-tested approaches in an attempt to work dynamically, create meaning and ultimately sustainable shifts in consciousness. The reader is invited to reflect on own experiences that left not only meaningful insights about group processes but transformed the way in which life is viewed and embodied after the event. In this way, this chapter presents a gallery of intentions – ODC approaches, modalities and interventions – to consider in designing efforts to unleash the gifts of self and others.

13.2 The Voice of an Elder that Did this Herself

On Learning To Just E"

Lynne Rutherford

Developing leaders is not an intellectual exercise. Are we actually developing leaders or are we creating an opportunity for individuals to become their future self, in whatever way they can or choose to be, to find their place in the world as partners, parents, community leaders and/or leaders at all levels in organisations?

After several decades "doing" leadership development in organisations ranging from retail to financial services, to NGOs and latterly in supply chain, in South Africa and then in Europe, Australia and the US, I myself have been on a journey. The catalyst, on reflection, was the Global Financial Crisis back in 2008, working in Financial Services in Europe, where I saw leadership at its worst, driven by greed, revenge and self-interest.

I chose to leave that world behind and joined a large supply chain organisation which attracted me in that they were giving me carte blanche to create an alternative approach to talent management, including development at all levels.

This is not just my story. It is the story of those wonderful people who put their trust in me to take them on a journey which in some (not all – one has to be open to change) transformed their lives and those around them. I didn't change them; they embraced the opportunities that we provided and went on their own personal journey of transformation. It is the story of my team, who started off thinking I was this crazy woman from South Africa with some "out there" ideas that wouldn't work in Europe, the US and Australia and who became my biggest supporters and wanted to learn more so that they too, could facilitate this change for people. It is the story of one consultant in particular, based in Johannesburg, Hein Schroder, who "got" what I wanted to do and who drove me to be even more courageous in my work. Oh, what an awesome partner he was, and still is, when I think of the brain dumps, Post-it notes and eventual experiences we co-created.

Where do I start? At the beginning I guess. I walked into an organisation which had just invested a couple of million USD on leadership assessments for their top 65 leaders. These assessments were sitting in files in a cupboard in my new office. So I started to read...

Blindingly Obvious?

Armed with highlighters and the facilitator's best friend, Post-its, I discovered 6 common themes:

- The organisation was excellent at recruiting very talented engineers, asset managers and logistics experts.
- As a leadership cadre, they were intellectually strong – really clever people.
- They were very good at "doing".
- What was missing was the self-awareness of their impact on others.
- They lacked the coaching skills to develop their teams (they saw that as the role of HR).
- They struggled to articulate their sense of purpose.

Why did this matter? Being a dominant player in most markets in over 60 countries, we were a successful organisation. However, my experience in Financial Services had taught me one thing – when the going gets tough, and everything starts to fall apart when we least expect it, self-preservation kicks in, and if we don't have that strong sense of purpose which acts as our moral compass even in difficult times, a lot of people can get hurt.

So, Where Do We Start?

Well, I spent two years working with this group, including the CEO. In fact, I told him if he was not prepared to be part of this journey, being the role model, open to new experiences, then it was doomed to fail. To his credit he threw himself into the "interventions" (I don't like that word but hesitate to use the word "programmes"), and he went on his own personal journey, he allowed himself to become vulnerable in front of others, realising that it created trust between himself and his extended leadership team.

To be honest, a lot of this work did centre around the more "traditional" approach to leadership development, working with my trusted business school partner in France and perhaps opening the eyes of these very talented and intellectual practitioners to new and different approaches to running an organisation. They were all introduced to their own executive coach and worked with them for a period of time, thus experiencing for themselves the value of coaching.

One of the biggest changes I made, and one of the most difficult, was repositioning the organisation's approach to Coaching. It was predominantly seen as a remedial "thing to do" to someone, with very little context or measurement of effectiveness. It was an easy solution, both for HR and line managers to "fix" someone. It took probably two years to reframe coaching as development for our most talented people in whom we wanted to invest, a partnership between the individual, their line manager and HR. We got there in the end, and lasting change was the outcome.

So what? You may ask. Exactly. I will share with you here that this group was not my ultimate target. All I was doing here was "preparing the soil" for what was to come, to unleash the potential, with their help, of the next generation.

Assessment Versus Development

A programme of sorts already existed for this next generation, in the form of a very thorough assessment centre (it was called a development centre, but to me it was an intellectual exercise in receiving feedback, some coaching and being unleashed back into the organisation).

How sustainable and transformative can this be, when we are not engaging with the whole person, with their hearts as well as their minds, providing experiences that will take them out of their comfort zone and develop a deep sense of who they really are in the world?

And so our Development Centre was created, back in 2009, with the first one being piloted in 2010. I still remember sitting with (Hein) in the sunshine on a rare warm summer afternoon in Kent, in the U.K., brainstorming what this next level of development might look like and ending up with bits of paper all over the table, with a plan starting to form.

Yes, we still had the psychometrics – but we were selective in which ones we used, as the main purpose was to increase awareness of self and one's impact on others in all aspects of one's life. After all, a leader is not just a part of a team, but a family member, a part of a community, and a member of society. To develop a leader, we needed to work with the whole, not just a part of the individual's role in life.

We wanted our participants to experience the new and unknown, to take them out of their comfort zone and to expand their minds. We interspersed feedback and coaching and self-exploration with silent walks in nature, tai chi and guided visualisation. To our delight, the engineers, asset managers and logistics experts embraced all of it and their emotional and creative sides were somehow unleashed. They learned how to "be" and not just "do".

One participant in particular stands out – he came to the development centre as an action-oriented head of sales, and as we partnered over the years on his development journey, he became one of our biggest advocates for becoming more self-aware as a leader, courageously giving and receiving feedback, and coaching and mentoring the talent that he had in his team. He is now on the Global Executive Team, running a $1.3 billion part of the business.

Horse Whisperers and Shakespeare

For me, it wasn't enough. There were still too many succession gaps, too much focus on experience vs. leadership potential. I just knew that we hadn't come near to unleashing that potential that was there and a step change in our approach was needed.

I had a vision of developing a cadre of the next level of leaders, developing the whole person, not just the technical and intellectual piece, but the emotional and spiritual as well. Can you teach self-awareness, empathy, resilience and comfort with ambiguity in a classroom? I did not and still do not believe so. This is something that is developed over time, in a supportive and experiential environment, and so my aim was to facilitate this environment in different ways.

With my trusted partners, we created a programme that took the leaders further and further into the unknown and the new. Through the experience of a theatre group, they entered into a world of upheaval, change, courage against all odds, through the powerful medium of storytelling. (Thank you, William Shakespeare, for The Tempest and Henry 5th).

We started and ended each day with a mindfulness practice, including yoga early each morning. We had poets telling stories, a socio-political economist giving insights around a campfire into world events such as the Arab Spring, Brexit and the first election of Donald Trump -expect the unexpected and how to deal with it as leaders.

We went into the stables nearby and witnessed a Horse Whisperer take a wild-eyed untrained horse and through a structured but respectful process gain the trust of the horse, allowing him to saddle him and sit on him.

Taking experiential learning to a new level, we took the groups to places like Johannesburg, Delhi and Sarajevo, where they interacted with incredible people who had gone through such trauma such as apartheid and ethnic wars, and who had come out the other side as strong, supportive communities, with a positive outlook on life despite their personal hardships. We used metaphors to debate what leadership means to them, and what they had experienced at a deeper level. There were tears, laughter, and a general unburdening of those things that were holding them back.

Each participant had access to an external executive coach to help them process their self-insights and to bring it back to their leadership journey and back into the organisation, and they all had a mentor from the organisation's executive team.

The journey took 18 months, with four groups participating over a period of five years. Was it transformative? Did it "work" ? Over 50% of the participants moved into bigger roles, moved internationally and cross-functionally. Some left – this was a transparent conversation I had with the Executive Team when I went to ask them for the investment, which was not insignificant. "You may find that some participants may leave the organisation as a result of the programme", I told them. That the experiences they would go through were so life-changing that some of them would start to question their values and their role in the organisation, wanting to contribute in a different way.

One of our most talented women left about a year after experiencing this development, saying that she had been inspired to use her leadership and experience to support and develop other women, specifically in the Trucking industry in the US, where there is a chronic shortage of drivers, and very little infrastructure to keep women safe when driving long distances. She started an academy for women truck drivers and became an advocate and lobbyist for them. In some ways, as the organisation is a large supply chain and logistics organisation, it benefitted from this as it was helping to alleviate this driver shortage!

Storytelling is a very powerful development tool. It engages the creative, the emotional and the imaginative side of our leaders. That is where the deep change happens, where minds are opened and it is passed on to the next generation, which is why I believe that taking a risk, and doing things differently, brings sustainable change at all levels of the organisation.

It's not easy, it's even a bit scary to be honest, as you never know how it will "land". But it's worth it, and I am proud of what we did. Every time one of those leaders has a successful career move, they send me a WhatsApp, thanking me for their development journey. That is my reward.

13.3 A Bundle of ODC Journeys

Below, a few journeys are described that can be considered. It all has a different flavour and maybe all must be experienced once in the development of a leader. The story of Lynne Rutherford above illustrates her novel approach to adult development and ODC. The journeys collected below like a bundle of short stories, may stimulate the reader and the practitioner to do self-development or incorporate some of the insights into own designs.

Reclaiming the Power of Life Force Energy

Helga Coetzer

In the pursuit of profound healing and self-discovery, alternative modality work invites us to reconnect with the vibrant, life-giving energy that flows through every living being. Life force energy is not merely a concept-it is the dynamic current that drives growth, evolution and the essence of who we are. Yet, fear-based resistance patterns within our nervous system can stifle this natural flow, leaving us disconnected from our innate potential for transformation.

The essence of life force energy

At its core, life force energy fuels our very existence, powering our physical, emotional, and spiritual well-being. The human body, as a natural conduit, channels this energy to foster expansion and evolution. However, as we navigate life's challenges and encounter both real and perceived threats, our primal needs for acceptance, belonging, and connection can be compromised. Over time, these experiences along with inherited ancestral patterns-create subconscious imprints that may obstruct the free flow of energy, manifesting as tension, emotional blockages or chronic stress. By integrating alternative modalities and somatic work into ODC practices, coaching and even group processes can reach deeper levels of awareness and result in lasting shifts in thinking, feeling and knowing.

Listening to the body's hidden language

Healing is far more than a set of techniques or holistic interventions-it is an embodied, lived experience. Our bodies communicate through subtle signals: the language of muscle responses, energy shifts, and stored memories. By engaging deeply with these sensations, we can access the wisdom of our physical being, allowing us to feel, process, and ultimately release unresolved emotional pain. This journey of reconnecting with our inner sensations is vital, as true transformation arises from being fully present to our energetic shifts rather than merely intellectualising our experiences.

Beyond conventional healing modalities

While traditional holistic therapies and medical interventions offer important support, the essence of healing lies in our capacity to be, feel, and experience transformation from within. Inspired by thought leaders such as Dr Gabor Maté and Dr Stephen Porges, this approach underscores that healing is an integration of mind, body and spirit. Techniques like Holotropic Breathwork and PSYCH-K® facilitate expanded states of consciousness, empowering us to break free from ingrained neural pathways and to embrace a more fluid, authentic state of being. These techniques can be incorporated in Personal Purpose and Self Mastery ODC interventions as supporting ways to become aware of new ways of perceiving.

Embracing the journey of transformation

As tension dissipates and the body releases its long-held burdens, a space is created for life force energy to flow unimpeded. This release not only softens our stress responses but also reveals a deeper, more authentic connection to our true selves. Complementary modalities such as Cranio-sacral Therapy, Energy Work, and Bodytalk further support this process by bypassing conditioned responses and restoring the natural rhythm of our energy. Ultimately, the journey is about reclaiming the power to trust our inner guidance, to feel our own energy flow, and to step into a state of inner calm and vitality.

The journey to T.H.R.I.V.E.®

An example of a programme that aims at integrating alternative modalities with consciousness work is the Journey to T.H.R.I.V.E.® This transformative programme meets the participant where they are honouring the nervous system's need for safety while guiding you step by step towards deeper healing, emotional freedom and personal empowerment. By integrating energetic release work, breathwork, and subconscious reprogramming, participants learn to dismantle limiting patterns and reconnect with their authentic power. In doing so, participants rewrite their story, shift from limitation to expansion, and embody the life they were meant to live.

This approach is a call to awaken the truth within-to listen to the silent language of the body and to reclaim the powerful, healing force that resides in every one of us. Embrace the journey, reconnect with your life force, and step into a future defined by clarity, vitality and boundless potential.

Supported by more traditional ways of dealing with group process facilitation and with assessments such as pre- and post-EQi measures, lasting shifts in leadership behaviour can occur.

Old Ways Explored in a Contemporary Way

Origins leadership journey - an epic expedition to the origin of human consciousness

Giselle Courtney

The ORIGINS LEADERSHIP JOURNEY is a groundbreaking organisational development intervention designed to activate human potential, deepen innovation and expand leadership consciousness by immersing participants in the primordial landscapes of human cognitive evolution. Embark on an epic expedition through southern Africa, retracing the footsteps of our ancestors to the dawn of modern human consciousness and the emergence of Homo sapiens, the species of wisdom.

By engaging with mythical sites, archaeological finds, megalithic structures, fossil records, deep time impact craters, prehistoric animals and ancient edible botanicals, this sensory-rich experience reconnects participants with the deep evolutionary forces that shaped human perception, creativity and problem-solving.

The intervention leverages primal intelligence, embodied learning and sensory activation to reignite innovative thinking, leadership resilience and deep intuition in modern organisations.

This is more than a leadership programme - it is an odyssey of self-exploration, unlocking the potential to lead with clarity, authenticity and vision.

Transformational journey anchored in systems psycho-analytic thought

The Hidden Dynamics of High Impact Leadership[xvii]

Dr Jean Cooper

A programme for middle management offered by The Institute for Leadership and Transformation and the Tavistock Institute, offers a unique self-directed programme to embark on a transformative journey is entirely your own. This programme invites you to embark on a journey of self-discovery and profound organisational impact. By integrating systems psychodynamics with real-world leadership challenges, you are empowered to create a ripple effect of high-impact leadership. This transformative programme is your gateway to not only breaking through invisible barriers but also reimagining your role as a leader-setting the stage for future success, whether within your current organisation or on your own entrepreneurial path. The modules offer a thorough analysis into leadership dynamics.

Module 1: Authority, role and system

Discover the intricate dynamics of authorisation and de-authorisation-upward, downward, lateral, and inward. Learn to navigate the pitfalls and seize the opportunities inherent in organisational roles and recognise the systemic forces that impact performance.

Module 2: Working with boundaries and organisational culture

Explore how task, role and authority boundaries shape organisational culture. Gain insights into transforming detrimental boundary habits and learn to strike the balance between rigidity and flexibility in your leadership approach.

Module 3: Social defences and organisational learning

Uncover the unconscious patterns that impede change and stifle innovation. Address blame cultures, bureaucratic constraints and defensive routines while developing strategies to convert resistance into creative engagement.

Module 4: Decision-making and uncertainty

Examine how unconscious forces influence strategic choices. Learn to cultivate anti-fragile teams capable of 'thinking under fire' and master the art of firm yet empathetic decision-making in high-pressure environments.

---

xvii The Hidden Dynamics of High Impact Leadership. https://jeanhenrycooper.com/the-hidden-dynamics-of-high-impact-leadership.html

Module 5: Group dynamics, power and influence

Delve into the emotional currents that drive group dynamics. Navigate systemic conflicts and power struggles, transforming groupthink into robust, collaborative teamwork that drives high performance.

Module 6: Middle managers as culture shapers

Embrace your role as a transformative leader and cultural shaper. Align your team with organisational purpose, foster spaces for reflective thinking and sense-making, and become a trusted thinking partner in strategic transformation initiatives.

The programme equips middle managers with the skills to read, respond to, and influence the hidden forces shaping organisational culture and performance. By applying systems psychodynamics thinking, participants develop the awareness, insight and courage to transform their leadership presence, creating extraordinary impact within their organisations or future ventures.

Collective Leadership Capacity – A Journey

Majoja[xviii] – Together (company specific name) -
A Transformational Odyssey for the Future

Rica Viljoen

In the ever-evolving landscape of leadership, the journey toward collective leadership is a multifaceted odyssey - one that begins within, expands through collaboration, and ultimately embraces a global perspective. The Organisational Development Journey described here develops in three phases. It was designed for an organisation as an advanced development initiative for emerging high-flyers and successors who are poised to lead in a future that values diversity, collective wisdom and strategic innovation.

Year 1: The I-space: Finding own voice

Every transformation begins at the core of the individual. In the first year, leaders step into the I-space - a dedicated realm for cultivating self-awareness, emotional intelligence and authentic leadership. Over a series of intensive three-day sessions, participants engage in reflective practices centred on authentic leadership, self-mastery, and personal purpose. This phase lays a robust foundation for growth by enabling leaders to understand their intrinsic strengths and unique contributions. The phase consists of three sessions spread over eight months. Each session lasted three days.

---

xviii Swahili word based on case study facilitated in Tanzania

Photo 13.1: Colour in mandalas during group process to further personal reflection

Year 2: The WE-space: Embracing strategic business thinking

Building on personal insight, the journey advances into the WE-space, where collective intelligence meets strategic collaboration. In the second year, leaders converge to tackle complex business challenges through the lens of systems thinking, scenario planning, design thinking and innovation. Working in small, diverse groups, they address real-world business problems and transform strategic ideas into actionable solutions. This phase highlights how individual brilliance is amplified by teamwork and shared vision. Systems thinking, design thinking and an action learning project form part of this journey. The same structure as in year one was followed.

Year 3: The ORG-space: Building a Global worldview and collective leadership

In the final year, the journey expands into the ORG-space, where leaders develop a global perspective and deepen their understanding of collective leadership. Participants explore world view theories and the dynamics of building an inclusive culture, supported by meta-theories discussed in this book. An international immersion experience further enriches this stage, offering firsthand insights into cross-cultural collaboration and the global challenges modern organisations face. Assessments quantify pre- and post-intervention ROI.

Some of the post-intervention feedback received includes:

"Excited to see these people in this room, we are friends now. I used to be a person that would react instantly to emotions or people. I overheard an employee gossip about me, she noticed I was there and heard her and when we eventually got together to talk about it, I handled it much better than I would've in the past, I have come a long way. I gained assertiveness and resilience in this course"

"I believe this course was specially sent for me. I would give all of myself in the past and then burn out. Now I know it's me first. I need to fill my cup first. Then I can tackle my day. I take 15 minutes every day to breathe to ensure my mind is clear. I feel so much more focused and level-headed.

"Beautiful people under stress are still the same beautiful people, this course has taught me that they just react differently. This helped me grow as a person and a leader. At this late stage in my life I know myself better."

Your legacy lives on through us. We have so much to give to our communities, locally and globally. I am your product, too.

Conclusion

Together, these three interconnected journeys form a comprehensive roadmap for developing well-rounded, future-ready leaders. Over the course of three transformative years - with each phase building upon the last - participants evolve into strategically agile leaders who are adept at navigating modern business complexities and committed to fostering inclusive environments. This initiative is more than a succession plan; it is a visionary blueprint for constructing collective leadership, minimising talent flight, and nurturing leaders who are ready to drive positive change across continents.

Transformational journey towards inclusivity

Kaleidoscope of differences – spiral dynamics in action®

Mandala Consulting

Second tier integral, functional and innate leadership can rely on the value systems that help them cope with an array of life conditions – from survival, to belonging; from belonging to having personal power; from regulating the uprising of personal power with standard operating procedures, compliance and ethics to achieving success; from self-drive for achievement and innovation to a more philanthropic way of attending to humanity and global needs. Typical questions that can be considered in a session of this nature include:

- Why am I here on earth now?
- And why in this body and time and context?
- What is the unique voice that needs to come through me?
- What is my myth?
- When will I become cynical and unfulfilled – and when will I feel I lived a life well lived?
- What is my own leadership philosophy?
- How can we connect to allow a more functional reality for all?
- And what must be discontinued?
- How can we do human better?

Structure of the journey

The journey is facilitated over 8 to 12 months with an array of various interventions that comprises of experiences deeply engrained in the ODC principles described in this book. Immersions are facilitated that assist participants in exploring the theories of African scholars like Credo Mutwa[xix] and Vusi Vilakati[xx]. A combination of interventions is crafted together to ensure that the developmental needs of the organisation or the leadership group are met. Assessments from the base of the exploration and a systemic ever-evolving dynamic experienced is created through rigorous and skilled facilitation of boundaries of content, space and time that create trust and meaning. Spiral Dynamics Integral infused experiences are tied together in an integral and purposive manner.

13.4 Interventions That Last

Designing and facilitating a dynamic way of connecting to sound, sight, touch, taste and smell helps participants to experience emotions and behaviours of self and others in an integral, authentic and holistic way. In crafting narratives for leadership, cultural transformation or strategic change in a sensory manner these narratives become more engaging, memorable and emotionally impactful.

Sight (Vision)

Creating the organisation in the mind of all: by creating a future state of self, a vision board or an idealised state of the organisation, sight is introduced in the intervention.

---

xix Vusamazulu Credo Mutwa /ˈkreɪdoʊ ˈmʊtwə/ (21 July 1921 – 25 March 2020) was a Zulu sangoma (traditional healer) from South Africa. He was known as an author of books that draw upon African mythology and traditional Zulu folklore.

xx Vusi Vilakati is an African scholar that conceptualised African Spiritual Consciousness in his Masters and Doctoral Studies at the University of Johannesburg

Metaphors are important in PURPLE-remembrance[xxi] – "a ship steering through a storm"; "let's not milk the cow dry". Visualising a future reality through scenario planning, Vision, mission and values frameworks and other interventions make the outcome more tangible. Storytelling, symbols and myths help significantly here. ODC interventions to consider are:

Art and drama

Leaders can craft sensory-rich narratives that make change more relatable. Instead of saying let's become more innovative one can say, "picture a team that walks in a workspace filled with energy – whiteboards full of ideas, rapid discussions over coffee and shared excitement of what is next." Visual storytelling creates memorable explorations of how dynamics play out in groups. One way is through working with art-based activities.

An organisation embarked on a journey of becoming second tier or YELLOW as their 5-year vision passionately stated. In a large group event, the team engaged in a ritual to illustrating their individual spiral dynamics values through making masks[xxii]. In a group activity various diversity of thought aspects was considered, and group gestalt work was used to facilitate an exploratory setting where it could be considered how these diversity dynamics manifest in the group and the organisation.

Photo 13.2: Spiral Dynamics Masks at a strategic session with Jet Educational Services

As a visual sign of the transformation the company also reallocated to a different office space.

This was a powerful signal in the shift in culture.

---

xxi Spiral Dynamics value systems described by colours are described in paragraph 3.3.

xxii A clip of the process of JET Education Services, is available at https://www.youtube.com/watch?v=e5JZpBEOYkU

Psychodrama and group constellations

A group process can be facilitated where the convenor plays with "the jazz" of the group. The dynamic interplay of individual and collective experiences creates a shared understanding of the phenomenon under inquiry. The unity and interconnectedness between participants are enabled, and the emersion of collective insight is allowed. Constellation work is a form of psychodrama where characters embody the energy of role players/actors in the field in an attempt to facilitate profound insights and rebalance forces within the field of consciousness.[314, 315]

Picture 13.3: Inclusivity at Constellation Event

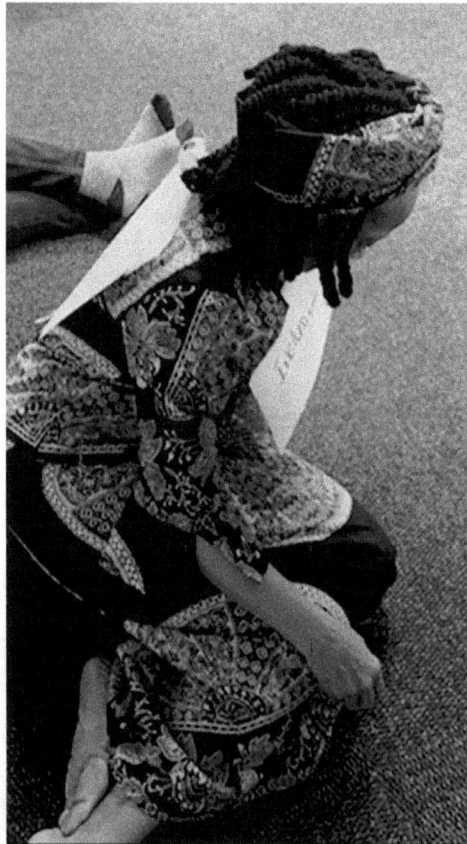

.During an event on the dynamics at play in the societal context, the actor playing INCLUSIVITY became fatigued and wearily rested on the ground. Zulu healing rituals often involve symbolic gestures, communal witnessing, and acknowledgment of past wrongs. Similarly, in constellation work, participants take on the roles of family members, embodying intergenerational dynamics in ways that transcend verbal articulation. This ritualistic enactment creates an embodied experience of systemic truths, facilitating healing at both personal and collective levels.[316]

Sound (Hearing) – The Power of Words and Silence

What does the organisation sound like? It may be full of debate or quiet fear.

The ability to sit with self and others in silence says something about the power dynamics in a group. The silence can also be quiet tension or fleeing behaviour. In Vision Quests, being with self often unleashes innate insights. The tone of leadership conversations, the rhythm of conversations and organisational silence. Jung's reminder that if something is suppressed as silence, it will come out as a cry[317] must also be considered. Speaking and not speaking impact in the emotional climate in the organisation. An ODC intervention to consider is:

The voice of sound: Drumming in ODC

Rooted in deep ancient traditions drumming creates a sense of connection and synchronisation – resulting in collective rhythm. This is an important part of high-performance teams. Drumming illustrates the importance of effective communication and fosters strong cohesion in teams. It results in social bonding and cooperation. A sense of belonging and unity is created. Individual rhythms need to be adjusted to that of the group in active participation. By incorporating drumming in ODC interventions, a space for collective expression is added to an intervention. Well-facilitated by the ODC practitioner can leave the group with an understanding of how to adjust to change, how to deal with organisational transitions and how to transcend artificial boundaries such as language and culture. The shared rhythmic experience leads to a sense of collective identity among diverse groups.

Picture 13.4: Drumming during group event

The sound of leadership matters. It can give trust and psychological safety. So is the art of listening to hear in ODC:

The art of listening with the intent to understand

To be honest, it's an interesting and proud opportunity to add my thoughts to Rica's book. The question is how to add value? I am an accountant; I am not nearly as skilled in psychology as is required to fully grasp the subtleties of interaction and organisational development and change, however I am a keen observer. To be fair, I have been involved in, and exposed to, a lot of businesses, from one-man bands to big corporates "and I have seen". I figure that is my contribution, a "layman's" perspective of how this book is relevant and important.

People talk about "business" but if you look beyond the façade, business is just about people. Serving customers, servings shareholders, paying staff, it all exists ultimately for the benefit of people.

When I say "benefit", things start to become interesting. What the business does is really determined by who controls it, and most often what is beneficial to them personally. I was once told, "that a boardroom doesn't vote for what is best for the company, the outcome is just where majority of common personal benefit overlapped". Now I am not saying that is an absolute truth, but it is a scary thought. Are there decision-makers "serving" the greater good or serving themselves, and how do you know, especially when its "white collar" and subtle.

From owner entrepreneur businesses where the shareholder holds himself as priority number one through the evolution to big corporates where the efficiency of size snowballs resulting in mega profits ("Fat") which in turn allows for inefficiency and political games that small business could not survive. I have also learnt that the "C Suite" is not necessarily the crème that has risen to the top, but sometimes just the floaters who place themselves there for employment. It's there to be seen, if you know what to look for, and reading a book like this will help you see.

If we really want to swing for the bleachers, we need to be brave enough to reflect on our own behaviour. Question where we are looking to protect ourselves at the cost of the greater good, and I think Organisational Development and Change practitioners have somewhat of a responsibility to help uncover this, otherwise on some level they are enabling. Consider what the business purpose should be, and who it should be serving? Only once we are clear on that can we look at how it needs to be designed, and "design" centres around finding the right people, and the right people includes those that can appreciate and work with each other's differences acknowledging the synergy that it brings. It is important to remember that the head has more impact than the tail, and so you need to choose the right leadership. They will, in turn create the right direction and culture. Culture can easily be pegged as a fluffy nice to have, however it is culture that will decide who is attracted to the business and who chooses to stay in it. The right culture will also cause the business to be self-sustaining, as "fit" employees will feel aligned, motivated, and act in terms of what is right for the company beyond rules and policy.

That is where people like Rica play an important role. They paint the human picture beyond what we can see. On occasion, I have chatted with Rica, and I chuckle to myself, because I explain things as I see them and at the same time, as she listens, I get the impression that Rica sees my story like Neo saw the matrix. Way beyond what I think I am sharing.

Touch (Tactile) – Feeling Culture and Change

What does the organisation feel like? Is the interaction arm or rigid?

Change is often felt before it is understood. It also needs to be experienced to be internalised. Workshops, prototypes, interactive sessions all help. How the CEO greats a newcomer may signal "We are in this together." Becoming acutely aware of the way in which touch impact us and others indeed valuable. An ODC intervention to consider is:

Your body is talking to you. Are you listening?

Crisna Ashforth

Kinesiology is a holistic therapy that looks behind the symptoms caused by stress. Kinesiologists use muscle testing as a feedback mechanism to access and assess information on your health and wellbeing. Muscle testing is a profound method that allows the Kinesiologist to "talk to your body" accessing conscious, subconscious and body memory. This provides a real-time evaluation of the mind, the body, the neurological systems, the endocrine and hormonal responses, the energy system and feelings, emotions, old negative behaviour patterns, and memories. More importantly, it shows the integration or lack of integration of the various systems in relation to each other.

When we are unable to respond to our stressful lifestyles in an appropriate way the signals between body and brain become unclear. This shows up as a change of muscle response that is abnormal via muscle testing. A Specialised Kinesiologist can detect this muscle response in a person and in so doing can find out where the person is not coping in their life.

By aligning bodily awareness with cognitive insights, individuals can develop a deeper understanding of their personal reactions to change, stress, and decision-making. Techniques such as breathing exercises, somatic regulation and energy-balancing practices can facilitate emotional resilience, enabling leaders to remain composed and adaptable in high-stakes situations.

Facilitating Embodied Decision-Making

Organisations often emphasise cognitive decision-making, but somatic cues-such as tension, posture, and breath-provide valuable, often overlooked, insights. Through kinesiology, individuals can learn to integrate bodily awareness into their decision-making processes, leading to more holistic and grounded choices. By developing the ability to "listen" to their bodies, leaders can better align their strategic actions with their intuitive understanding of complex organisational dynamics.

Reducing stress and enhancing adaptability

> Change initiatives within organisations often evoke resistance and stress. Kinesiology offers a set of practical tools for mitigating stress responses and improving adaptability. Simple movement-based interventions, such as grounding exercises and tension release techniques, can help employees manage uncertainty and maintain a sense of balance amid transformation.
>
> The incorporation of ODC and kinesiology further amplifies these benefits by fostering self-awareness, strengthening emotional intelligence, and equipping individuals with embodied tools to navigate change. As organisations and communities continue to seek deeper, more meaningful engagement, these interdisciplinary approaches stand as compelling methodologies for unlocking potential, fostering connection, and shaping the future in ways that transcend the limits of conventional discourse.

Personal presence is critical in leadership. Alternative modalities are really helpful in creating experiences that stretch on the one side yet provide valuable practices on the other.

Taste (Gustation) – Flavouring Experience

What is the 'taste' of change? Exciting or hard to swallow?

Change has a flavour to it. We often say, "sweet success", "bitter resistance", "the bitter tase of failure in our first transformational attempt to make the ultimate success even sweeter". The culture can be "nurturing". "The smell of fresh coffee starts the executive meeting" – it is like a ritual. A new leadership style can be "a breath of fresh air" and impact the "stench of outdated policies". An ODC intervention to consider is:

> Culinary experiences where groups prepare dishes from different cultures to share; cooking together as part of a team building or searching for ingredients in a survivor-like experience provide spaces from communication where "we can share bread" and have meaningful connections. In spaces like this role and position the authority it holds falls away and relationships are forged that linger long after the intervention.

Taste results in satisfaction. It describes psychological reactions to shifts. "is the change experience fulfilling?", "Was the meeting distasteful?", "employees digest new ways and culture shifts".

Smell (Olfaction) – Scent and Memory in Culture

Scents trigger deep emotional and memory-based reactions and responses. "we have a fresh start" and "the toxic environment" are metaphors that reflect real psychological experiences. An ODC intervention to consider is:

The greatest garden on earth - South African Fynbos®. A sensory connection to origin.[xxiii]

Giselle Courtney

The wildflower biome at the southern tip of Africa is the greatest natural garden on earth, not only because of its unsurpassed floral diversity, breathtaking scenery and novel flavours that the world is only now discovering, but also because it holds the 'seeds' of human consciousness. Unearthed in Cape coastal caves is some of the world's earliest archaeological evidence of human creativity and abstract thought dating back 160 000 years. Fynbos vegetation already covered the landscape at the time of the emergence of innovation in homo sapiens, 'sapiens' meaning of wisdom.

By experiencing the ancient flavours of Fynbos today, it could be said that we reach into the depths of time and sense the first flowering of symbolic thought, the origin of consciousness.

This can be combined with AN ANCIENT FLAVOUR TRAIL[xxiv]

During this intervention leaders embark on an ancient flavour 'trail' of aromatic infusions made from eleven of the 7000 species in the Fynbos biome. Lunch is an experimental tapa accompanied by the South African Fynbos® range of seasonings and botanical infusions. Crafted to activate creativity and innovation and recommended as a prelude to strategy sessions, as a team building experience and for exploring change and diversity. The setting for this unforgettable connection to terroir is a private haven for critically endangered Swartland Renosterveld in the scenic Cape Winelands valley of Wellington.

13.5 Reflection of The Impact of Journeys

My Personal Journey in Jungian Coaching: A spiral dynamics application in Change Consulting, Organisational Dynamics, and Transforming Toxic Work Environments

Bedelia Theunissen

Jungian coaching has been a transformative and deeply personal journey for me. Following a significant personal trauma, I sought healing and clarity, and it was

---

xxiii The greatest garden on earth - South African Fynbos®. https://www.southafricanfynbos.com

xxiv Cape Town Fynbos Experience® - A MIXOLOGY OF VELD & FLOWER through Jungian coaching that I found the tools and insights necessary to navigate my inner world. Rooted in the depth psychology of Jung, this approach allowed me to explore the unconscious mind, engage with archetypal energies, and move toward individuation-a journey of self-discovery and integration that ultimately led to my healing and growth.

The foundations of my healing through jungian coaching

At the heart of my experience with Jungian coaching was the belief that each individual has an innate drive toward individuation-the process of becoming one's true self. After my trauma, I felt lost, fragmented, and disconnected from my inner self. I felt helpless. Through Jungian coaching methods, I began the process of integrating unconscious material, understanding personal and collective archetypes, and balancing the conscious and unconscious aspects of my psyche. Unlike traditional therapeutic models that focus on symptom relief, Jungian coaching allowed me to delve deeply into my soul's narrative, uncovering hidden wounds and the wisdom they carried.

Engaging in shadow work was one of the most powerful aspects of my healing. By confronting and embracing the parts of myself that I had previously repressed, I could transform deep-seated fears and limiting beliefs. The Jungian process provided a space for me to engage in dialogue with my inner world, allowing insights to emerge that had previously been obscured. Dream analysis, too, became an essential guide, revealing symbols and messages that helped me make sense of my journey and facilitated deep transformation.

The role of the RED approach in spiral dynamics

As I worked through my healing journey, I found that the RED approach of Spiral Dynamics played a crucial role in my transformation. The RED approach, characterised by strength, self-assertion, and raw personal power, allowed me to reclaim aspects of myself that had been suppressed due to trauma and limiting beliefs. I realised that my wounds had left me feeling powerless, hesitant to assert my needs, and disconnected from my own authority. For a long time, I blamed myself and had recurring thoughts of what I did to cause the situations and what I could have done differently.

By embracing the RED energy, I learned to stand in my power and express myself unapologetically. This phase of my journey was about breaking free from self-imposed limitations, setting firm boundaries and honouring my primal instincts. Instead of viewing assertiveness as aggression, I reframed it as self-empowerment, an essential step toward reclaiming my life. This newfound strength complemented my work with Jungian coaching, providing the courage needed to fully integrate my shadow and embrace my authenticity.

The transformation that followed

As I continued this process, I noticed profound changes in my perception of myself and the world around me. My trauma had initially left me feeling powerless, but through Jungian coaching and the Red approach of Spiral Dynamics, I reclaimed my sense of agency and inner wisdom. One of the most pivotal moments was realising that my pain held meaning-it was not just something to be overcome but an initiation into a deeper level of self-awareness and resilience.

For example, I discovered through archetypal exploration that I had been embodying the "Wounded Healer" archetype, a profound realisation that reshaped how I viewed my suffering. Rather than seeing myself as broken, I began to understand my experiences as a source of strength and insight, allowing me to support others on their own journeys.

Applying this to my role as a change consultant

As a change consultant, my personal journey through Jungian coaching and Spiral Dynamics has provided me with profound insights into human transformation. Change, whether individual or organisational, is rarely linear and often involves deep psychological resistance. My understanding of Jungian principles allowed me to recognise the unconscious fears, archetypes and collective patterns that influence resistance to change.

By integrating shadow work into my consulting practice, I help organisations and leaders uncover hidden cultural and emotional blocks that hinder transformation. The Red approach in Spiral Dynamics teaches me the importance of balancing authority with empathy-helping leaders to step into their power while fostering trust and collaboration.

Moreover, my experience with individuation informs my approach to change management. I see organisational change as an individuation process on a collective scale-one that requires integrating past challenges, embracing new identities, and aligning conscious strategies with deeper, often unconscious, cultural values.

Through this lens, I bring a unique and holistic approach to change consulting, guiding individuals and organisations through transitions with a deeper understanding of the psychological dynamics at play. Jungian coaching has not only been my personal healing tool but also a professional framework that allows me to facilitate sustainable, meaningful transformation in the corporate world.

Applying this to team dynamic workshops

Besides change consulting, I apply these principles to team dynamic workshops, helping teams navigate interpersonal relationships, leadership styles and collective growth. Understanding team dynamics through Jungian coaching and Spiral Dynamics provides a powerful framework for addressing conflicts, improving communication, and fostering collaboration.

I found shadow work is particularly useful in teams, as unaddressed individual and collective shadows often manifest as workplace tensions and power struggles. By guiding teams through structured exercises to identify their unconscious patterns, I help them create more transparent and cohesive working relationships. Recognising team archetypes, such as the "Hero," "Caregiver," or "Trickster," allows members to appreciate diverse strengths and contributions while addressing underlying tensions.

The Red approach in Spiral Dynamics also plays a critical role in leadership development within teams. Encouraging individuals to step into their personal power while maintaining respect for others fosters a healthy balance between assertiveness and collaboration. This approach is particularly beneficial in high-pressure environments where decisive leadership and strong interpersonal dynamics are essential for success.

By integrating these methodologies into my team workshops, I create transformative experiences that enhance not only professional relationships but also personal growth. Teams that engage in this deep work emerge with a stronger sense of trust, accountability and resilience, leading to more effective and harmonious workplaces.

Transforming toxic work environments

Toxic work environments often stem from unresolved conflicts, power struggles and a lack of psychological safety. Using Jungian coaching and Spiral Dynamics, I help organisations uncover the root causes of toxicity, addressing both individual and collective shadows that perpetuate dysfunction.

Shadow work can reveal underlying fears, insecurities, and suppressed emotions that lead to toxic behaviours such as micromanagement, passive-aggressiveness, or resistance to change. By bringing these unconscious patterns to light, individuals and teams can work toward healthier interactions, fostering a culture of transparency and trust.

The Red approach is particularly useful in shifting toxic environments, as it empowers employees and leaders to assert healthy boundaries, take ownership of their roles, and address issues with confidence rather than avoidance. When balanced with other Spiral Dynamics levels, this creates a workplace culture where direct communication, mutual respect and collaboration thrive.

By applying these methodologies, I facilitate deep, lasting change within organisations, helping them transition from dysfunction to resilience, empowerment and productivity.

Embracing the Journey Forward

Jungian coaching and Spiral Dynamics have become more than just tools for healing - it has become a way of living. The depth of self-awareness I gained continues to shape how I move through life, fostering greater authenticity, resilience and connection. My journey was not just about recovering from trauma; it was about emerging with a new, integrated sense of self.

Now, as I continue to refine my understanding of Jungian psychology and Spiral Dynamics, I am dedicated to sharing this wisdom with others who seek healing and transformation. Whether in individual coaching, team workshops or organisational change efforts, these principles offer a path to wholeness, authenticity and sustainable success.

13.6 Final Thoughts

As we stand at the culmination of this exploration into the diverse, intricate, and deeply transformative landscape of Organisational Development and Change (ODC), one truth emerges: growth is not a singular journey but a convergence of many paths. Much like a carefully curated smorgasbord, each approach, modality and intervention presented in this chapter is an offering-an invitation to explore, to taste, to integrate what resonates and to leave behind what does not serve.

The voices captured here, from the wisdom of elders to the stories of contemporary transformation, remind us that ODC is not simply about methodologies; it is about human experience, the unfolding of potential, and the shaping of consciousness. Whether through systems psychoanalysis, sensory-based interventions, or deeply embodied leadership journeys, the underlying principle remains the same-lasting change is not imposed; it is cultivated, nurtured, and ultimately embraced by those who embark upon the path.

In leadership, as in life, there is no single prescription for transformation. What works in one context may not work in another. And yet, the essence of ODC-the ability to awaken, to challenge, to reveal, and to heal-remains universal. It is found in the silences between words, in the energy that moves through bodies and organisations, in the resilience of those who dare to see differently, and in the courage to step into the unknown.

As this chapter concludes, the invitation extends beyond these pages. The smorgasbord does not end here. It continues in practice, in lived experiences, and in the spaces where leaders, practitioners and seekers co-create the future. The question is no longer simply how we facilitate change, but who we become. In the end, the most profound interventions are not those that dictate solutions but those that open doors-doors to deeper awareness, authentic leadership, and ultimately, to a way of being that is more aligned, connected, and whole.

Chapter 14

The Evolving World of Work, Standards of Good People Practices, and ODC

Dr Ajay Jivan

14.1 Introduction

There is much conjecture on how the world of work is evolving and forecasting of how it will continue to evolve into the future. The wide range of available white papers, advisories, and thought leadership prescribe how organisations are to make sense of, and respond to, the future. These speak of best practices for the future. In this chapter we will stand back to reflect on how we situate ourselves in the evolving world of work and consider the place of good and ethical people practices. We will first explore how the evolving world of work is being framed, particularly the ideas of a new world of work and a new normal. We will then consider a thematic approach to understanding our evolving context and the world of work. Following this we will ask how we can position standards of good people practices in this evolving context and world of work. We will cite the example of the People Practices and Governance Standard published by the South African Board for People Practices (SABPP) on good ODC practices.

14.2 Evolving and New World of Work

There is a gallery of available images and narratives trying to capture what, in essence the evolving world of work is. The predominant theme or the golden thread that seems to run through the various images and narratives is that of disruption, particularly technology-based disruption. This is the disruption – in the sense of interruption, undoing, and breaking down - of what is characterised as the traditional organisation and world of work. Thus, we hear of the new world of work or the 'new normal', implying a transition to a completely different and transformed organisation and an overhaul of the way work, workers, and the workplace are organised and managed. The COVID-19 pandemic brought a sense of urgency in our reckoning with the new world of work or new normal. The pandemic certainly disrupted across the globe, on a large scale, our experience of continuity in every aspect of our lives, whether our working, social, or personal lives. And it interrupted our sense of direction and progress. It made real what is termed as the BANI world – the brittle, nonlinear and incomprehensible world provoking a constant state of anxiety.

We need to pause and reflect, though, on the various images and narratives of the new world and the sense of urgency and the urge for the immediacy of action. This is not a call for passiveness, procrastination or paralysis. Rather, it is a call for deliberative reflection and action that is contextualised, sound, and informed. This is important when organisations undertake ODC interventions to respond to these shifts in world views and realities. And it is critical when considering an ODC approach and the range of interventions from the perspective of good and ethical people practices, which we will discuss in the next section.

If we pause for a moment, we then realise that the term 'new normal' is itself not new. It has been used previously to distinguish times of significant social, economic and political change and uncertainty.[318, 319] An example of this is its used to mark the 2008 financial crisis. In the present it is used to demarcate the significant interruptions and changes to how we work, play, make meaning, and relate to others post-COVID. There is much conjecture on how the way we work, play, make meaning, and relate will change and take shape in this new normal.[320 321] There are a wide range of descriptions of, and prescriptions for, the new normal. These vary from a narrow focus on remote and flexible working to broader perspectives on building effective hybrid and distributed teams as well as reimagining the business and operating models of organisations. The question we need to pose is what is new, what is normal, and whether we have arrived in a sense to a new status quo.

If we pause further, we begin to appreciate that the way organisations had responded and adapted to the COVID-pandemic and the so-called post-COVID new normal was not like a light switch. Organisations did not simply flip a switch and then instantly and seamlessly everything within changed to a new normal. Organisations needed to contend with its social and technical systems, for example, including the complexities of each system and the complexities from how these systems relate to and influence each other. In ODC we recognise and understand these complexities from, for example, a socio-technical systems, human relations or human work interaction design perspective. We critically analyse the various systems and how these are embedded and related within broader ecosystems. We see the organisation as an ecosystem, and that it is itself located within other ecosystems. We consider how the organisation needs to take form and shape given its internal ecosystem and the external ecosystems within which is it is located and wherein it sustains itself.

As we pause and consider our perspectives or lenses, we can then revisit the body of knowledge of ODC and that of people practices more broadly. However, this is not to say that we just apply the previously tried and tested off before. We need to also re-examine and reconsider the body of knowledge given the current exigencies and contingencies as well as the significant shifts and changes in our worldviews and realities. In the next section we will turn our attention to the body of knowledge of people *practices*. Specifically, we will consider the previous HRM Standards and the revised Standards that were launched in September 2023 as the People Practices and Governance Standards (PPGS).

14.3 Standards of Good People Practices in The Evolving World of Work

The SABPP National HRM Standard (HRMS) was developed in 2013 to serve as the professional grounding for the HR community and improve people practices and outcomes within organisations. The HRMS was developed by HR or people professionals to enable professionalisation based on clear standards and to enhance the people profession. The HRMS was compiled through a series of consultative workshops where the HR or people professionals outlined what are good people practices. It distils and consolidates the body of knowledge of *practice*. There are thirteen Standards comprising a practice definition, a set of outcomes defined as objectives, a process diagram and an application guideline to achieve these outcomes. The HRMS does not aim to resolve or reconcile the various philosophical and theoretical perspectives and issues within HRM and HRD. Its focus is on practices and articulating good and ethical people practices.

The HRMS is based on a conceptual model, which is referred to as the HR Management Systems Model, and it draws on the quality management and systems perspectives. The Model attempts to integrate the various aspects of people practices. It structures these in terms of the phases of quality management practice: these are the phases of prepare, implement, review, and improve. Aligned with these phases is the work of strategic alignment, building the HR architecture, undertaking service delivery, and the measurement of these. The HRMS also meant to provide a framework to integrate the fields of academia, research and practice.

Since its launch in 2013, the global and local contexts and the world of work have evolved and continue to evolve, with significant changes to work, the workplace and the workforce. There is also the shift in terminologies, for example, the shift from 'HR function' to 'people function' and from Chief HR Officer to Chief People Officer. Organisations are also shifting from the traditional divide of HRM and HRD, with the emphasis on building integrated services that are outcomes-focused such as good employee experience. The COVID-19 pandemic accelerated some of these changes; however, we see many organisations struggling with navigating and adapting to these in terms of developing long-term organisational design and development solutions. Consider the many debates and conflicts on the 'return to office' mandates by employers, which have now gained the acronym 'RTO'.

Two questions confronted us, given the evolving and changing world of work. The first is the question of how our context and the world of work are evolving. The second is the question of how we position the standards of good people practices in this context. There was a need to respond strategically to these changes and to ensure that the organisation's duty of care to employees and the broader stakeholders, as per the King Code IV of good governance for example, is implemented.[322] To take account of the many changes over the period to the external and internal contexts of HRM and HRD work and changes within the HR profession, the HR Management Standard was formally reviewed. Consultative workshops and specialist working groups were used to help review the HR Management Standard approach and the contents of each Standard. This was to determine to what extent good practice had changed over the decade and how we should position the Standards in the evolving world of work. The review addressed two questions: how we can understand our evolving context and the new world of work and how we continue to set standards of good people practices for this context and world of work. As previously noted, the review resulted in the launch of the second edition of the Standards, namely, the People Practices and Governance Standard. The revised naming of the Standard acknowledges the shifts in our vocabulary and ways of thinking about HRM and HRD.

A framework of people strategy themes was developed as part of the review to help HR practitioners navigate and make sense of the evolving context and new world of work. The themes can be pictured as four spokes with a centre. The four spokes are embracing and shaping new futures; holding purpose in an ever-changing world; addressing diversity, inclusion, equity, and belonging in the new futures; and building resilient and sustainable organisations. The 'centre of gravity' of the four themes is being people centred. That is being people centred as we embrace and shape the future, and consider the purpose, governance, diversity, inclusion, belonging, resilience, and sustainability of our organisations. The diagram below illustrates the themes and how we can build on these as we engage with the evolving world of work and our evolving contexts.

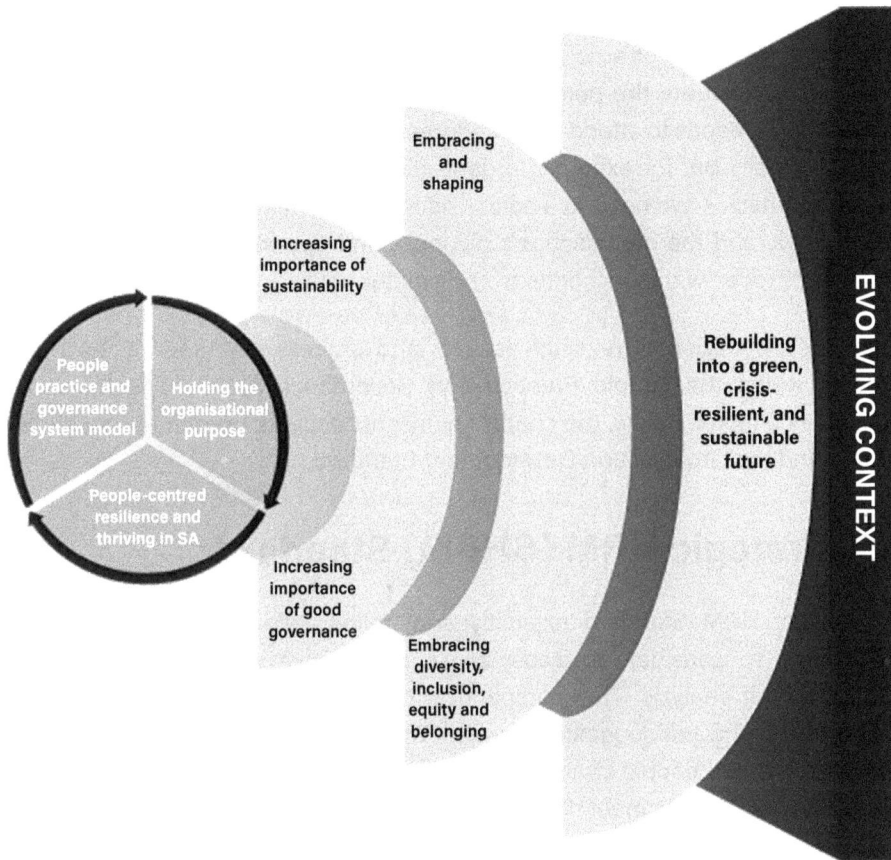

Figure 14.1: Standards in the ever evolving context[323]

14.4 Standards and ODC In The Evolving World of Work

The People Practices and Governance Standard (PPGS) comprises of thirteen standards that speaks to business and people strategy alignment, the related people management architecture, the HR value creation and delivery platform, and the monitoring and evaluation platform. The PPGS draws attention to the ecosystems within an organisation as well as the ecosystems that the organisation is itself embedded and sustained within. For example, the internal and external workforce and talent ecosystems, as well as the local and global ecosystems for learning and development. It follows then that ODC needs to pay attention and address the various ecosystems at different levels. That is, ODC needs to attend to the ecosystems within the organisation and attend to the organisation itself as a whole ecosystem that is embedded within other meso and macro levels of ecosystems. We can use, for example, the metaphor of a container that is used in systems and psychodynamic approaches to illustrate the point. As much as ODC addresses what is within the container, it also needs to attend to and address the container itself within its context. A focus internally on, for example, organisation design that is jobs focused looks within the container. We need to also consider the business landscape, the evolving world of work, and the organisation's business and operating models for how it is itself fit for purpose within its contexts and creates value.

A complete discussion of relevant aspects and process diagrams of the thirteen standards within the People Practice and Governance Standard is beyond the scope of this chapter. Below, the chapter highlights aspects from the Strategic HRM Standard and the Organisation Development Standard.

14.5 Strategic HRM (SHRM) Standard

The Strategic HRM Standard explicitly and deliberately points to the need for organisations to consider an ecosystem's perspective and the ecosystems at various levels of analysis. This perspective, the appreciation of the various levels of ecosystems, and the suggested analysis of the external and internal contexts is meant to inform the people strategic agenda of the organisation and how HRM and HRD will be leveraged to meet this agenda and create HR value. Thus, there is a shift beyond the traditional HR binaries to consider the people strategic agenda and how the outcomes thereof can be met in a systemic and systematic manner. Relatedly, another outcome of the SHRM Standard is to determine an appropriate and relevant structure of the people function to deliver on the people strategic objectives. Here, we could consider the recent discussions on taking an outside-in approach to the design of the people management structure, where the business strategy, aligned people strategy and meeting of stakeholder needs informs the structure and capabilities of the people management function.

The Standard provides an example of a maturity model comprising of two tracks. One track focuses on the people function and the other track on the organisation in terms where it is positioned regarding people-centred high performance. The factors related to high performance include the organisational leadership and culture and levels of engagement and accountability. The organisation needs to clearly and deliberately articulate its philosophy on how it will harness the contribution of its people who create value in a sustainable manner, and how it will manage the various stakeholders and their preferences and priorities. For example, the preferences and priorities of its people, its customers and that of the organisation.

14.6 Organisation Development (OD) Standard

The Organisation development (OD) Standard points to the need for an evidence-based approach to address the organisation and its ecosystems in terms of their capabilities, relationships, effectiveness, resilience and sustainability. It refers to the importance of systemic and systematic organisational responses to address these. ODC thus plays an important role in developing a common vision of the future and determining the related people strategy and agenda. The Standards process diagram speaks to the importance of linking and optimising the following elements: organisational purpose, organisational design, organisational culture and people effectiveness. Thus, organisations need to consider their organisational design principles carefully to support the organisation's purpose and strategy. And they need to consider the relevant OD capability required within and/or outside of the organisation.

Some of the outcomes specified in the OD Standard include the following:

- ensuring the organisation has identified a clear sense of its purpose, its related values and culture, and vision of the future;
- facilitating alignment within the organisation and across the various stakeholders in the value chain with the organisational purpose and values (in keeping with the ecosystem perspective of the PPGS);
- identifying relevant organisation design principles that effectively support the organisational purpose and strategy as well as business and operating models;
- enabling stakeholder engagement and collaboration in all OD processes;
- identifying organisational effectiveness factors through an evidence-based approach;
- improving effectiveness at various levels of the organisations to meet organisational objectives; and
- developing a relevant OD capability that can manage the OD process from entry, contracting, and diagnosing to analysis, designing and implementing the range of required OD interventions, and the evaluation of these. The OD capability needs to also speak to innovation within itself and within the organisation in alignment with the organisational objectives. This includes innovation of the organisation as a whole and its purpose, strategy and business and operating models. Thus, it is innovation within the organisation and of the organisation itself as a container as previously discussed. It is a question of whether the current organisation – as a container, vehicle or agency – is fit for purpose for holding the purpose of the organisation and creating value.

14.7 HR Governance, Risk and Compliance (HR GRC) Standard

As we consider the future, the purpose and value creation of the organisation, and the internal and external ecosystems, we need to pay attention to the duty of care of the organisation and good corporate governance and citizenship. The HR GRC Standard sets a clear objective for the people strategy to develop a diverse and inclusive ethical culture that is sustainable, and that meets governance and ethics outcomes. These outcomes are aligned with codes of good corporate outcomes such as the present King Code IV. It includes an ethical culture, ethical and effective leadership, effective control, good performance and legitimacy.[324] It requires integrated thinking, which sees the organisation as an integral part of society and embedded and interconnected within ecosystems. Aligned with this is stakeholder inclusivity which appreciates the interconnectedness of the organisation and its different stakeholders. This then demands good corporate citizenship that pays attention to the rights, obligations and responsibilities of organisations.

14.8 Final Thoughts

The chapter explores the evolving world of work and the place of standards of good people practices and duty of care. It points to the importance of good people practices and cites the example of the SABPP People Practice and Governance Standard. The Standard provides the professional and critical space to pause and reflect on our practices and the body of practices that informs it, and it can provide us the 'scaffolding' to consider how best we serve our respective organisations in an ethical manner and in alignment with good governance. The chapter points to the need to attend to the organisation from within and without, undertaking ODC interventions to address the ecosystems within the organisation and the organisation itself as an ecosystem. This requires an OD capability, and a people function that is designed from the outside-in and speaks to the strategic agenda and objectives of the organisation, going beyond traditional binaries.

Chapter 15

Conclusion of Book

As we reach the final pages of this consideration, it is fitting to return to the essence of what it means to conclude – a word that, in its very nature, holds both an ending and a beginning. As Jung reminds us, "What we do not make conscious appears in our lives as fate." To conclude is not simply to finish but to gather the wisdom of the journey and carry it forward into the unknown, transformed by the insights we have uncovered.

Throughout this book, we have ventured into the deep exploration of human complexity, embracing the multiplicities of identity, the tensions of belonging, and the fluidity of transformation. In this inquiry, inclusivity has emerged not merely as a value or an abstract principle but as a living, breathing, evolving process – a process that requires continual engagement, self-reflection, and, above all, the courage to be fearlessly true to self and others. Inclusivity is not an end goal but an ongoing practice, a perpetual unfolding of shared humanity.

The book challenges us to step beyond the passive acceptance of difference and into the active co-creation of environments where difference is not just tolerated but celebrated. This requires more than policy or rhetoric; it calls for a profound psychological and cultural shift in social systems. It invites us to recognise the ways in which exclusion is often not an external act but an internalised narrative - a shadow that lurks in our unconscious biases, in our fears, in our inherited scripts. Only through conscious engagement can we renarrate these scripts and forge a more expansive, expectant and functional future.

And so, in the spirit of Jungian thought, we return to the idea that the deepest work of transformation begins within. Just as the psyche must integrate its shadow to achieve wholeness, so too must our organisations, communities and societies embrace the full spectrum of human experience. To deny any part of ourselves or others is to fracture the possibility of true unity. The archetype of integration – be it within the individual or the collective – demands a reckoning with what has been silenced, with what has been cast aside. True inclusivity is not about erasing difference but about amplifying the voices that have been historically muted and bringing them into the light of shared recognition.

Endings, then, are never truly final. They are portals, thresholds, moments where the past and the future meet in dialogue. In ancient traditions, rites of passage mark the end of one phase and the beginning of another, emphasising that transformation is not linear but cyclical. The wisdom we gather here will not remain static; it will evolve, shape-shifting in response to new challenges, new awakenings, new encounters.

This book does not conclude in the conventional sense but rather extends an invitation. An invitation to continue the work of deep listening, to hear the unsaid, to foster spaces where all voices are heard, and to remain vigilant against the insidious pull of exclusionary comfort. It is an invitation to embrace the complexities of identity with humility and grace, to recognise that every individual carries within them a universe of experience, and to honour that complexity as sacred.

It calls for heroes, as echoed so intensely by David Bowie in the song with the same name – Heroes. Lurie[325] compared this song to the process of alchemy and said:

> "We may be average and regular in the present moment, but we have the potential, at any time, for heroic thought and action – even if only for one day. The transformation can be brought about by an external event or through an internal change in perspective".

The book calls for exactly that – to change our outlook to a more integral, hopeful stance in an attempt to do human better.

Jung[326] wrote that "the greatest and most important problems of life are all fundamentally insoluble. They can never be solved but only outgrown." Inclusivity, then, is not a problem to be solved but a consciousness to be expanded. It is a path, not a destination, one that winds through our collective psyche and demands of us a commitment to constant evolution. Integral leadership is a leadership philosophy that attempts this.

May this journey continue beyond these pages. May it live in the spaces between words, in the silent understandings we cultivate, in the courage to challenge and be challenged. And may we always remember that true transformation is not measured by what we finish, but by what we dare to begin anew.

> *A journey, after all, neither begins in the instant we set out, nor ends when we have reached our doorstep once again. It starts much earlier and is really never over, because the film of memory continues running on inside of us long after we have come to a physical standstill. Indeed, there exists something like a contagion of travel, and the disease is essentially incurable.*
>
> *Ryszard Kapuściński*
>
> *Travels with Herodotus*

References

Aboobaker, N., Edward, M. & Zakkariya, K.A. (2020). Workplace spirituality and employee loyalty: An empirical investigation among millennials in India. *Journal of Asia Business Studies*, 14(2), pp.211–225.

Acemoglu, D. & Restrepo, P. (2019). Automation and New Tasks: How Technology Displaces and Reinstates Labour. *Journal of Economic Perspectives*, 33(2), pp. 3–30.

Ackoff, R. L. (2003). Iconoclastic Management Authority, Advocates a "Systemic" Approach to Innovation. *Strategy & Leadership*, 31(3), pp. 19–26.

Ackoff, R.L. (2003). Iconoclastic management authority advocates a "systemic" approach to innovation. Strategy & Leadership, 31(3), pp.19–26.

Adeyemi, A. (2021). Hybrid Change Models in African Organisations: Integrating Indigenous Wisdom and Agile Practices. *Journal of African Business Transformation*, 12(1), pp. 45–63.

Adizes, I. (1974). Industrial democracy: Yugoslav style. New York: Free Press.

Alipour, A. (2019). The conceptual difference really matters: Hofstede vs GLOBE's uncertainty avoidance and the risk-taking behavior of firms. *Cross Cultural & Strategic Management*. Published online ahead of print. doi: 10.1108/CCSM-04-2019-0084

Anderson, R. (2020). Dialoguing as a Catalyst for Organisational Resilience, *Journal of Management Studies*, 57(4), pp. 689–710.

Ashmos, D.P., & Duchon, D. (2000). Spirituality at work: A conceptualization and measure. *Journal of Management Inquiry, 9*(2), 134-145.

Associates in Process Improvement. (2020). *The Model for Improvement*. [online] Available at: http://www.apiweb.org [Accessed 20 Jun. 2025].

Athos, A.G. & Gabarro, J.J. (1978). *Interpersonal Behavior: Communication and Understanding in Relationships*. Englewood Cliffs, NJ: Prentice-Hall.

Atkins, P. W. & de Paula, J. (2006). *Physical Chemistry* (8th ed.). Oxford: Oxford University Press.

Baldwin, R. (2016). *The Great Convergence: Information Technology and the New Globalisation*. Boston: Harvard University Press.

Barnett, B.G., Basom, M.R., Yerkes, D.M., & Norris, C.J. (2000). Cohorts in educational leadership programs: Benefits, difficulties, and the potential for developing school leaders. *Educational Administration Quarterly*, 36(2), 255-282. doi: 10.1177/0013161X00362005.

Bar-On, R. & Parker J. D. (2000). *The Handbook of Emotional Intelligence: Theory, Development, Assessment, and Application at Home, School, and in the Workplace*. San Francisco: Jossey-Bass.

Bar-On, R. (2018). *reuvenbaron.org*. [Online] Available at: http://www.reuvenbaron.org/wp/the-5-meta-factors-and-15-sub-factors-of-the-bar-on-model/ [Accessed: 08 May 2019].

Bar-On, R. (2006). The Bar-On model of emotional-social intelligence (ESI). Psicothema, 18(Suppl.), pp.13–25.Bar-On, R. (2010). *New US Air Force Study: EQ to Save $190 Million*. Available at: [Assessed on 1 March 2025]. Study conducted with MHS (Toronto).

Barrett, R. (2000). *Liberating the Corporate Soul: Building a Vision for Your Organisation's Future*. San Francisco: Jossey-Bass.

Bass, B. M. (1985). *Leadership and Performance Beyond Expectations*. Los Angeles: The Free Press.

Beck, D. (2013). *The Master Code. Spiral Dynamics Integral Accreditation*. Course notes. Santa Barbara: Adizes Business School.

Beck, D. E. & Cohen, C. C. (1996). *Spiral Dynamics: Mastering Values, Leadership, and Change*. Cambridge: Blackwell.

Beck, D. E., Solonin, S., Larsen, H. T., Viljoen, R. C. & Johns, T. (2017) *Spiral dynamics in action. Humanity's master code*. New Jersey: Wiley Publishers.

Beck, D.E. & Linscott, G. (2011). The Crucible. Forging South Africa's Future. In Search of a Template World. Maryland: Perfect Publishing.

Beckhard, R. (1969). *Organization development: Strategies and models*. Reading, MA: Addison-Wesley.

Bernstein, E.J., Bunch, N.C., & Michael L. (2016). Beyond the Holacracy Hype: The Overwrought Claims – and Actual Promise – of the Next Generation of Self-Management Teams. *Harvard Business Review*. 94(7-8). pp. 38–49.

Bion, W.R. (1961). *Experiences in Groups And Other Papers*. London: Tavistock, pp. 139-189.

BIOSS, n.d. *BIOSS: Understanding work and the capability of people*. [online] Available at: https://www.bioss.com [Accessed 20 Jun. 2025].

Blackie, S (2024). *The Rooted Woman Oracle*. California: Hay House

Blackman, J.S. (2004). 101 defenses: How the mind shields itself. New York: Brunner-Routledge.

Block, P. (2009). *Community: The Structure of Belonging. Oakland:* Berrett-Koehler Publishers.

Blumer, K. P. (1969). *Symbolic Interactionism: Perspective & Method*. Englewood Cliffs, New Jersey: Prentice Hall.

Bohm, D. (1998). *On Dialogue*. New York: Routledge.

Bollas, C. (1987). The shadow of the object: Psychoanalysis of the unthought known. London: Free Association Books.

Bolton, R. (1983). *People Skills: How to Assert Yourself, Listen to Others, and Resolve Conflicts*. New York: Simon & Schuster.

Booysen, L., & Nkomo, S. (2006). Think manager – think female: A South African perspective. *ACSG Conference, 14 - 16 March 2007, Belville, Stellenbosch*.

Breslin, L., McMenamin, L., & Galvin, M. (2018). Leadership for inclusion: The art of developing leadership for inclusion in schools. Dublin: Centre for Inclusive Pedagogy.

Breuer, J. & Freud, S. (1955). *Studies in Hysteria. In The Standard Edition of the Complete Psychological Works of Sigmund* 2. pp. 1–307.253. London: Hogarth Press.

Brown, J. & Isaacs, D. (2005). *The World Café: Shaping Our Futures Through Conversations That Matter*. San Francisco: Berrett-Koehler Publishers.

Brown, P. & Green, A. (2021). Currency Decline and Economic Policy in the 21st Century. *Journal of Economic Perspectives*, 35(3), pp. 45–60.

Brown, T. (2008). Design Thinking, *Harvard Business Review*, 86(6), pp. 84–92.

Brunner, L.D. & Villari, B.A. (2004). The Leicester model: Group relations training and its impact on organisational and social life. London: Karnac Books.

Brynjolfsson, E. & McAfee, A. (2014). *The Second Machine Age: Work, Progress, and Prosperity in a Time of Brilliant Technologies*. New York City: W. W. Norton & Company.

Brynjolfsson, E., Horton, J. J., Ozimek, A., Rock, D., Sharma, G. & Ye, H.-Y. (2020). COVID-19 and Remote Work: An Early Look at US Data, *National Bureau of Economic Research*, Working Paper 27344.

Buck, M.L. (2004). Mentoring: Creating a legacy of leaders. In: C. McCauley & E. Van Velsor (eds), The Center for Creative Leadership handbook of leadership development. 2nd ed. San Francisco: Jossey-Bass, pp. 537–568.

Burke, W.W. & Litwin, G.H. (1992). A causal model of organizational performance and change. *Journal of Management*, 18(3), pp.523–545.

Burns, T. & Stalker, G.M. (1961) *The Management of Innovation*. Tavistock, London.

Burton, R. M., Obel, B. & Håkonsson, D. D. (2020). *Organisational Design: A Step-by-Step Approach*. Cambridge University Press.

Bushe, G. R. (2013). The Appreciative Inquiry Model: A Constructive Approach to Organisational Change, *Journal of Organizational Change Management*, 26(3), pp. 411–421.

Cameron, K. S., & Quinn, R. E. (2011). *Diagnosing and Changing Organizational Culture: Based on the Competing Values Framework*. New Jersey: Wiley Publishers.

Campbell, J. (1949). *The Hero with a Thousand Faces*. New Jersey: Princeton University Press.

Cascio, J. (2020). Facing the Age of Chaos. *Distinguished Fellow, Institute for the Future.*

Cavaghan, R., & Elomaki, A. (2022). Dead Ends and Blind Spots in the European Semester: The Epistemological Foundation of the Crisis in Social Reproduction. *Journal of Common Market Studies, 60*(4), pp. 445-902.

CIPD (2020). Reskilling and Workforce Transformation: Embracing the New World of Work. CIPD Report. Available from. [Accessed 23 Feb 2025].

Clayton, K., & De Braine, R.T. (2023). Performance management process changes on the work identity of employees during COVID-19. *SA Journal of Industrial Psychology, 49*, pp. 2090.

Coghlan, D. & Brannick, T. (2014.) *Doing Action Research in Your Own Organization. Edition: Fourth Edition.* Washington DC: SAGE Publishers.

Cohen, B., & Meinl, L. (2016). *Healing through the field: The evolution of systemic constellations*. Cambridge: Cambridge University Press.

Cohen, M.Z. Kahn, D.L. & Steeves, R.H. (2000). *Hermeneutic Phenomenological Research: A Practical Guide for Nurse Researchers*. Thousand Oaks, CA: Sage.

Collins, J., & Porras, J. I. (1994). Built *to Last: Successful Habits of Visionary Companies*. New York: Harper Business Publishers.

Collins, P. H. (2000). *Black Feminist Thought: Knowledge, Consciousness and the Politics of Empowerment*. Oxfordshire: Routledge.

Cooper, J.H. (2025). Consultancy Training Groups. Available at: [Accessed on 2 March 2025].

Cooper, J.H. (2025). The Hidden Dynamics of High Impact Leadership. [Accessed on 2 March 2025].

Cooper, R.K. & Sawaf, A. (2019). Executive EQ: Emotional intelligence in leadership and organizations. New York: Penguin Putnam.

Cooperrider, D., Whitney, M. & Stavros, J. (2003). *Appreciative Inquiry: A Positive Revolution in Change*. San Francisco: Berrett-Koehler Publishers.

Coopersmith, K. (2021). Personal development planning and vertical leadership development in a VUCA world. *Journal of Values-Based Leadership, 15*(1), pp. 10.

Covey, S. R. (1989). *The 7 habits of highly effective people: Powerful lessons in personal change.* New York, NY: Simon & Schuster.

Cox, D. (2020). Unmasking the Unconscious: Systems Psychoanalytic Approaches to Organisational Change. *Journal of Management Studies,* 57(6), pp. 789–812.

CranioSacral Therapy Association. (2022). What is craniosacral therapy? Assessed from. [23 Feb 2025].

Crede, M., Jong, J., & Harms, P. (2019). The generalizability of transformational leadership across cultures: A meta-analysis. *Journal of Managerial Psychology,* 34(3), 139-155. doi:10.1108/JMP-11-2018-0506

Crenshaw, K. (1989). *Demarginalizing the Intersection of Race and Sex: A Black Feminist Critique of Antidiscrimination Doctrine, Feminist Theory and Antiracist Politics.* University of Chicago Legal Forum.

Cross, L., Bazron, B. J., Dennis, K. W. D. & Isaacs, M. R. (1989). *Towards a Culturally Competent System of Care.* Available from . [Accessed 28 Feb 2025].

Cummings, T. G. & Worley, C. G. (2019). *Organisation Development and Change.* Cape Town: Cengage Learning.

Dawkins, R. (1976). *The selfish gene.* Oxford: Oxford University Press.

De Jager, W. (2003). *Dialogue: The Process of Shared Understanding in Organisations.* Cape Town: University of Cape Town Press.

Deming, W. E. (1987). *A Theory of a System for Educators and Managers: The Deming Library Volume XXI Expert-Knowledge Systems,* Inc. [Online]. Available from [Accessed 28 Feb 2024].

Deming, W. E. (1993). Deming Four Day Seminar. Course handout. Phoenix, Arizona, February.

Deming, W. E. (1994). *The New Economics for Industry, Government, Education.* Cambridge, Massachusetts: Massachusetts Institute of Technology, Centre for Advanced Engineering Study.

Deming, W. E. (2018). *Out of the Crisis.* Cambridge: The MIT Press.

Deming, W.E. (1982). Out of the crisis. Cambridge, MA: Massachusetts Institute of Technology, Center for Advanced Educational Services.

Denning, S. (2020). The secret language of leadership: How leaders inspire action through narrative. Hoboken, NJ: Wiley.

DiMaggio, P. J. & Powell, W. W. (1983). The Iron Cage Revisited: Institutional Isomorphism and Collective Rationality in Organisational Fields. *American Sociological Review,* 48(2), pp. 147–160.

Dolan, S. L. & Kawamura, K. M. (2015). *Cross Cultural Competence: A Field Guide for Developing Global Leaders and Managers.* Bingley: Emerald Group.

Donaldson, L. (2001). *The Contingency Theory of Organisations.* Washington DC: SAGE Publications.

Du Plessis, M. (2023). Trait emotional intelligence and flourishing: The mediating role of positive coping behaviour. *SA Journal of Industrial Psychology,* 49, pp. 2063.

Dulchinos, D. & Viljoen, R.C. (2023). The Clare Graves Archives; Pillars of Integral Thought – Origins of the Second Tier 'Beige' and 'Purple', Presentation at Integral Europe Conference, May 2023. Clare Graves Foundation Dispatch

Dulchinos, D., Johns, T.Q., Parstorfer, B., Viljoen, R.C. and Viljoen, R.A. (2023). Insights from a pioneer of integral thought. Integral Leadership Review, 22(2). Clare Graves Foundation Dispatch #1. [Accessed 14 Feb. 2025].

Edmondson, A. C. (1999). Psychological safety and learning behaviour in work teams. *Administrative Science Quarterly*, 44(2), pp. 350-383.

Edmondson, A. C. (2019). *The Fearless Organisation: Creating Psychological Safety in the Workplace for Learning, Innovation, and Growth.* New Jersey: Wiley Publishers.

Ellis, C. (2004). *The Ethnographical I.* Walnut Creek: CAL AltaMira Press.

ENISA (2021*). Cybersecurity Challenges in a Digitally Connected World.* Available from: [Accessed 22 February 2025].

Erikson EH. (1968). *Identity, psychosocial, in Encyclopedia of the social sciences*, edited by DR Sills. New York, Macmillan & Free Press: 61-65.

EYQ. (2020). How do you build a 'better normal'? EYQ: EY's think tank for business insights. [online] Available at: https://www.ey.com/en_gl/megatrends/how-do-you-build-a-better-normal [Accessed 22 February 2025].

Freeman, M. (2017). *Modes of thinking for qualitative data analysis.* New York: Routledge.

Freire, P. (1970). *Pedagogy of the Oppressed. Herder and Herder.* New York: Continuum Books.

French, R. & Simpson, P. (1999). Learning at the edge: Political and poetic discourse in organizational learning. *Management Learning*, 30(1), pp.39–56.

French, W.L. & Bell, C.H. (1999). Organization development: Behavioral science interventions for organization improvement. 6th ed. Upper Saddle River, NJ: Prentice Hall.

Freud, S. (1910). The Origin and Development of Psychoanalysis. *The American Journal of Psychology*, 21(2), pp. 181-218.

Freud, S. (1921). *Group psychology and the analysis of the ego, in A general selection from the works of Sigmund Freud*, edited by J. Rickman. London: Hogarth, p195.

Freud, S. (1933). *New Introductory Lectures on Psychoanalysis* (Vol. 2). Middlesex: Pelican Freud Library.

Freud, S. (1964). *Jokes and Their Relationship to the Unconscious.* New York City: Norton Publishing.

Friedman, T. L. (2005). *The World is Flat: A Brief History of the Twenty-first Century.* New York City: Farrar, Straus and Giroux.

Friend, A. (n.d.) *Organic Intelligence: Regenerated* [Online]. Desert Trax. Available at: [Accessed 19 Jun. 2025].

Frontiers (2020). *How Normal is the New Normal? Individual and Organisational Implications of the Covid-19 Pandemic. Frontiers in Psychology.* Available from. [Accessed 20 Feb 2025].

Gabriel, Y. (2021). *The storytelling organisation: Narrative as a form of organisational sensemaking.* 2nd ed. Oxford: Oxford University Press.

Galbraith, J. R. (2014). *Designing Organisations: Strategy, Structure and Process at the Business Unit and Enterprise Levels.* New Jersey: Wiley Publishers.

Garcia, R. & Patel, S. (2020). World Café Methodology in Co-Creating Organisational Strategy: A Case Study, *International Journal of Management*, 38(4), pp. 345–364.

Gardner, H. (1983). Frames of Mind: The Theory of Multiple Intelligences. New York: Basic Books.

Gilchrist, H. (2019). *Future Work: How Businesses Can Adapt and Thrive in the New World of Work*. London: Palgrave Macmillan.

Glaser, B. & Strauss, A. (1967). *The Discovery of Grounded Theory*. New York: Aldine de Gruyter.

Glaser, B. (1992). *Basics of Grounded Theory Analysis*. Mill Valley, California: Sociology Press.

Glaser, B. G. (1998). *Doing Grounded Theory: Issues and Discussions*. California: California Sociology Press.

Goleman, D. (1995). *Emotional Intelligence: Why It Can Matter More Than IQ*. New York City: Bantam Books.

Goleman, D. (1999). Working with emotional intelligence. London: Bloomsbury.

Gooden, W.R. (2016). Maturing leadership: How adult development impacts leadership. London: Routledge.

Gordon Lawrence Foundation, n.d. *Social Dreaming*. [online] Available at: [Accessed 19 Jun. 2025].

Goren-Bar, A. (2021). *An introduction to Jungian Coaching*. London: ⊠Routledge. ISBN-10. 0367367998 ; ISBN-13. 978-0367367992

Gosling, J., & Case, P. (2014). Social Dreaming and Eco-centric Ethics: Sources of non-rational insight in the face of climate change. *Organization*, (20)5 p. 705-721.

Gould, L.J. (1993). Contemporary psychoanalytic perspectives on organizations: The psychodynamics of individuals, groups and organizations. In: L. Hirschhorn and C.K. Barnett, eds. *The Psychodynamics of Organizations*. Philadelphia: Temple University Press, pp.44–66.

Goulding, C. (2002). *Grounded Theory: A Practical Guide for Management, Business and Market Researchers*. London: Sage Publications Ltd.

Graves, C. (1974). Human Nature Prepares for a Momentous Leap. *The Futurist*, April, pp. 72–87.

Grof, S. (2000). Psychology of the future: Lessons from modern consciousness research. Albany, NY: State University of New York Press.

Hall, E. (1983). *The Dance of Life: The Other Dimension of Time*. New York: Doubleday.

Hanna, T. (1988). *Somatics: Reawakening the Mind's Control of Movement, Flexibility, and Health*. Boston: Da Capo Press.

Harrison, N. E. (2000). *Constructing Sustainable Development*. Albany: SUNY Press.

Heifetz, R. A. (1994). *Leadership Without Easy Answers*. Boston: Harvard University Press.

Hellinger, B. (2001). *Acknowledging What Is: Conversations with Bert Hellinger. Zeig, Tucker & Theisen.*

Hill, C. W. L., Jones, G. R. & Schilling, M. A. (2014). *Strategic Management: Theory: An Integrated Approach*. Cape Town: Cengage Learning.

Hinshelwood, R.D. (2001). Thinking about institutions: Milieux and madness. London: Jessica Kingsley Publishers.

Hofstede, G. (1984). *Culture's Consequences: International Differences in Work-related Values*. Beverly Hills: Sage.

Hofstede, G. (1991). *Cultures and Organisations: Software of the Mind*. New York: McGraw-Hill.

Hofstede, G. (1994). Images of Europe: Past, Present and Future (in P. Joynt & M. Warner, eds.), *The Netherlands Journal of Social Science*, 30(1), pp. 63-82.

Holcomb-McCoy, C. C. & Meyers, J. E. (1999). Multicultural Competencies and Counsellor Training: A National Survey. *Journal of Counselling and Develop*ment, 77, pp. 294–300.

Huffington, C., Armstrong, D., Halton, W., Hoyle, L. & Pooley, J. (2004). *Working Below the Surface: The Emotional Life of Contemporary Organisations*. London: Karnac Publishers.

Huss, A. (2004). Authenticity in Storytelling: The Critical Role of Narrative in Organisational Transformation, *Journal of Organizational Change*, 15(2), pp. 89–104.

ILO (2021a). *The Future of Work in a Post-COVID-19 World. International Labour Organisation.* Available from [Accessed 23 Feb 2025].

ILO (2021b). *The Future of Work: Trends and Challenges.* Available from [Accessed 24 Feb 2025]

Institute for Healthcare Improvement. (2003). *The Breakthrough Series: IHI's Collaborative Model for Achieving Breakthrough Improvement.* Cambridge, MA: Institute for Healthcare Improvement. Available from: [Accessed 27 Feb 2025].

Institute of Directors Southern Africa (IODSA) (2016). *King IV Report on Corporate Governance for South Africa.* Available from:. [Accessed 24 Feb 2025]

Jackson, T. (2004). *Cross-Cultural Theory and Methods: Management and Change in Africa.* London: Routledge.

Jaques E. (1997). *Requisite organization: a total system for effective managerial organization and managerial leadership for the 21st century.* Arlington: Cason Hall.

Jaques, E. (1976). A general theory of bureaucracy. London: Heinemann.

Jaques, E. (1989). Requisite organization: A total system for effective managerial organization and managerial leadership for the 21st century. Arlington, VA: Cason Hall.

Jivan, A. & Abbott, P. (2023). Setting Standards for Our Evolving Context: Revising the HRM System Model and Standard. *SABPP Fact Sheet*, October/November 2023. Available from . [Accessed 14 Feb 2025]

Johnson, B. (1996). P*olarity Management: Identifying and Managing Unsolvable Problems.* Worcester: HRD Press.

Johnson, P. & Edwards, T. (2022). Co-creating Organisational Futures: Longitudinal Perspectives on Appreciative Inquiry, *Leadership & Organization Development Journal*, 43(2), pp. 145–163.

Jung, C. G. (1954). *Man and His Symbols.* New York: Doubleday.

Jung, C. G. (1959*). The Archetypes and the Collective Unconscious.* Princeton University Press.

Jung, C. G. (1963*). Mysterium Coniunctionis.* Princeton University Press.

Jung, C. G. (1968). *Man and His Symbols.* Dell Publishing.

Juran, J.M. (1986). *The quality trilogy: Quality planning, quality control, and quality improvement.* Quality Progress, 19(8), pp.19–24.

Kamoche, K. & Harvey, M. (2007). *Management in Africa: Context, Challenges, and Strategies. Journal of International Management Studies*, 8(3), pp. 89–105.

Kelle, U. (1995). Theories as Heuristic Tools in Qualitative Research. In I. Maso, P. A. Atkinson, S. Delamont & J. C. Verhoeven (eds.), *Openness in Research: The Tension Between Self and Other* (pp. 33–50). Assen: Van Gorcum.

Kets de Vries, M. F. R. & Cheak, A. (2014). *Psychodynamic Approach. In Leadership: Theory and Practice* (7th ed., pp. 365–384). Washington DC: Sage.

Kets de Vries, M. F. R. (2001). *The Leadership Mystique*. London: Prentice Hall.

Kets de Vries, M. F. R. (2014). The Shaman, the Therapist, and the Coach. SSRN *Electronic Journal*, 16(1), pp. 1–18.

Khan, H., Rehmat, M., Butt, T.H. (2020). Impact of transformational leadership on work performance, burnout and social loafing: a mediation model. *Future Business Journal*. 6, pp. 40.

Kim, D.A. (1995). Archetypes as dynamic theories. *The Systems Thinker*, 6(6):6-9.

Klein, M (ed.) (1975). Evvy and Gratitude and Other Works 1946-1963. Cambridge: The Free Press.

Klein, M. (1946). Notes on Some Schizoid Mechanisms. *The International Journal of Psychoanalysis*, 27, pp. 99–110.

Koortzen, P. and Cilliers, F. (2002). Working with conflict in teams: The CIBART model. HR Future, 6(4), pp.36–41.

Kotter, J. P. (1996). *Leading Change*. Boston: Harvard Business School Press.

Kouzes, J. M., & Posner, B. Z. (2002). *The Leadership Challenge: How to Make Extraordinary Things Happen in Organizations*. New Jersey: Wiley Publishers.

Kouzes, J. M., & Posner, B. Z. (2017). *The Leadership Challenge: How to Make Extraordinary Things Happen in Organizations*. New Jersey: Wiley Publishers.

Krupat, A. (2023). *Ethnocriticism: Ethnography, History, Literature* (in Spanish). Berkeley: University of California Press. Available at: https://www.ucpress.edu/book/9780520334434/ethnocriticism [Accessed 13 May 2024].

Laidler, K. J. (1987). *Chemical Kinetics* (3rd ed.). New York City: Harper & Row.

Laloux, F. (2014). *Reinventing Organizations*. Toronto. Nelson Parker.

Langley, G.J., Moen, R.D., Nolan, K.M., Nolan, T.W., Norman, C.L. and Provost, L.P. (2009). The improvement guide: A practical approach to enhancing organizational performance. 2nd ed. San Francisco: Jossey-Bass.

Langley, G.J., Moen, R.D., Nolan, K.M., Nolan, T.W., Norman, C.L. and Provost, L.P. (2013). The improvement guide: A practical approach to enhancing organizational performance. 2nd ed. San Francisco: Jossey-Bass.

Lather, P. & St. Pierre, E. A. (2013). Post-qualitative research. International. *Journal of Qualitative Studies in Education*, 26(6), 629–633.

Laubscher, L. I. (2013). *Human Niches: Spiral Dynamics for Africa*. Available from   [Accessed 15 Nov 2024].

Lawrence, W.G. (1999). Exploring individual and organisational boundaries: A Tavistock open systems approach to the study of organisations. Karnac Books.

Lawrence, G. (2003). Social Dreaming as Sustained Thinking. *Human Relations* 56(5) p. 609-624.

Lawrence, W. G. (2005). *Introduction to Social Dreaming: Transforming Thinking*. London: London: Routledge.

Lawrence, W.G., Bain, A. & Gould, L. (1996). *The Fifth Basic Assumption. Free Associations*, 6(37), pp. 1–20.

LeBaron, M. (2005). *Creating the Space for Dialogue in Organisational Learning*. London: Sage.

Lencioni, P. (2002). *The Five Dysfunctions of a Team: A Leadership Fable*. San Francisco: Jossey-Bass.

Levinson, H. (1981). *Executive*. Cambridge, MA: Harvard University Press.

Lewin, K. (1951). *Field Theory in Social Science. New York City*: Harper & Row.

Lewin, K., (1947). Frontiers in group dynamics: Concept, method and reality in social science; social equilibria and social change. Human Relations, 1(1), pp.5–41.

Lewis, R. (2019). The Symbolic Dimensions of Change: Psychoanalytic Insights into Organisational Transformation. *Leadership Quarterly*, 30(4), pp. 456–475.

Lloyd, R. (2018). Quality health care: A guide to developing and using indicators. 2nd ed. Burlington, MA: Jones & Bartlett Learning.

Long, S. (2016). *Transforming Experience in Organisations: A Framework for Organisational Research and Consultancy.* London: Karnac Publishers.

Long, S. and Manley, J. (2009). Social dreaming: A critique. In: S. Long, ed. Socioanalytic methods: Discovering the hidden in organisations and social systems. London: Karnac, pp.85–102.

Long, S., & Manely, J. (Eds.). (2019). *Social Dreaming: Philosophy, Research, Theory and Practice* (1st ed.). Routledge, Oxford.

Lurie, R.D. (2018). Through the (Stained) Looking Glass: David Bowie & the Berlin Trilogy. Blurt. Archived from the original on 20 September 2022. [Accessed 13 April 2025 via Rock's Backpages].

Mandala Consulting (2014a). *Qualitative Research Report: NM and UM (interim Oct 2014) Leading the Company A Way,* Johannesburg, RSA.: Mandala Consulting (Available on request).

Mandala Consulting (2014b). *Company A: Patient Care Co-operative Inquiry FINAL report presentation 04 April 2014,* Johannesburg, RSA.: Slide presentation (Available on request).

Mandala Consulting (2015). *Qualitative Research Report: NM and UM (interim Sept 2015). Leading the Company A Way,* Johannesburg, RSA.: Mandala Consulting (Available on request).

Mandala Consulting (2016). *Qualitative Research Report: NM and UM post Leading the Company A Way,* Johannesburg, RSA.: Mandala Consulting (Available on request).

Manley, J. (2014). Gordan Lawrence's Social Dreaming Matrix: Background, Origins, History, and Development. *Organisational and Social Dynamics.* 14(2), p 322-341.

Margulies, A. (1989). *The Empathic Imagination*. London: W.W. Norton & Company, p3.

MarketLine. (2017). *PESTLE Country Analysis Report: South Africa.* London, U.K.: MarketLine.

Martinez, L. & Jones, T. (2021). Comparative Analysis of World Café and Open Space Technology, *Management Learning,* 52(2), pp. 122–139.

Martins, N., Martins, E. C. & Viljoen, R. C. (2017). *Organisational diagnostics.* Bryanston: Knowres, ISBN: 978-1-86922-673-2.

Mayer, J.D. & Salovey, P. (1997). *Emotional Development and Emotional Intelligence: Educational Implications.* New York, NY.: Basic Books.

Mbigi, L. (2000). The Emergence of African Management Thought. *Journal of African Business,* 1(1), pp. 15–29.

McComb, H. and Barnard, M. (2024). Understanding early object relations: The infant mind and development. Cape Town: Institute Press.

McCormick, S. & Ross, J. (2021). Digital Transformation and Organisational Change: An Appreciative Inquiry Approach, *Journal of Organizational Change Management*, 34(1), pp. 98–116.

McLuhan, M. (1964). *Understanding Media: The Extensions of Man*. New York: McGraw-Hill.

McNamee, S. (1988). Accepting Research as Social Intervention: Implications of a Systemic Epistemology. *Communication Quarterly*, 36(1), pp. 50-68.

Mijolla, A. (2019). *International Dictionary of Psychoanalysis*. London: Karnac Books.

Mikolajczak, M. (2009). Going beyond the ability-trait debate: The three-level model of emotional intelligence. E-Journal of Applied Psychology, 5(2), pp.25–31.Mintzberg, H. (1979). *The Structuring of Organizations: A Synthesis of the Research*. New Jersey: Prentice Hall.

Mohanty, C. T. (2006). *Feminism Without Borders: Decolonising Theory, Practising Solidarity*. Carolina: Duke University Press.

Mostert, M. (2024). *Executive Futures: A Quest for Quantum Curriculum*. Bryanston: Knowledge Resources.

National Geographic. (2019). Why elephants are considered a keystone species. *National Geographic*. [online] Available at: https://www.nationalgeographic.com [Accessed 13 June 2025].

Nell, S. (2023). Developing leadership capacity in nursing: A longitudinal study of cultural transformation using the BeQ. PhD.

Newman, L. S., Duff, K. J. & Baumeister, R. F. (1997). A New Look at Defensive Projection: Thought Suppression, Accessibility and Biased Person Perception. *Journal of Personality and Social Psychology,* 72(5), pp. 980–1001.

Norman, C. L., Nolan, T. W., Moen, R., Provost, L. P., Nolan, K. M. & Langley, G. J. (2013). *The Improvement Guide: A Practical Approach to Enhancing Organizational Performance*. San Francisco: Jossey-Bass.

Nurick, A.J. (1985). Participation in organizational change: The TVA experiment. New York: Praeger.

Nurick, A.J. (2020). The good enough manager: The making of a GEM. 2nd ed. Chapter 6. *New York: Routledge.*

Obholzer, A. & Roberts, V. Z. (2019). *The Unconscious at Work: A Tavistock Approach to Making Sense of Organisational Life* (2nd ed.). Oxfordshire: Routledge.

Ogden, T. H. (1979). On Projective Identification. *International Journal of Psychoanalysis*, 60, pp. 357–373.

Okafor, E. (2022). Ubuntu and Adaptive Leadership: Rethinking Organisational Transformation in Africa. *African Journal of Management*, 18(2), pp. 77–94.

Olkowicz, J.U., Jarosik-Michalak, A., & Kozlowski, A. (2024). The Role of a Leader in Shaping Employee Behaviour in the VUCA/BANI world. *Journal of Modern Science*, 2(562), pp. 503-534.

Orr, D.W. (2002). The nature of design: Ecology, culture, and human intention. Oxford: Oxford University Press.

Owen, H. (1997). Open space technology: A user's guide. San Francisco: Berrett-Koehler Publishers.

Owen, H. (2008). Open space technology: A user's guide. 3rd ed. San Francisco: Berrett-Koehler Publishers.

Owen, M. & White, D. (2019). Facilitative Strategies in the World Café: Enhancing Collaborative Engagement in Organisations, *Journal of Organizational Communication*, 45(3), pp. 210–228.

Owen, M. and White, D. (2019). Facilitative strategies in the World Café: Enhancing collaborative engagement in organisations. Journal of Organizational Communication, 45(3), pp.210–228.

Patel, R. & Smith, L. (2020). Creating Resilient Organisations: The Role of Appreciative Inquiry in Change Management, *International Journal of Management Reviews*, 22(4), pp. 567–585.

Pawar, B.S. (2016). Workplace spirituality and employee well-being: An empirical examination. *Employee Relations, 38*(6), 974-995.

Pearson, C. (1991). *Awakening the Heroes Within: Twelve Archetypes to Help Us Find Ourselves and Transform Our World*. San Francisco: HarperOne.

Pink, D.H. (2005). *A Whole New Mind: Moving from the Information Age to the Conceptual Age.* New York: Riverhead Books.

Pink, D.H. (2009). *Drive: The Surprising Truth About What Motivates Us.* New York: Riverhead Books.

Plato (1974). Theaetetus (G. M. A. Grube, Trans.). In J. M. Cooper (ed.), *Plato: Complete Works* (pp. 483–524). Indianapolis: Hackett Publishing.

Plummer, K. (2001). Documents of life 2: *An invitation to a critical humanism.* United Kingdom: SAGE Publications Ltd. https://doi.org/10.4135/978184920888.

Porges, S.W. (2011). *The Polyvagal Theory: Neurophysiological Foundations of Emotions, Attachment, Communication, and Self-Regulation.* New York City: W.W. Norton & Company.

Porges, S.W. (2017). *The Pocket Guide to the Polyvagal Theory: The Transformative Power of Feeling Safe.* New York City: W.W. Norton & Company.

Porter, M. E. & Kramer, M. R. (2011). 'Creating Shared Value', Harvard Business Review, 89(1/2), pp. 62–77.

Powell, W. W. (1990). *Neither Market nor Hierarchy: Network Forms of Organization. Research in Organizational Behavior*, 12, pp. 295–336.

Prinsloo, A. (2021). Enhancing healthcare delivery through a framework that integrates inclusivity and quality improvement science. Modderfontein: Da Vinci Institute.

Prinsloo, A., Viljoen, R.C. Provost, L. (2024). Improving management through quality improvement and inclusivity in Haas E.J. (ed). *Mine Safety & Health: Approaches from the Field*. Englewood, CO: Society for Mining, Metallurgy & Exploration., pp. 107-126.

Provost, L.P. (2016). Using data for improvement. Healthcare Executive, 31(2), pp.46–49.

PSYCH-K Centre International. (2021). PSYCH-K: A user-friendly way to reprogram the subconscious mind. Available from. [Assessed 3 Feb 2025].

Ramose, M. B. (2002). African Philosophy through Ubuntu: A Tool for Organisational Transformation. *Journal of African Studies*, 20(4), pp. 55–70.

Ramose, M.B. (2000). *Dialoguing and the Crisis of Meaning: Critical Perspectives on the African Experience.* Johannesburg: Ravan Press.

Rioch, M.J. (1970). The work of Wilfred Bion on groups. Psychiatry, 33(1), pp.56–66.

Robertson, B. J. (2015). *Holacracy: The New Management System for a Rapidly Changing World.* New York: Henry Holt and Company.

Rogers, C.R. (1951). *Client-Centered Therapy: Its Current Practice, Implications, and Theory.* Boston: Houghton Mifflin.

Rogers, C.R. (1961). On becoming a person: A therapist's view of psychotherapy. Boston: Houghton Mifflin.

Rogers, E. M. (2003). *Diffusion of Innovations,* 5th Edition. New York: Simon and Schuster.

Rogers, E.M. (1995) Diffusion of Innovations. 4th Edition, New York: The Free Press, New York.

Rosenbaum, S. C. (2004). Group-as-Mother: A Dark Continent in Group Relations Theory and Practice. *Group Relations Reader 3.* Jupiter, FL: A. K. Rice Institute.

Roth, W.-M., Lawless, D. & Tobin, K. (2000). *Dialogue in Education: Releasing the Power of Collaborative Inquiry.* New York: Teachers College Press.

Saenz, H., Anderson, N., Ledingham, D. & Supko, M. (2020). The "New Normal" is a Myth. The Future Won't be Normal at All. Available from https://www.bain.com/insights/the-new-normal-is-a-myth-the-future-wont-be-normal-at-all/ [Accessed 08 November 2020].

Salovey, P. & Mayer, J.D. (1990). Emotional Intelligence. *Imagination, Cognition and Personality,* 9(3), pp.185–211.

Saunders, M.N.K., Lewis, P., & Thornhill, A. (2019). *Research Methods for Business Students* (8th ed.). New York: Pearson.

Scharmer, O. (2009). Theory U: Leading from the future as it emerges. San Francisco: Berrett-Koehler Publishers.

Schein, E. H. (1999). *Process Consultation Revisited: Building the Helping Relationship.* Reading: Addison-Wesley.

Schein, E. H. (2010). *Organisational Culture and Leadership.* San Francisco: Jossey-Bass.

Schön, D. A. (1983). *The Reflective Practitioner: How Professionals Think in Action.* New York: Basic Books.

Scoville, R. and Little, K. (2014). Comparing lean and quality improvement. IHI White Paper. Cambridge, MA: Institute for Healthcare Improvement. Available at: http://www.ihi.org/resources/Pages/IHIWhitePapers/ComparingLeanandQualityImprovement.aspx [Accessed 20 Jun. 2025].

Senge, P. M. (1990). *The Fifth Discipline: The Art and Practice of the Learning Organisation.* New York: Doubleday.

Shapiro, E.R. and Carr, A.W. (2012). Lost in familiar places: Creating new connections between the individual and society. New Haven: Yale University Press.

Shapiro, M., Green, P. & Walters, J. (2021). Unconscious Dynamics in Organisational Transformation: A Systems Psychoanalytic Perspective. *Journal of Organizational Change,* 34(2), pp. 102–123.

Sisodia, R., Wolfe, D.B. & Sheth, J.N. (2007). *Firms of Endearment: How World-Class Companies Profit from Passion and Purpose.* Upper Saddle River, NJ: Wharton School Publishing.

Slattery, J. and Wylie, R. (1999). Future Search Conferences: A powerful method for aligning diverse stakeholders. Journal of Applied Behavioral Science, 35(3), pp.377–393.

Smith, J. & Johnson, K. (2019). Storytelling and Organisational Identity: A Narrative Approach to Change, *Strategic Management Journal,* 40(2), pp. 123–145.

Smith, J. (2022). Geopolitical Tensions and Global Economic Disruptions: The Russia–Ukraine Conflict, *International Affairs Journal*, 98(2), pp. 112–130.

Smuts, JC. (1930). *Africa and Some World Problems*. Oxford: Clarendon Press

Sneader, K. and Singhal, S. (2021). The next normal arrives: Trends that will define 2021— and beyond. McKinsey & Company. [online] Available at: https://www.mckinsey.com/featured-insights/leadership/the-next-normal-arrives-trends-that-will-define-2021-and-beyond [Accessed 20 Jun. 2025].

Snowden, D. J. & Boone, M. E. (2007). A Leader's Framework for Decision Making. *Harvard Business Review*, 85(11), pp. 68–76.

Sparkes, A.C. (2002). Telling tales in sport and physical activity: A qualitative journey. Champaign, IL: Human Kinetics.

Stapley, L.F. (2006). Individuals, groups, and organisations beneath the surface: An introduction. London: Karnac.

Stein, S.J. & Book, H.E. (2013). *The EQ Edge: Emotional Intelligence and Your Success*. 3rd ed. Mississauga, Ontario: Jossey-Bass.

Stein, S.J. and Book, H.E. (2011). The EQ Edge: Emotional intelligence and your

Stokes, J. (2019). The unconscious at work in groups and teams. In: A. Obholzer and V.Z. Roberts, eds. The unconscious at work: A Tavistock approach to making sense of organisational life. 2nd ed. Abingdon: Routledge, pp.19–27.

Sweller, J. (1988). Cognitive load during problem-solving: Effects on learning. *Cognitive Science*, 12(2), pp. 257-285.

Tavers, T. (2025) 3 Signs That You Are 'Psychospiritual', Forbes.com. [Accessed on 1 March 2025].

Taylor, S. (2019). The Role of Free Dialogue in Fostering Transformative Change in Organisations, *Organisational Dynamics*, 48(2), pp. 113–122.

The BodyTalk System. (2023). Understanding energy-based healing modalities. Available from on 28 Feb 2025].

The Knowing Field. (2022). Systemic Awareness and the Power of Group Facilitation. *The Knowing Field Journal, 31*, 89-103.

Tiller, W.A., Dibble, W.E., & Kohane, M.J. (2001). *Conscious Acts of Creation: The Emergence of a New Physics*. Pavior Publishing.

Trist, E. & Bamforth, K. (1951). Some Social and Psychological Consequences of the Longwall Method of Coal-getting. *Human Relations*, 4(1), pp. 3–38.

Trompenaars F. (1994) *Riding the waves of culture: understanding diversity in global business*. Burr Ridge: Irwin.

Tshetshe, Z. (2023). A Framework for Aligning Corporate Strategy and Organisational Culture to Promote Business Effectiveness: The Case of a South African Construction Enterprise. DBL Thesis. Available at. [Accessed 2 March 2025]. DOI:

Tshetshe, Z., & Viljoen, R. (2024). A framework for aligning corporate strategy and organisational culture to promote business effectiveness: The case of a South African construction enterprise. *Future X Journal*, pp. 34-53.

Tuckman, B. (1965). Developmental sequence in small groups. *Psychological Bulletin*, 63, pp. 384-399.

Turner, J. & Kim, H. (2022). The Impact of Inclusive Dialogue on Strategic Planning: Evidence from the World Café Approach. *Strategic Change*, 31(1), pp. 75–88.

Turner, V. (1969). *The Ritual Process: Structure and Anti-Structure*. Venice: Aldine Press.

Turquet, P.M. (1974). Leadership: The individual and the group. In: G.S. Gibbard, J.J. Hartman and R.D. Mann, eds. Analysis of groups. San Francisco: Jossey-Bass, pp.337–367.

Tushman, M. L. & O'Reilly, C. A. (1996). Ambidextrous Organizations: Managing Evolutionary and Revolutionary Change. *California Management Review*, 38(4), pp. 8–30.

Tutu, D. M. (1999). *No future without forgiveness*. New York, NY: Doubleday.

Ulrich, D., Smallwood, N. and Sweetman, K. (2009). The leadership code: Five rules to lead by. Boston, MA: Harvard Business Press.

USA Today. (2011). Starbucks CEO: Social conscience key to future success. *USA Today*, [online] 21 March. Available at: https://usatoday30.usatoday.com/money/industries/food/2011-03-21-starbucks-ceo-howard-schultz_N.htm [Accessed 13 June 2025].

Van Rensburg, G. (2007). *The leadership challenge in Africa*. Johannesburg, South Africa: Van Schaik.

Vilakati, M.V, Schurink, W.J. & Viljoen, R.C (2013). *Exploring the concept of African Spiritual Consciousness. Academy of Management Proceedings*.

Viljoen R. & Laubscher L. I. (2015b). Spiral dynamics. *Integral polity: Integrating nature, culture, technology and economy*. Lessem, R. & Abouleish, I. (Eds.). Gower. Farnham, U.K. 978-1-31711.

Viljoen, R. C. & Drotskie, A. (2017). Courageous leadership in multi-cultural environments — a South African case. In B. Vogel, *Developing leaders for positive organizing: A 21st century repertoire for leading in extraordinary times*. Emerald, ISBN: 978-1-78714-241-1

Viljoen, R. C., Van Zyl, H., Toendepi, J., & Viljoen, S. (2018). *Co-determination: The answer to South Africa's industrial relations crisis*. Bryanston: Knowres. ISBN: 9781869227555.

Viljoen, R.A. (2024a). On Coaching. Unpublished article. Available at Mandala Consulting.

Viljoen, R.C. & Laubscher, L.I. (2015a). African spiritual consciousness at work. In C. Piller & R. Wolfgramm (Eds). *Indigenous spiritualties at work: Transforming the spirit of business enterprise*. Charlotte, NC: Information Age Publishing. ISBN: 978-1-68123-156-3.

Viljoen, R.C. (2008). *Radical Organisational Transformation through Inclusivity*. Unpublished doctoral thesis. Unisa.

Viljoen, R.C. (2014a). *The Phenomenon of Caring. Implementation Plan*. Randburg, RSA.: Mandala Consulting.

Viljoen, R.C. (2014b) *Inclusive organisational transformation: An African perspective on human niches and diversity of thought*. Gower, ISBN 10.0367738880.

Viljoen, R.C. (2015). Organisational change and development: An African perspective. Bryanston: Knowres. ISBN: 978-1-86922-540-7.

Viljoen, R.C. (2016). Engagement in multi-cultural environments: Reflections and theoretical development. In: H. Nienaber & N. Martins, eds. Employee engagement in a South African context. Bryanston: Knowres, pp. 33-52.

Viljoen, R.C. (2018) Interstate bus lines: A tribal centre of gravity in need of functional blue. *Integral Leadership Review*. 14(1).

Viljoen, R.C. (2021). *BeQ Accreditation Manual: Level B*. Randburg, RSA.: Mandala Consulting. pp. 281

Viljoen, R.C. (2024). *Pearls from Graves – insights on Adaptive Intelligence of Social systems.* Unpublished paper presented at the Integral Conference of North America. Denver. May.

Viljoen, S.C. (2024b). Sustainable organisational transformation through integral leadership. Unpublished MBA dissertation. Rivonia: Henley Business School Africa.

Viljoen-Terblanche, R.C. (2008). *Ensuring Sustainable Organisational Transformation through Inclusivity*. Unpublished Doctor of Business Leadership Thesis. Johannesburg, RSA.: Graduate School of Business Leadership (UNISA).

Walsh, C. and Prinsloo, A. (2019). Building capacity for quality improvement: A hospital group's approach to reducing mortality. South African Medical Journal, 109(6), pp.432–436.

Walton, M. (2000). The Deming management method. New York: Perigee Books.

Watkins, M. (2007). Your next move: The leader's guide to successfully navigating major career transitions. Boston, MA: Harvard Business Press.

Weber, M. (1947). *The Theory of Social and Economic Organization*. Oxford: Oxford University Press.

Weick, K. (1995). *Sensemaking in Organizations*. Thousand Oaks, CA: Sage.

Weisbord, M.R. (1976). Organizational diagnosis: Six places to look for trouble with or without a theory. Group & Organization Studies, 1(4), pp.430–447.

Weiss, J.W. (2009). *Business Ethics: A Stakeholder and Issues Management Approach*. 5th ed. Mason, OH: South-Western Cengage Learning.

Weiss, J.W. (2014). *Business Ethics: A Stakeholder and Issues Management Approach*. 6th ed. San Francisco, CA: Berrett-Koehler Publishers.

Wells, L. (1980). The Group-as-a-Whole: A Systemic Socio-Analytic Perspective on Interpersonal and Group Relations. *Advances in Experiential Social Processes*. 2. pp. 1-35.

Wheatly, M. (2005). *Finding Our Way: Leadership for an Uncertain time*. San Francisco CA: Berrett-Koehler Publishers.

WHO (2020). *Coronavirus Disease (COVID-19) Dashboard*. Available from. [Accessed 22 February 2025].

Wilber, K. (2020). *Integral theory in action: Applied, theoretical, and critical perspectives on the AQAL model*. Boulder, CO: Shambhala.

Winnicott, D.W. (1953). Transitional objects and transitional phenomena—a study of the first not-me possession. *International Journal of Psychoanalysis*, 34, pp.89–97.

Winnicott, D.W. (1990). Playing and Reality. London: Routledge.

World Economic Forum. (2004). *Global Competitiveness Report 2004–2005*. Geneva: World Economic Forum. Available at: https://www3.weforum.org/docs/WEF_GCR_2004-05.pdf (Accessed: [insert date]).

Zahavi, D. (2019). Getting it quite wrong: van Manen and Smith on phenomenology. *Qualitative Health Research*, 29(6), pp.900–907.

Endnotes

1	Graves, 1974.	38	Bar-On, 2006.
2	ILO, 2021b.	39	Beck, Solonin, Larsen, Viljoen & Johns, 2017.
3	Kotter, 1996.		
4	Scharmer, 2009.	40	Viljoen, 2014, 2024.
5	Kotter, 1996.	41	Orr, 2002.
6	Viljoen 2016.	42	Freeman, 2017.
7	Viljoen, 2015.	43	Beck, et al, 2017.
8	Bion, 1961.	44	Freeman, 2017.
9	Jung, 1954.	45	Beck, et al., 2017.
10	Jung, 1954.	46	Graves, 1974.
11	Erikson, 1968	47	Beck, et al., 2017.
12	Jung, 1954.	48	Beck & Cowan, 1996.
13	Freud, 1921, p195.	49	Viljoen, 2015.
14	Bion, 1961.	50	Scharmer & Viljoen, 2014.
15	Graves, 1974.	51	Beck & Cowan, 1996.
16	Beck & Cohen, 1996.	52	Beck, et al., 2017.
17	Senge, 1990.	53	Beck, et al. 2017.
18	Jaques, 1989.	54	Viljoen, 2014.
19	Graves, 1974.	55	Viljoen, 2014.
20	Viljoen, 2016.	56	Viljoen, 2014.
21	Lather & St. Pierre, 2013.	57	Viljoen, 2014.
22	Krupat, 2023.	58	Viljoen, 2014.
23	Zahavi, 2019.	59	Laloux, 2014.
24	Wilber, 2020.	60	Jung, 1954.
25	Smuts, 1930.	61	Schein, 2010.
26	Cohen, Kahn & Steeves, 2000.	62	Laloux, 2014.
27	McNamee, 1988.	63	Hofstede, 1994.
28	Viljoen, 2008.	64	Trompenaars, 1994.
29	Dawkins, 1976.	65	Graves, 1974.
30	Viljoen, 2024.	66	Beck, et al., 2017.
31	Beckhard, 1969.	67	Viljoen, 2014.
32	Lewin, 1947.	68	Jung, 1954.
33	Burke & Litwin, 1992.	69	Jung, 1954.
34	Viljoen, 2008,2014, 2024.	70	Viljoen, 2023.
35	Burke & Litwin, 1992.	71	Senge, 1990.
36	Viljoen, 2008,2014,2016.	72	Beck, et al, 2017.
37	Jung, 1954.	73	Kotter, 1996.

74   Jung, 1954.

75   Jung, 1954.

76   Scharmer, 2009.

77   Goren-Bar, 2021.

78   Viljoen, 2015.

79   Kets de Vries, 2014.

80   Viljoen, 2015.

81   Scharmer, 2009.

82   Goren-Bar, 2021.

83   Viljoen, 2016.

84   Viljoen, 2015.

85   Kets de Vries, 2014.

86   Scharmer, 2009.

87   Goren-Bar, 2021.

88   Kets de Vries, 2014.

89   Viljoen, 2015.

90   Goren-Bar, 2021.

91   Scharmer, 2009.

92   Goren-Bar, 2010.

93   Viljoen-Terblanche, 2008.

94   Jung, 1968.

95   Viljoen, 2024b.

96   Viljoen, 2024b.

97   Adizes, 1974.

98   Gooden, 2016.

99   Viljoen, 2019.

100 Viljoen, 2013.

101 Viljoen, 2014.

102 Covey, 1989.

103 Weisbord, 1976.

104 Viljoen, 2018.

105 Senge, 1990.

106 Kim, 1996.

107 Ackoff, 2003.

108 Senge, 1990.

109 Mostert, 2024.

110 Mostert, 2024.

111 Jaques, 1997.

112 Jaques, 1974.

113 BIOSS, (n.d.).

114 Robertson, 2015.

115 Laloux, 2014.

116 Bernstein et al., 2016.

117 Laubscher, 2013.

118 Khan, Rehmat, Butt., et al.,2020.

119 Nell, 2023.

120 Nell, 2020, p237.

121 Nell, 2020, p151.

122   Nell, 2023.

123 Nell, 2023.

124 Nell, 2023, p206.

125 Viljoen, 2014b.

126 Plummer, 2001

127 Goleman, 1995.

128 Gardner, 1983.

129 Goleman, 1998.

130 Salovey & Mayer, 1990, pp.185–211.

131 Mikolajczak, 2009.

132 Goleman, 1995.

133 Stein and Book, 2011.

134 Winnicott, 1953, pp.89–97.

135 Nurick, 2020, p28.

136 Nurick, 2020.

137 Erikson, 1968, p138.

138 Ulrich, Smallwood & Sweetman, 2009.

139 Buck, 2004.

140 Watkins, 2007.

141 Goleman, 1999.

142 Bollas, 1987.

143 French & Simpson, 1999.

144 Stein & Book, 2013.

145 Margulies, 1989, p3.

146 Gould, 1993, p50.

147 Pink, 2005, p91.

148 Winnicott, 1990.

149 Bolton, 1983.

150 National Geographic, 2019.

151 McLuhan, 1964.

152 Pink, 2005, p20.
153 Levinson, 1981, p19.
154 Athos & Gabarro, 1978.
155 Weiss, 2009.
156 Weiss, 2014.
157 Stein & Book, 2011, p25.
158 Stein and Book, 2011, p133.
159 Gilchrist, 2019.
160 Sisodia, Wolfe & Sheth, 2007.
161 USA Today, 2011.
162 Gould, 1993, p 62.
163 Nurick, 1987, pp 100-101.
164 Cooper & Sawaf, 2019.
165 Tavers, 2025.
166 Blackie, 2024.
167 Blackie, 2024.
168 Blackie, 2024.
169 Blackie, 2024.
170 Jung, 1954.
171 Friend, (n.d.).
172 Rogers, 1951.
173 Rogers, 1961.
174 Viljoen, 2024a.
175 Viljoen, 2024a.
176 Bion, 1961.
177 Hinshelwood, 2001.
178 Long & Manly, 2009.
179 Manley, 2014.
180 Gordon Lawrence Foundation, (n.d.).
181 Long & Manly, 2009.
182 Gosling & Case, 2014.
183 Long, 2019.
184 Manley, 2014.
185 Long & Manly, 2009.
186 Lawrence, 2003.
187 Lawrence, 2003.
188 Owen, 1997.
189 Edmondson, 1999.
190 Sweller, 1988.
191 Beck, et al. 2017.
192 Bion, 1961.
193 Turner, 1969.
194 Heifetz, 1994.
195 Schön, 1983.
196 Cooper, 2025.
197 Turner, 1969.
198 Barrett, 2000.
199 French & Bell, 1999.
200 Barrett, 2000.
201 Bushe, 2013.
202 Cooperrider et al., 2003.
203 Lewis, 2019.
204 Smith, 2020.
205 McCormick & Ross, 2021.
206 Johnson & Edwards 2022.
207 Patel and Smith, 2020.
208 Bohm, 1998.
209 de Jager, 2003.
210 LeBarOn, 2005.
211 Anderson, 2020.
212 Taylor, 2019.
213 Ramose, 2000.
214 Brown et al., 2005.
215 LeBarOn, 2005.
216 Viljoen, 2014.
217 Weick, 1995.
218 Smith & Johnson, 2019.
219 Gabriel, 2021.
220 Denning, 2020.
221 Huss, 2004.
222 Jung, 1954.
223 Wheatly, 2005.
224 Brown & Isaacs, 2005.
225 Turner & Kim, 2022.
226 Martinez & Jones, 2021.
227 Owen & White, 2019.
228 Coghlan and Brannick, 2014.
229 Owen, 2008.

230 Slattery & Wylie, 1999.

231 Obholzer & Roberts, 2019.

232 Huffington et al., 2004.

233 Obholzer & Roberts, 2019.

234 Brunner & Villari, 2004.

235 Rioch, 1970.

236 Freud, 1910.

237 Freud, 1933.

238 Kets de Vries, 2014.

239 Stapley, 2006.

240 Long, 2016.

241 Stapley, 2006.

242 Klein, 1946.

243 McComb & Barnard, 2024.

244 Stapley, 2006.

245 Newman, Duff, & Baumeister, 1997.

246 Huffington et al., 2004.

247 Huffington et al., 2004.

248 Blackman, 2004.

249 Freud, 1910.

250 Ogden, 1979.

251 Stapley, 2006.

252 Blackman, 2004.

253 Blackman, 2004.

254 Mijolla, 2019.

255 Stapley, 2006.

256 Stapley, 2006.

257 Blackman, 2004.

258 Stapley, 2006.

259 Freud, 1910.

260 Mijolla, 2019.

261 Blackman, 2004.

262 Stapley, 2006.

263 Blackman, 2004.

264 Blackman, 2004.

265 Stapley, 2006.

266 Blackman, 2004.

267 Wells, 1980.

268 Rosenbaum, 2004.

269 Rosenbaum, 2004.

270 Huffington et al., 2004.

271 Bion, 1961.

272 Stokes, 2019.

273 Stapley, 2006.

274 Shapiro & Carr, 2012.

275 Bion, 1961.

276 Turquet, 1974.

277 Lawrence, Bain & Gould, 1996.

278 Koortzen & Cilliers, 2002.

279 Kets de Vries & Cheak, 2014.

280 Koortzen & Cilliers, 2002.

281 Koortzen & Cilliers, 2002.

282 Koortzen & Cilliers, 2002.

283 Lawrence, 1999.

284 Turquet, 1974, p. 357.

285 Koortzen & Cilliers, 2002.

286 Lawrence, Bain & Gould, 1996.

287 Lawrence et al., 1996.

288 Norman et al., 2013, p13.

289 Norman et al., 2013, p5.

290 Sparkes, 2002.

291 Walton, 2000.

292 Deming, 2018.

293 Juran, 1986a.

294 Provost, 2016.

295 Langley et al., 2013.

296 Langley et al., 2009, p25.

297 Langley et al., 2009.

298 Langley et al., 2009, p24.

299 Lloyd, 2018b.

300 Scoville & Little, 2014.

301 Deming, 1982: 52.

302 Viljoen, 2015a.

303 Associates in Process Improvement, 2020.

304 Viljoen, 2015a.

305 Prinsloo, 2021.

306 Prinsloo, 2021.

307 Viljoen, 2015b.

308 Viljoen, 2008.

309 Viljoen, 2015a.

310 Walsh & Prinsloo, 2019.

311 Breslin et al., 2018, p108.

312 Viljoen, 2018.

313 Beck, et al., 2017.

314 Grof, 2000.

315 Gánte, 2021.

316 Cohen & Meinl, 2016.

317 Jung, 1954.

318 EYQ, 2020.

319 Frontiers, 2020.

320 Saenz, Anderson, Ledingham & Supko, 2020.

321 Sneader & Singhal, 2021.

322 Jivan & Abbott, 2023.

323 Jivan & Abbott, 2023.

324 IODSA, 2016.

325 Lurie, 2018.

326 Jung, 1953.

Index

www.ingramcontent.com/pod-product-compliance
Lightning Source LLC
Chambersburg PA
CBHW080519220326
41599CB00032B/6131